AWAKEN
YOUR
PSYCHIC
ABILITY

AWAKEN YOUR PSYCHIC ABILITY

UPDATED EDITION

*Learn how to
connect to the
spirit world*

DEBBIE MALONE

ROCKPOOL

A Rockpool book
PO Box 252
Summer Hill
NSW 2130
Australia

rockpoolpublishing.com
Follow us! f ⊙ rockpoolpublishing
Tag your images with #rockpoolpublishing

1st edition published in 2016 by Rockpool Publishing as *Awaken your psychic
abilities*, under ISBN: 9781925017953

This updated edition published in 2022, by Rockpool Publishing
ISBN: 9781922579546

Design and typsetting by Sara Lindberg, Rockpool Publishing
Edited by Heather Millar

A catalogue record for this
book is available from the
National Library of Australia

NATIONAL
LIBRARY
OF AUSTRALIA

Printed and bound in China
10 9 8 7 6 5 4 3 2 1

CONTENTS

INTRODUCTION

HAVE YOU EVER felt that there is more to the world than your eyes can see?

Have you experienced déjà vu or had prophetic dreams that came true?

Do you ever see, feel, know or hear things that nobody else does?

Have you ever thought that you might be psychic, but didn't know what to do about it?

If this is the case, then you have picked up the right book as you are about to go on a journey of spiritual discovery. Throughout this book each chapter will explain the different types of psychic gifts we have within us.

I have included exercises and meditations that will help you to practise and strengthen your hidden psychic talents.

When I discovered my spiritual gifts I didn't realise that there were so many different ways that people could connect to the spirit world. It wasn't until I explored my gifts further that I began to understand the different ways that the spirit world can make its presence known to us.

The main spiritual gifts are:

- Psychic ability
- Mediumship

- The 'psychic clairs' known as:

  - Clairvoyance
  - Clairaudience
  - Clairsentience
  - Clairempathy
  - Clairtangency also known as psychometry
  - Claircognisance
  - Clairgustance
  - Clairalience

Don't be alarmed if you don't have all of these abilities working at the present time. You may discover that you can reawaken all of the gifts included in this book or you may find that you only utilise some of these abilities. It is important to understand that there is no right or wrong way to work with spirit. What is most important is that you are able to make a connection to the higher spiritual realms to continue your spiritual growth.

When I began to work with spirit, I didn't have all of my gifts working on a consistent level. My abilities would be intermittent and would work when I least expected them to. It was as if I didn't have a constant energy supply to sustain the connection and I had a loose wire in my spiritual connection circuit.

I discovered that the more I tried to get my abilities to 'work on demand', the more frustrated I would become and the less control I had.

Being angry or thinking negative thoughts would also interfere with my psychic connection. Fear has a great influence while working with spirit. The more frightened I became of working with the spirit world the more frightening and out of control my connection to spirit became.

I totally understood how Harry Potter felt when he was trying to master the ability to ride the 'Nimbus 2000' broomstick. When Harry first sat on the broom, he had many challenges and obstacles that tried to throw him off his path. Remember, mastering any ability takes time, dedication, trust, belief, patience and most of all practise.

An Olympic athlete doesn't just wake up one day and win a gold medal. The athlete has many trials and tests before ever being chosen to be part of the Olympic team. Being part of a spiritual team you will experience many ups and downs, disappointments and achievements but with dedication and persistence you will achieve your goals.

It is also important to realise that each Olympian has a gift that is their own particular strength. Some athletes enter more than one area of competition, while the majority will discover that they have one gift that is their greatest strength.

If you can keep this in mind when you begin your spiritual journey and focus on what is your greatest strength, you will discover a wonderful insight into a world we share with unseen spiritual beings.

These beings have a greater insight into the world around us. They are there to guide and assist you in your everyday life. Once you are working with these higher beings, you will view the world from a completely different perspective. The more you learn about the spiritual realms, the more you will want to discover what other gifts your spiritual teachers want to share with you.

It is now time to uncover what spiritual gifts lie within you. Take your time with the exercises, be patient and most of all believe in yourself and your connection to spirit. Your spiritual helpers will only give you as much as you can handle so, if at times you don't feel you are making a connection, take some time out and re-centre yourself.

I believe in you like your spiritual helpers, spirit guides and angels do. Let's begin your journey of a lifetime.

Love & light,

Debbie Malone

PSYCHIC MEDIUM

ACKNOWLEDGEMENTS

I WOULD LIKE to thank my husband Warwick for his patience while I have undertaken my spiritual journey. My three beautiful children Ryan, Blake and Shannon, you have taught me more than I could ever have taught you. You are the greatest gifts spirit has given me. Together we have experienced a spiritual journey like no other. I look forward to our future adventures together.

To my spirit guide Running Horse and my beautiful angels, together we have come so far. You have taken me on journeys I find hard to put into words.

My many near-death experiences have certainly changed my perspective on life. They have allowed me to access higher knowledge I only dreamt existed. I am thankful that through these journeys I have found my connection to you. I am also very grateful that it wasn't my time to leave this earth just yet.

Last but not least, to my beautiful spirit helpers who have inspired and guided me from above. Nanna and Poppa Gee for your love and support from spirit, I thank you. To Robert Malone, my beautiful father-in-law who passed while I was writing this book – thank you for giving me inspiration while you were alive and now from spirit.

Thank you everyone for showing me how to believe in my gifts so I could share them with others.

Remember to:

- Be kind to yourself.
- Know in your heart that you are a spiritual being, who is reigniting your natural-born spiritual gifts.
- Be patient with your progress, don't force your connection to spirit.
- Accept that anything is possible, be open to receiving.
- Understand that the information you are given is not just wishful thinking or your imagination.
- Be aware of the signs and symbols that surround you.
- Look at life through new eyes. You have been looking, but not seeing. It is time to refocus.
- Do not allow ego to overshadow your connection.
- Believe in yourself and be in awe of the spiritual abilities that you possess.
- You are a spiritual being, living an earthly experience. It is time to stand in your own light.

From the words of Hilma af Klint (Swedish spiritual visionary artist and medium):

> *'The phenomenon we are trying to explain*
> *is truly bewildering.*
>
> *What is this phenomenon, you ask?*
>
> *Well, beloved, it is that which we want to call the*
> *secret growing.'*

CHAPTER 1

YOUR PSYCHIC GIFTS – WHAT ARE THEY?

YOU ARE AN INCREDIBLE SPIRITUAL BEING who is currently living an earthly experience. Some of us are aware of our psychic gifts from childhood while others may discover these psychic abilities at a later time in their life. That being said it doesn't mean that you are any less psychic than the next person.

Some people are inquisitive and look to open their psychic gifts, others might be aware of them but are too frightened to explore them further, some people deny their abilities for fear of being ridiculed or thought to be different or strange. Others may have experienced a loss or a trauma that has put them on their spiritual path of psychic discovery. In whatever form you came to be on this journey, I wish to welcome you and I look forward to our journey of psychic discovery together.

As you work your way through this book, I will go through what the different psychic abilities are and teach you how you can connect to your natural born spiritual GPS (Global Psychic System).

The most common psychic gifts are:

- Psychic – a person who can see into the past, present and future.
- Medium – a person who can see and communicate with spirits, beings and loved ones in the spirit realms.
- Clairvoyant (clear seeing) – a person who can see via their normal senses using their third eye to see signs, symbols and beings in the spirit realms.
- Clairaudient (clear hearing) – a person who hears via their normal senses and uses their sixth sense to hear messages, guidance and voices of beings in the spirit realms.
- Clairsentient (clear physical feeling) – a person who receives messages from the spirit realms via their feelings, usually in their solar plexus chakra that is located in their stomach.
- Clairempath (clear emotional feeling) – a person who experiences the emotions, thoughts and symptoms of another person or their heart chakra. Also known as an empath.
- Clairtangent (clear touching – also known as psychometry) – a person who is able to receive information from inanimate objects such as a watch, ring, photograph or an antique item.
- Claircognisant – a person who experiences a light bulb moment where they just simply know things about something or someone. Claircognisance is not connected to the other psychic clairs, such as sight sound, sensations or psychic touch.
- Clairalient (clear smelling) – a person who receives information through smell, such as fragrances, cooking smells or odours.
- Clairgustant (clear tasting) – a person who receives psychic information through the sense of taste, without actually having the item in their mouth.

Preparing for your spiritual journey

Before you undertake any journey, it is always important to be prepared for what lies ahead. If you were going to take a trip to the moon, you would take the time to gather the correct tools and do the relevant training so that you are prepared to land on the moon safely and in one piece. You would also look at all of the ways to protect yourself in order for you to make a safe return home to planet Earth.

I want you to think of this book as your psychic guide to what is possible and for you to see what gifts lie within yourself. It will give you the knowledge and understanding of what each psychic tool is, how to activate it, how to practice and strengthen it and most of all how to be the master of your gifts.

It is extremely important that you learn how to exercise your psychic muscles and strengthen them along this journey, so in time you will be in control of your gift and gain insight to what a truly special spiritual psychic being you are.

You will experience times of frustration, disappointment and perhaps even anger that things do not always happen as quickly or easily as you would like. A word that will come up regularly throughout this book will be 'PATIENCE'.

Yes, this word is something I am sure you will hear again and again, even if you don't want to. What you need to remember is that this word will present itself to you for a reason. Spirit will only give you as much as you can handle at a time. If you rush the exercises and don't learn the lesson, then you will not understand how each gift links into the next.

You may also find that some of the exercises will be much easier to follow than others, while you may feel you just don't get some of them at all. Do not despair, by the time you work your way through the whole book you will discover things will start to make more sense.

I recommend that if there are any psychic gifts that did not resonate in the beginning, go back over the exercises and try doing them again. You may surprise yourself with how you have opened up.

When I began my journey, I did not have all my psychic gifts working together at once. The only way I could see clairvoyantly was when I was in a dream state or when I meditated. If I tried to connect to the spirit world when I was awake, nothing happened. Now, over 30 years later, I have access to all of the psychic clairs and they are second nature to my daily life. You too will have the same opportunity to let your gifts unfold. All you need to do is be patient, believe and persevere. Now let's begin.

What is your psychic tool kit?

As we go through this book, I will be talking about different tools that will be introduced to you along the way.

As I mentioned in the introduction, when you undertake a journey you need to gather the right equipment. Doing psychic spiritual work is also a journey that must be taken seriously. You will be working with the seen and the unseen forces, so it is important to be able to trust that you will always be in safe hands along your journey.

Tool checklist

You – You are the most important psychic spiritual tool throughout this entire journey, as it is you who spirit will come to, communicate with, blend with and utilise as a vessel to communicate messages from the other side. You, as the vessel, need to look after yourself; you need to be balanced; you need to feel safe, protected and in control of your surroundings and the connections you will make throughout this journey. While doing a reading for others, you actually need to take the 'you' out of the equation and put yourself into the sitter's shoes.

Psychic protection and white light – Learning to white light yourself is a vital tool that you should never proceed without. Would you take a trip to the moon and not be protected by the right type of flight suit or correct space craft? Of course, you wouldn't. This is why, before you start any spiritual work, you must put on the right protective equipment in order for you to be safe. If you are not protected and do not have an understanding of opening and shutting the door to the spirit realms you may not always have access to the right spiritual frequency or vibration.

Throughout this book I will speak about frequency and vibration as there are many different levels (frequency or vibrations) on which good and bad spirits reside. Putting it simply, when a human being passes over to the spirit realm they do not automatically get a set of wings and become an angel. On the human realm there is good and bad in life, and in the spirit realms, there is also the same frequency of good and bad.

Learning to understand what frequency or vibration resonates with you on a positive level and what doesn't resonate with you on a negative level is a vital tool of understanding. This will help you to learn when a spirit is good, bad, malevolent or simply lost and in need of assistance. Surrounding yourself daily with white light and lifting your vibration should become part of your practice. You need to understand what psychic protection is and what a psychic attack is and you need to know how to shut the latter down.

The psychic clairs – The word 'clair' comes from the French word meaning clear. We, as human beings, measure life with what we are told are the five physical senses: touch, taste, smell, sight and sound. However, we are not taught about the innate spiritual senses that we also possess within us.

These underestimated abilities are part of our eight 'clair' senses that connect us to the unseen spiritual realms surrounding us. We all possess these gifts, but it is only when we tune in and activate these gifts that we can begin to unlock these hidden abilities. When you are open to working with these senses, there is a whole other spiritual world that you can only dream could exist.

In the following chapters, I will discuss the differences between the eight psychic clairs in further depth.

Spiritual activation – How to turn it on and how to turn it off. Working with spirit is a wonderful blessing and a gift. However, if you are not in control of it and not working on the higher frequencies, it can also feel like a curse. Learning how to turn on and off your abilities at will is most important.

When I initially started to do readings, I was constantly open and receiving messages from anywhere and everywhere. This, as a psychic medium, can be draining because you are constantly being bombarded with messages from the human and spirit realms.

It wasn't until I progressed with my journey that I learnt that it was possible to tune in and tune out.

Auras and chakras – These two vital energy forces contained around and within the body are part of our psychic tools. Auras and chakras help us to protect ourselves, and to see, feel, balance and heal ourselves and others. Some of you will have the gift of seeing auras around the body, while some of you will be able to feel auras around someone's body.

When you are not in balance cracks can appear in your aura or energies can become attached to your aura. When your chakras are not aligned you may feel out of balance and ungrounded, and you may experience illness within your body. Learning how to balance, clear and align your auras and chakras is a part of your psychic protection routine.

Creating a sacred space – The more you connect with the spiritual realms, the more important it will become for you to create a sacred space in which to do so. Your sacred space can be a physical space or a space within your mind's eye. It is not important how you create your sacred space; what is important for you is to have access to your sacred space in order to connect with the higher spiritual vibrations when you are doing your spiritual work.

Your spiritual journal and psychic symbology – Once you undertake your spiritual journey, you will be given many messages, signs, symbols, colours and sounds. I strongly advise that as part of your psychic tool kit you create a spiritual journal to record all of the information that you download from spirit. In the future, you will discover what an invaluable tool this is to refer back to. We will go into these symbols later in the book.

Working with your angels – When we decide to incarnate into the earth realm, we are accompanied by our own personal guardian angel. This special being will accompany us throughout our entire life helping and guiding us.

We also have access to other angels from many different realms. I will help you to understand what their roles are in your life.

Spirit guides – As spiritual beings, we also have access to our spirit guides. Spirit guides are different to our angels in that they are spiritual beings who actually lived on the earth plane, whereas many of the angels from the angelic realms have not lived as physical beings. Spirit guides are here to accompany us during our lifetime here on Earth.

Divining tools – Many people like to use divining tools such as pendulums and dowsing rods to help them to divine answers from spirit. These tools can be used to receive 'yes' and 'no' answers to questions you ask spirit. They can be used to locate lost objects, measure the aura and divine for water.

Numerology – Numerology can be used to assist you to understand different personality traits, birth force numbers and the numerological cycles that people experience during their life. Numerology is a valuable tool that can be used in conjunction with your psychic clairs.

Psychic etiquette (do's & don'ts) – Working as a spiritual being who is of service to others on the physical realm is an absolute privilege. If you decide to work with spirit you should always keep in mind what a huge responsibility it is. We will discuss this further throughout the book.

CHAPTER 2:

JOURNALLING AND CREATING YOUR PSYCHIC REFERENCE GUIDE

ONE OF THE IMPORTANT ASPECTS OF DEVELOPING your psychic ability is the understanding and bond that you will have with your spirit team. During this book and while working with the exercises in each chapter you will discover that certain signs, sounds, colours, feelings, numbers and visions will pop into your head.

At first this may feel a little confusing and at times overwhelming, that is why I want you to start to journal every part of your journey. You will understand your journal's importance in documenting your spiritual journey in years to come. This will be an important gift to yourself to refer back to for future reference.

I know when I was suddenly thrust into the psychic spiritual realms, I was quite frightened and didn't understand what was happening to me. My early introduction into the other side was not a chosen path; it was something that happened to me through many of my near-death experiences.

To be honest I was a very reluctant psychic student. I truly never wanted to embark on this journey in the initial stages of my abilities awakening. I actually tried to hide from them, shut them down and ignore them. During this quite traumatic time of my life, trying to run away from the psychic person that I was born to be actually heightened my abilities. I found that being fearful actually stopped me from having any control of when I would see visions, hear and see dead people, or receive messages from the other side. This is one of the reasons that I wanted to write this book.

When my journey began there wasn't the same freedom and openness that we experience today about the psychic and spiritual realms. Thirty years ago books such as this were classed as occult books and were often kept under the counter at bookshops or hidden and kept to the side.

I am so thankful that times have changed, and we can now openly discuss these incredible gifts we are all born with.

To this day, I look at the scraps of paper and notes I made during my early spiritual journey, and I am amazed at how far I have come and how important the initial images and messages I received from spirit actually were.

My one disappointment is that I didn't keep better records of all of my spiritual guidance. This is why I want you to begin the journey with the right tools to assist you along the way.

When I first began working with law enforcement, I was asked to keep a journal of all of my visions. The officer in charge of the taskforce I was working with asked me to write everything I saw down. He advised that I should just record what the date was and the information I received. He told me not to over-think what I saw nor try to rationalise it, as this is

when the rational minds steps in and may distort the true meaning of what I was receiving.

At first, I thought if I did exactly that, he would think I was some crazy person with a distorted mind. What I later realised was that the information was not for me to judge – it was given to me to pass on to the officer, it was not for me to try and make sense as it was not a personal message to myself.

What is important to remember is that working with the spirit world is not always something to be taken literally. For instance, one case I worked on with the police, I was given an image of a woman in a foetal position in the dark, and I saw a car driving south of Sydney through the Royal National Park heading towards a town called Wollongong. I then heard the word 'breakdown' very clearly.

I initially thought that the missing woman was staying down in Wollongong and may have had a mental breakdown and was in the dark, and she had driven through the Royal National Park to get to Wollongong.

I wrote all of this information down and passed it onto the police. It wasn't until the woman's body was later found and the case went to court that my visions made sense.

Yes, the woman was in a car in a foetal position in the dark; her killer had placed her in that position in the boot of her car. He drove the car through the Royal National Park on his way to Wollongong to dump her body when the car broke down in the national park.

As you can see, the information I picked up was correct, but it was in a different context to what my rational mind had thought it was.

Sometimes when I am doing a reading, I may see that someone I am doing a reading for is having issues with a car. When the car is a constant problem, I always see the colour of the car to be lemon. When I initially saw this colour, I didn't understand what it meant, as I knew that the owner did not have a yellow-coloured car. Over time I came to understand that something being called a lemon is a metaphor for an object that is defective or faulty.

Other examples of understanding your guide's messages may come in the form of repetitive signs or symbols. I have discovered through working with my spirit team that I will receive repetitive messages while doing readings for different people.

Each reading will be unique to the client I am reading, however at times the meaning that I am being shown relates to a similar situation in that persons' life. For example: I may see someone rubbing a female's stomach, or I may see a loved one in spirit holding a new-born baby in their arms. The rubbing of the female's stomach indicates to me that the person is pregnant, or they are very fertile and will be pregnant in the not-too-distant future. If a loved one is holding a new-born baby, the baby will usually be wrapped in either a blue or pink baby blanket to indicate to me what the sex of the child will be.

Over the years, I have kept track of all of these repetitive signs and symbols, so that when I tune into someone to do a reading, as soon as I see that image or symbol, I know immediately what area of the client's life I am focusing in on.

I have written a deck of reading cards based on messages from my guides called Psychic Reading Cards.

Through paying attention to the details your guides share with you, you too will be able to understand the image your spirit team shows you immediately.

It's also important to remember that just because one person sees an image or symbol and relates to it in one way, it doesn't mean that it will mean the same thing to you. In some cases, it may make total sense, while in other situations it may not.

By journalling everything you see, hear, feel, experience, smell or dream, you will be able to understand what your spirit teams want you to know.

Steps to begin your journalling

Purchase a journal. The journal doesn't need to be an expensive book, it could simply be a notebook. However, I would recommend the book has a tough cover and spine. As this journal is going to accompany you on many adventures, it needs to be able to withstand being by your side constantly.

Create headings. You may wish to split the journal into different sections for different signs, as well as having a daily page to write on. I would suggest you purchase a journal with at least 200 pages and use one half for the daily messages, and then turn the book upside down and use the other side for your headings section. Add headings like:

- Symbols
- Guides and guardian angels
- Names
- Number sequences
- Colours
- Affirmations
- Fragrances
- Drawings
- Psychic phenomenon
- Feelings
- Sounds and songs.

Once you purchase your book you may also like to use it to practise automatic writing with your spirit team. It is totally up to you how you utilise your journal – the main thing is to record everything you experience through all of your psychic senses.

Doing a dedication to spirit and asking them to work with you and your journal will strengthen your connection. Tell your spirit team that when you are writing things in the journal, it is their time to make contact.

I find doing the same thing on a daily basis helps me create a routine for when and if I am ready to work with spirit.

Just remember before you start your journalling always record the date and perhaps the time if you think it is important. This will show you when you have your greatest connection to your spirit helpers. You may find the morning is your best time to make contact, or it may be when you are winding down at the end of your day that your connection is best.

Try starting off your day by asking spirit what is your word for the day? Better still ask what is your affirmation for the day? Your spirit team may decide they will give you a sign for the day instead. I have found on many occasions the word they have given me – such as the word 'believe' – has popped up all through the day on which I received it. I could be listening to the radio and a song would play with the word 'believe' jumping out at me. I could be driving and an advertisement on a billboard or a bus would have 'believe' on it. I would pull out an affirmation card message for the day and the word 'believe' would be there again. When this happens, it is confirmation that spirit wants you to pay attention to their messages and is reaffirming you are on the right track.

Once you make a habit of journalling, you will soon discover how quickly the messages your spirit team shares with you resonate and make sense.

In time your journal will become your own psychic bible. Treat it with respect as this is something sacred between you and your spirit team. It will become your key to unlocking many hidden treasures.

Journal dedication

Divine and infinite spirit, I ask that we work together as a team. I dedicate this journal to you and wish to use it as a tool that allows us to reach the highest vibration possible when we connect with each other during our spiritual work. This journal will be a source of knowledge, guidance, inspiration and a connection to source energy. I thank you for the connection and I look forward to our future connections. Together we work as one.

CHAPTER 3:

CREATING YOUR SACRED SPIRITUAL PLACE

WHEN YOU BEGIN WORKING WITH the spirit world, it is always a good idea to create a sacred place to do your work. This can be achieved in one of two ways: by creating a physical sacred space or an internal imaginary sacred space you enter during your meditation and spirit work.

To begin you need to pick a location that you can dedicate to your spiritual work. This place may be in your home or office. The space you create needs to be somewhere you can retreat from the outside world so that you can make contact with your inside world in peace.

Your sacred space doesn't need to be an entire room – it could be just a corner of the room, or it could be as simple as picking a specific chair or a place where you can put cushions on the floor to sit on. You may even choose to have a sacred space outside in your garden, balcony or courtyard where you can connect with your spirit guides by being amongst nature.

Your internal sacred space

Creating an internal sacred space is great for those people who don't have room to dedicate an area to work in. Why not think outside of the square when you choose to create your sacred space. You may decide that your sacred space is a place you access in your mind instead of a dedicated physical space.

An internal space can be used when you are away from home or your office and can be easily accessed by just a thought or through meditation. You may find that using specific affirmations or mantras can also be of assistance in accessing your internal space.

Before I had a room in my home to dedicate to doing my spiritual work, I would sit in a comfortable position in my lounge room and meditate with some of my special crystals or talismans.

I have a very unusual amethyst crystal ball that has a double hexagon inside of it. The hexagon acts as a doorway for me to connect to my spirit guides and guardian angels. When I sit and meditate with the crystal ball, I visualise the hexagon becoming a spiritual doorway that opens up. When I do this the density of the crystal ball changes, and I feel like I am shrinking down and walking through into an amethyst crystal cave inside the ball. I always feel safe and secure when I do this and have been extremely blessed to communicate with many enlightened souls in this sacred space.

You may choose a special crystal that you use to connect to your inner space with or you may have a special guided meditation or ambient music that helps you to connect. Everyone has their own way of connecting and working with their guides, angels and ascended masters. Through time and practise you will be able to determine what works best for you.

Ideas for decorating your sacred space

I would suggest that you decorate your space with things that you find enhance your connection to the spirit world. You may wish to use some of the following items or none at all; always go on what feels right within your soul. Some people find that they have a better connection if they have some of the following items:

- Crystals
- Books
- Your spiritual journal to record any contact with your guides and guardian angels
- Angel, oracle, tarot or divination cards
- Angel or deity statues
- A small water feature, which is great for lifting the vibration of the room and keeping the energy flowing
- Affirmation or mandala charts for your walls
- A wind chime so that you are made aware when those in spirit arrive
- Animal totems, if this is more your preference
- A comfortable chair or lounge where you can sit or lie down and relax and do your meditations
- An oil burner or infuser for your essential oils
- Candles and/or incense
- Spirit guide drawings if you have any of your guides.

As you progress with your spiritual growth this sacred place will become an important place for you to enter and make contact. The most important thing to remember is that this place is where you will endeavour to lift your vibration to connect to the higher energies of your angels and guides. When you are in a relaxed and calm environment, anything is possible.

I have found that the longer I have worked in my office, the higher the vibration has risen in my office environment. Many people enter the office and tell me how peaceful they feel as soon as they enter the room. This is because spirit and I both know that this space is where we need to do very important work.

Have you ever entered a library and felt the peace and tranquillity? This is because the energy of the library is that of receiving knowledge. It is as though the books on the shelves are waiting to instil their wisdom within you.

Working in your sacred place is similar, as the sole purpose of you working in the space is to resonate on the same frequency as those in spirit. Your angels and guides in spirit wish to instil you with their knowledge, wisdom and guidance.

Clearing negative energy

Once you have chosen your space, it is a good idea to clear the area you have chosen of any negative energy. This way you can invigorate the room by lifting the vibration to begin your spiritual work.

In many Eastern cultures, clearing negative energy is of utmost importance for the home and environment. When you are working with psychic power, it is important that you ensure that your home or sacred space is free of any negative energies that come from the physical and spiritual world.

Here are a few suggestions to help clear negative energy:

- Lighting candles made from essential oils is an excellent way to ward off negative energy. Purchase some fragrant tea-light candles and put a candle in each corner of the room and light them, allowing them to burn until they extinguish. You may choose to say affirmations or mantras asking any negative energies or entities to leave and not return.

- Burning incense is a common way to cleanse your home or sacred space. Sandalwood is the most commonly used cleansing incense. Lavender and sage incense are also popular choices.

- Chanting the mantra of 'om' is highly beneficial in cleansing a room and raising the vibration of the room. You may have a CD that you can 'om' along with or you may choose to 'om' on your own. The 'om' vibration is used as part of meditation routines and is used to help clear the mind of thoughts.

- Clapping your hands loudly with the intention to break up and remove any negative energy in a room or space is another common way to cleanse a room. While you are clapping, you can say affirmations asking any negative energy to leave the space.

- Singing bowls, bells and chimes are often used to clear the negative energy from homes or offices. If using a singing bowl to clear your sacred space, home or office, do so by playing your bowl as you move throughout your entire area. Make sure that you include any cupboards and corners to ensure that you disperse any stagnant or negative energy. You may choose to use chimes or bells in the same manner to clear the space. At the end of your clearing, demand that any negative energy left behind is to leave and not return.

- House clearing sprays made from essential oils or crystal essences are a wonderful way to cleanse your space. The great thing about clearing your space this way is that your space will smell great when you finish. These types of sprays can be purchased at New Age stores or online.

- Sage cleansing is a ritual I use to cleanse my home and office, as I find it works best for me. You may wish to experiment with different ways of cleansing to find out which works best for you.

How to cleanse using sage

Purchase a sage smudge stick, which can usually be found at spiritual stores. I usually use white sage. You can also use dried sage purchased at a continental delicatessen. I don't find that there is much difference between the two.

Before you begin, find a bowl or plate to hold the sage over as you don't want any embers catching light in your house. (Traditionally an abalone shell is used for this). Have a cup of water to extinguish the sage in when you have finished your smudging ritual, and a lighter or box of matches to ignite the sage. You may wish to have your favourite protective crystal with you when you perform the cleansing. Placing the crystal in your pocket is adequate.

Sometimes, it is hard to get the sage to ignite, so as a standby I always have some pure lavender oil at hand. I sprinkle a couple of drops onto the sage and this helps to ignite the sage, plus it makes it smell nicer as well.

Open all of the windows in the room or space you are smudging. If you have any roof fans, you may wish to turn them on also, to help the smoke reach every corner of the room. If you have blinds or curtains, open them all up as you want to have as much light streaming into the room as possible.

If you wish to smudge your whole home or office at the same time, begin your cleansing ritual at the lowest part of the house or office. If you have a garage or laundry downstairs, start there first.

Light the stick, and when it catches fire, blow it out and allow the embers to begin to smoke (the same way you do when you are lighting incense).

Now, this is the most important part of the whole process. You need to set your intention of cleansing and dedicating your room to your spiritual work.

Call in your guides and ask for assistance from the highest and purest white light possible. Ask for any negative energies or entities to leave your space and surround them with white light. Visualise them leaving via the open windows.

You may have a prayer you wish to say. I usually say the Lord's Prayer as this lifts the vibration of the room and activates your chakra points.

I walk around the room in a clockwise direction ensuring the smoke from the sage drifts into all the corners of the room, along the walls and up to the ceiling. I imagine the smoke dispersing any negativity or problems that may have occurred in the room and disappearing as the smoke floats out the window.

If the smoke floats straight up to the ceiling, it is an indication that the room is clear. However, if the smoke starts to turn into shapes or faces, it is a sign that negative energy is still present in the room. If this occurs, I then do another lap of the room to ensure that the stubborn negative energy leaves.

Before I leave the room, I visualise a beautiful shaft of white light appearing through the centre of the ceiling and filling the room with positive protection.

If you are going to clear the rest of your home or office, continue on the lowest level and then progress to the upper level if there is one. I do the same ritual as described above in each room until all rooms have been cleansed.

When I am finished, I move to the centre of the room, or if you are doing an entire house or office, move to the centre of the entire space.

I then visualise an even bigger shaft of light coming through the centre of the entire area, and a dome of protective light surrounding the entire area from above.

Next, turn in a clockwise direction and surround yourself with the sage smoke to give yourself a sage shower to dissipate any energy that may be attached to you.

Thank your guides and the higher beings that have helped you to cleanse your space of any negativity. Extinguish your smudge stick in some water.

You may wish to repeat this ritual in the future if you feel you need to clear any build-up of energy.

Have a shower to wash the smell of the smoke away. It also helps to finalise the cleansing process you have just undertaken.

After you have set aside an area for your sacred place, cleansed it and decorated it just as you wish, the next thing to do is to dedicate it.

There are a number of different ways that you can dedicate the space. Lighting a candle, burning incense or burning your favourite essential oils in an oil burner is a wonderful way to lift the vibration and fill the room with your favourite scent.

Sacred space meditation

- Before starting your meditation, ensure that you have your spiritual journal and a pen close at hand to record any messages you may receive from your spirit team during the meditation.

- Sit quietly and relax in a position that allows you to feel most comfortable. Gently close your eyes and take in a deep breath, now as you slowly exhale, visualise breathing out any negative thoughts or worries. Take in another deep breath, only this time, visualise breathing in beautiful white light – when you exhale, allow yourself to feel the peace that is surrounding you. While you are inhaling your next breath, feel the light becoming brighter and glowing within you. Visualise the light from within you expanding to every corner of your room and surrounding you.

- Ask your spirit team, consisting of your guides, guardian angels and loved ones in spirit, to be drawn to this beautiful, uplifting spiritual light to allow them to connect with you from this point forward in your special sacred space. Visualise the roof above your space disappearing, and in your mind's eye, look up and see the clouds above. Feel yourself lifting up into the clouds and feel totally at peace. Slowly look around you and see who has come to meet with you from your spirit team while you are up amongst the heavens.

- While you are in this special place, ask your spirit team to help you to dedicate your sacred space. Ask them to bless the space with their love and guidance. Communicate to your team that in the future they can find you in your sacred space to further develop your spiritual awareness.

- Listen to any messages they may have for you. They may give you guidance about what the next step is in your spiritual journey and how to proceed forward. Or they may simply make their presence known to you so that you can reunite at a future time. When you have received your message, thank your spirit team and slowly allow yourself to return your consciousness back to the room or space you are positioned in.

AFFIRMATION

I am protected and at peace while I am in my
sacred space. I acknowledge the spiritual guidance
I receive from my spirit team is for my highest
good. Together we work as one!

CHAPTER 4:

WHAT IS AN AURA?

THE WORD 'AURA' originates from a Greek word meaning '*breeze*' or '*air*' (*air* emanating from the body). The aura is connected to our subtle body and it surrounds us like a forcefield. While our chakras contain the seven colours of the rainbow within the body our aura contains the seven colours of the rainbow outside of the body.

Our aura contains information about our past, present and future within it. It is connected to our inner and outer emotions on a physical and spiritual level. Have you ever noticed how different colours can affect your moods and emotions? Do you ever feel that you are drawn to different colours yet repelled by others? Colours can have a significant effect on your body both internally and externally.

As you become more sensitive and connected to your auric field, you will understand what colours you need to surround yourself with. Some days you will need to wear red for example, as you need to be grounded and assertive in your work. Other days you may feel drawn to the colour pink as you are feeling sensitive and need to be nurtured. Referring to the chart in this chapter will assist you with determining which colours represent areas you need to focus on in your life.

So, what is our aura and what does it consist of? Our aura is made up of seven layers surrounding our body. The layers are also known as the 'auric layers' or 'subtle bodies'. An aura is an electromagnetic field that surrounds all living things. We, as human beings, have the ability to feel and in some cases see the aura. The human aura is a forcefield of light that surrounds our entire body. The multiple layers of the aura interact with our body relaying information throughout the body's seven chakra energy centres.

Each layer of our aura is connected to our physical, emotional, mental and spiritual feelings. Our aura is like a filing cabinet for all of our thoughts, feelings, spiritual awareness, health and past experiences to be stored.

Plants and animals also have auras.

It is possible to photograph an image of the aura using Kirlian photography. Have you ever been to a psychic fair and had your aura photographed? You will notice that the image is made of a number of different colours. Each colour represents a different part of the body. An aura photograph can indicate if there are any health or emotional issues surrounding a person at the time the photograph is taken.

Some people have the ability to see the auric colours around people with the human eye, while others are more likely to feel them. With perseverance and practise, you could also be able to see and feel the aura. (We will do some exercises later in this chapter.)

Have you ever stood in a line at the supermarket and felt like the person next to you was standing too close to you? If you have experienced this feeling you have felt someone else's aura touching yours. Many of us pick up on this type of feeling without realising you have experienced something happening to your aura.

Many of us pick up on the energy of other people without realising it. Children under the age of ten are generally very gifted with seeing the auras around people. Many children draw colourful pictures of people, plants and animals with rainbow colours surrounding the subject without even knowing what they are drawing.

What are the auric layers?

The first layer of the aura is known as the 'etheric body', and it is connected to our vital organs, glands and meridians. It relates to the health of our physical body. This layer is connected to the root/base chakra. The etheric body is in constant connection and movement with our physical body. The etheric body emanates approximately 1 to 6 cm (.5 to 2 inches) from our physical body.

The etheric layer can be seen by some individuals as a bluish-white glow that moves along the energy field of the physical body.

The second layer of the aura is known as the 'emotional body', and this layer is connected closely with our feelings and emotions. This layer is connected to the sacral chakra and reflects our current moods; it also stores any unsettled emotions like fear, loneliness and resentment.

This layer is different to the etheric body as it is more fluid in appearance and can be seen as different colours connected to different parts of the physical body. The emotional body extends approximately 2 to 10 cm (2 to 4 inches) from the physical body.

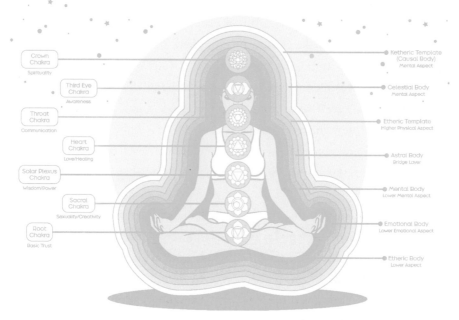

Chakras & Auric Layers

Crown Chakra
Spirituality

Third Eye Chakra
Awareness

Throat Chakra
Communication

Heart Chakra
Love/Healing

Solar Plexus Chakra
Wisdom/Power

Sacral Chakra
Sexuality/Creativity

Root Chakra
Basic Trust

Ketheric Template (Causal Body)
Mental Aspect

Celestial Body
Mental Aspect

Etheric Template
Higher Physical Aspect

Astral Body
Bridge Layer

Mental Body
Lower Mental Aspect

Emotional Body
Lower Emotional Aspect

Etheric Body
Lower Aspect

The third layer of the aura is the 'mental body'. This layer extends beyond your emotional body and is connected to your mental and thought process. The appearance of this layer can be seen as a bright yellow or golden light that emanates around the head and shoulder regions, extending around the entire body. The mental body extends approximately 7.5 to 20 cm (3 to 8 inches) from the physical body. This layer is connected to the solar plexus chakra.

The fourth layer of the aura is the 'astral body' or 'bridge layer'. This layer is 20 to 30 cm (8 to 12 inches) away from the physical body, and is connected to the three lower and three higher auric layers acting as a bridge between the more solid and spiritual energies. The astral body is considered the layer of love, as this is where we understand and express our emotions about our relationships with others. This layer is connected to the heart chakra.

The fifth layer of the aura is the 'etheric template body'. This layer is 30 to 60 cm (1 to 2 feet) away from the physical body, and is connected to the throat chakra. This layer is at the seat of our higher consciousness, sound communication, creativity and vibration. It acts as a carbon copy of our physical body on the spiritual plane. Energies from the spiritual and physical plane make contact on this plane, allowing both worlds to make contact.

The sixth layer of the aura is the 'celestial body'. This layer is 60 to 120 cm (2 to 3 feet) away from the physical body, and is connected to the third-eye/brow chakra. It connects us to intuitive knowledge, spiritual awareness, dreams, memories and the emotional level of the spiritual plane. Through this spiritual plane we can access knowledge that is greater than ourselves.

The seventh layer of the aura is the 'ketheric template' or 'causal body'. This layer is 76 to 106 cm (2.5 to 3.5 feet) away from the physical body. This layer is connected to the crown chakra, allowing you to access the knowledge that anything is possible. It is the outer layer that protects and holds all of the auric layers together, and it contains the spiritual blueprint of your soul's experiences and spiritual records.

What do the different colours of the aura mean?

Each of the colours of the aura have different meanings. The colours can indicate our state of health and emotions. I have included a brief description of what each colour indicates and what chakra they are aligned with. If the colour is dull or dirty looking it indicates the negative meaning of the aura.

Colours of the aura and their meanings

COLOUR	CHAKRA	MEANING	NEGATIVE
RED	Base	Strength, passion, vitality, energy, leadership, grounded	Anger, hyperactive, over-sensitive
ORANGE	Sacral	Open-minded, happiness, vitality, confidence, warmth	Stress, addictions
YELLOW	Solar-plexus	Optimism, inspiration, wisdom, intuition, sensitivity, clairsentient	Fatigue, stress
GREEN	Heart	Healing, love, health, balance, growth, nature, calm	Jealousy, victim, insecurity
BLUE	Throat	Communication, speech, caring, intuitive, spiritual, clairaudience	Fear of communication
INDIGO	Third-eye	Intuition, inner wisdom, imagination, creative, visual, clairvoyance	Nightmares
VIOLET	Crown	Enlightenment, visionary, psychic, artistic, inspirational, spiritual	Day dreamer, lack of focus

WHITE	Crown	Angelic qualities, purity, healthy, auric vision, psychic medium	Dirty white – illness
PINK	Heart	Romantic, affection, strong spirituality, compassion	Overly sensitive
BROWN	No specific chakra	Grounded, generous, calm, organised	Greedy, self-absorbed, close-minded
BLACK	No specific chakra	Unforgiving nature, past life issues, grief, health issues	Illness, depression, negative energy
GOLD	No specific chakra	Spiritual protection, enlightenment, wisdom, inner peace	None

How to feel your aura

Many people have felt the aura of others while standing in a crowd without even realising it. Have you ever wondered how to activate your aura and to feel the energy that is flowing within and around you?

With patience and practice you will be able to feel the energy of your aura within your hands.

Find a comfortable position within your sacred space. Lift up both of your hands and open your palms and fingers. Next, place both of your hands together palm on palm and finger to finger.

Gently and slowly rub your hands together ensuring that the middle of your palms touch; twist your hands side to side and ensure you have constant contact with the palms of your hands.

You should start to feel a warmth and energy build up between your palms. You may experience a buzzing, tingling, pulsing warm or hot sensation start to activate within your palms. Take your time and really focus on the energy as it builds. When you feel that there has been a significant energy shift, slowly start to pull your hands apart. Keep both of your palms facing each other as you do this.

Now, start to experiment and see how far you can separate the palms of your hands before you feel the energy disperse. Breathe calmly and focus on the energy within your palms. Visualise a ball of light or a ball of energy bouncing between your palms. With practice, you will be able to feel the energy as if it is a rubber ball or a ball of putty between your hands. Personally, it feels to me like I have a pair of magnets between my hands: if I put my hand one way the energy attracts and almost wants to stick together, if I turn them in a different direction, it feels like the energy is repelling itself in the same manner magnets do.

How to expand and contract your aura

Learning to expand and contract your aura is a useful tool. It can help you to push your aura out to expand your spiritual protective bubble so that you don't feel that others are in your space. Have you ever been in a crowd and felt like everyone else's energy was all over you? Have you felt claustrophobic and uncomfortable in other people's energy? Have you been on public transport, such as a train, plane or bus and felt the person beside you was in your space? I am sure you have all felt uncomfortable at some time in your life with this type of experience.

If you want someone to remove themselves from your energy, the following method will help you to understand how to expand your aura.

Firstly, close your eyes and breathe in slowly through your nose. As you do this, imagine your breath moving up from your nose and then moving up through to the top of your head and flowing out of your crown chakra. The easiest way to visualise this is to imagine you are a dolphin and you have a blowhole on the top of your head. Just as a dolphin exhales its breath through its blowhole, imagine yourself doing the same. As the breath leaves your body imagine it surrounding your entire being and expanding out to become a powerful forcefield of protection. By practising this exercise you will be able to expand your aura with each breath. Whenever you feel the need to protect yourself, use this visualisation method.

How to see your aura

Many people have felt the aura of others while standing in a crowd without even realising it. Have you ever wondered how you could tune in and really see the energy field of your aura?

As we have already discussed, there are seven auric layers. When you first try to tune into seeing your aura, you will see the outer layers. With patience and practise, you will be able to tune into the other layers as well.

Enter your sacred space. Subdue the light in the room – if you have blinds or curtains, close them slightly.

Sit comfortably where you will not be disturbed.

Do not sit in direct sunlight or have the light turned on in the room.

Breathe in and out three times, each time breathing in positive energy and light and exhaling any negative thoughts or fears.

Rub your hands together, ensuring that you consciously rub your palms together. Keep rubbing your hands together until you feel the warmth forming between your hands.

Turn both of your hands over so that your palms are facing you. Hold your hands approximately 30 cm away from your face. If possible, have a blank wall in front of you so that your eyes will not be distracted.

Gently spread your fingers apart and stare at your hands, focusing on the gap between your fingers.

It doesn't matter if you are drawn to your right or left hand, just let your eyes be drawn to whatever hand feels right.

You may feel if you are right-handed that you are drawn to your right hand or vice-versa if you are left-handed.

Sit quietly focused on the gap between your fingers. Be patient and watch as a fuzzy blue/white outline appears between your fingers. It can look a little like a mirage appearing before your eyes. What you are seeing is your auric field. If you continue to practise this exercise, you will be able to tune into the other auric layers.

It is also possible to measure the aura with divining rods. Please visit chapter 19: Divining with Pendulums and Dowsing Rods for more on this.

CHAPTER 5:

WHAT ARE CHAKRAS?

CHAKRAS ARE THE ENERGY SYSTEM contained within our bodies. There are seven major chakras located from the base of the spine to the top of the head. There are 21 minor chakras that are found throughout the body, predominantly along the trunk of the body, hands, head, knees and feet.

The word 'chakra' comes from an ancient Indian Sanskrit word meaning spinning wheel, vortex or circle. Chakras are the internal energy sources that assist in keeping the connection between our mind, body and spirit functioning properly. If any of our chakras are out of alignment and not in complete balance, our physical health can suffer as a consequence.

Each chakra has a different colour and frequency aligned to specific parts of the body. We will work through where each chakra is located, focusing on the colour and influences it has on the body. By being aware of your chakras and what they do for you, you will have a greater understanding of your emotions, thoughts and health issues.

Base/root – first chakra

Colour: red
Location: base of the spine (perineum)
Sense: smell
Crystals: garnet, ruby, bloodstone, red jasper
Element: earth
Glands/organs: kidneys, adrenals, spinal column, colon

Function: The base/root chakra is important to keep the body grounded and connected to the earth. The base/root chakra is connected to survival, physical body, safety and material matters. This chakra is what we access when we are in survival mode or physical danger. It influences our immune system, instincts, impulses and energy.

When functioning properly, the root chakra stimulates activity, gives us energy to exercise and gives us motivation. If you think this chakra is not functioning properly, you will not be grounded and you will feel scattered and disconnected. It can also cause you to feel tired, unmotivated and overly cautious about safety.

Sacral – second chakra

Colour: orange
Location: below naval
Sense: taste
Crystals: amber, citrine, coral
Element: water
Glands/organs: reproductive system, spleen, bladder and lower back

Function: The sacral chakra governs the emotional body. It influences our creativity, feelings, emotions, relationships and sexuality.

When this chakra is functioning properly, you will feel creative, imaginative, healthy and passionate about life. If the sacral chakra is not functioning properly, it can result in reproductive issues, bladder and kidney issues and addictive behaviour.

Solar plexus – third chakra

Colour: yellow

Location: above the navel, below the chest

Sense: sight

Crystals: yellow citrine, gold topaz, amber, tiger's eye

Element: fire

Glands/organs: liver, spleen, gallbladder, pancreas, stomach, nervous system

Function: The solar plexus is connected to personal power, confidence, energy and emotions. The solar plexus is where we connect to our psychic gift of clairsentience – gut feeling. It is also where we store our negative or positive emotions. Our solar plexus has an inner warning system that comes in the form of inner knowing and guidance. Psychic warnings can come in the feeling of butterflies or heaviness in the stomach.

When functioning properly, this chakra gives you the ability to believe in yourself and accomplish your goals. It helps you to be organised, able to cope with change and see life from a positive perspective. If the solar plexus chakra is not functioning properly, you will feel worried, nervous and negative. If unbalanced, this chakra can lead to health issues such as stomach ulcers, liver, pancreas and digestive problems. Emotional issues can manifest in anger and frustration.

Heart – fourth chakra

Colour: green (secondary colour is pink)

Location: centre of chest

Sense: touch

Crystals: emerald, green jade, malachite, green and pink tourmaline

Element: air

Glands/organs: heart, thymus gland, circulatory system, lungs, arms, hands

Function: The heart chakra is the connection to the physical and spiritual body. The primary feeling with the heart chakra is that of love, allowing us to give and receive unconditional love. It influences our spirituality, empathy, compassion, forgiveness and trust in others.

When functioning properly, this chakra gives you the ability to feel balanced and connected, allowing you to give unconditional love to others. It helps you to feel inner peace, joy and happiness. If this chakra is not functioning properly, you will have difficulty forgiving and feel unloved, unstable, emotional or suspicious. If the heart chakra becomes unbalanced, it can manifest in health issues such as heart problems, circulatory issues, lung problems and breathing issues.

Throat – fifth chakra

Colour: sky blue

Location: throat

Sense: speech

Crystals: turquoise, blue topaz, lapis lazuli, aquamarine

Element: ether/spirit

Glands/organs: thyroid, parathyroid, throat, mouth, teeth and immune system

Function: The throat chakra is connected to communication, self-expression, speech, sound and the psychic ability of clairaudience. This chakra assists with communication, dreaming, truthfulness, artistic and creative expression. People who are gifted speakers, writers, singers or are creative have a strong connection to their throat chakra.

When functioning properly, this chakra gives you the ability to be centred and happy. It assists you to connect to your higher self through meditation for spiritual guidance and gives you the strength to express yourself. If the throat chakra is not functioning properly, you can experience issues with communication, sore throats, earaches, thyroid problems, chronic fatigue, tiredness and depression.

Third eye (brow) – sixth chakra

Colour: indigo (dark blue)

Location: centre of the forehead between the eyebrows

Sense: intuitiveness and clairvoyance

Crystals: lapis lazuli, azurite, sapphire, fluorite, sodalite, clear quartz

Element: light

Glands/organs: pituitary gland, eyes

Function: The third-eye chakra is how we connect to our imagination, inspiration, psychic ability, intuition, higher self and inner guidance. The third eye gives you the ability to see inner visions through psychic insight and helps to connect you to your spirit guides and higher self. Through the practice of meditation, your third eye can open you up to the spiritual realm. This chakra gives you the ability to see that you have a higher purpose.

When functioning properly, this chakra enables you to be guided, connected and focused in your life. You have the ability to look at life with a bird's eye view, seeing life from a higher perspective. You will feel peaceful and be able to concentrate. If the third-eye chakra is not functioning properly you will feel unbalanced, suffer from headaches, migraines, eye problems, nightmares, forgetfulness and worrying unnecessarily.

Crown – seventh chakra

Colour: violet

Location: top of the head

Sense: extra sensory perception (ESP)

Crystals: amethyst, purple fluorite, clear quartz, diamond

Element: cosmic energy/spirit

Glands/organs: pineal gland, central nervous system

Function: The crown chakra is the central link to the spiritual universe and higher consciousness. It allows you to access spiritual wisdom and light connecting you to the Divine.

When functioning properly, this chakra allows you to feel balanced, free of ego and able to trust in the inner guidance from your higher self and spirit guides. This chakra links you to the connection of knowledge from the universe. It allows you to be at one with the Divine and guided in all you do. If the crown chakra is not functioning properly, you may experience issues with ego, fear and anxiety. You may suffer lack of inspiration, depression, self-doubt and frustration. Physical problems can manifest in the body as headaches, immune disorders, mental issues and anxiety.

Chakra alignment meditation

- Sit or lie down in a comfortable position. Gently close your eyes and focus on your breathing. Now, inhale slowly, and as you do this, imagine you are breathing in pure white spiritual light. As you exhale, imagine breathing out any negativity or stressful energy you may have been holding onto. Inhale slowly and visualise you are breathing in pure white protective spiritual light. As you exhale, imagine you are clearing yourself of any issues that are blocking your energy flow.

- Once again, inhale slowly and visualise you are breathing positivity and light to cleanse any blockages within you. Now, visualise that you are connected to Mother Earth and watch within your mind's eye as the earth beneath softens and your feet start to sprout like tree roots helping you to feel centred and grounded.

- Visualise light moving up from the earth beneath you and watch as the light enters through the soles of your feet moving up through your body. Visualise the light moving along your legs, up to your thighs and watch as it ignites a spinning ball of light in your base chakra. As the light reaches your base chakra, it turns a brilliant red.

- The spinning ball of light now glows brighter and brighter as it continues its journey up to your sacral chakra and turns into a brilliant orange.

- Now visualise the spinning ball of light moving up to your solar plexus and turning into a brilliant yellow.

- Feel the spinning ball of light moving up to your heart chakra and watch as it turns into a brilliant green ball of light.

- The energy of the spinning ball of light now moves up to your throat chakra and turns into a brilliant blue.

- Feel the energy of the spinning ball of light continuing to move up to your third eye, turning into a brilliant indigo.

- Visualise the energy of the spinning ball of light reaching your crown chakra and turning into a brilliant violet.

- Pause here for a moment and visualise the energy ball of light continuing to come up from your feet and moving through your entire body. Watch as all the colours of the rainbow expand and rotate as they flow throughout your body, and the energy moves and circulates throughout each and every space and cell within your being.

- Visualise as all the light expands and exits through your crown chakra. Feel the light connecting and grounding you to the earth, and feel it coming up through each of your chakra points clearing any blockages, negative thoughts, energies, or feelings you may have been harbouring within yourself.

- Feel any unwanted energy cascading away from within you as it spills out from your crown chakra. Watch as the energy evaporates into the ether as it clears all your chakras of any unwanted energy.

- Feel the energy around you now changing and you are bathed in a brilliant white light full of energy from above. This energy is such a brilliant white that it is hard to look at; the energy is warm, comforting and protective. Please take a few moments to stay in this place so that you can feel the connection you have with the light and the spiritual beings surrounding you.

• When you are ready allow the energy to surround you as you bring your awareness back into your sacred place.

• Remember this connection so that you can return to this sacred place at any time when you feel your chakras are blocked or unaligned.

• Be settled with the knowledge that whenever you need to realign your chakra points with this energy, you have the spiritual awareness to do so.

AFFIRMATION

My chakra points are all vibrating at the correct frequency, I am in perfect alignment with the universe.

CHAPTER 6:

WHAT IS PSYCHIC PROTECTION?

ONE OF THE MOST IMPORTANT THINGS to understand before doing any spiritual work is to undertake a process called 'psychic protection'. The more you progress with your spiritual journey the easier this process will become. With practice, protecting yourself with positive energy from the higher spirit realms will become second nature and in time you won't even have to think about it.

Psychic protection is an important step to stop you picking up any unpleasant entities or dark energies while you are doing psychic work. It will also help to prevent you from being overwhelmed with all of the energies you will receive from other people and the natural vibrations of the world.

If you don't protect yourself properly before undertaking any spiritual work, you could develop some of the following symptoms:

- Feeling emotionally drained and physically exhausted
- Feeling depressed
- Physical ailments arising, such as migraines, upset stomach

- Experiencing nightmares or negative thoughts
- Feeling angry without reason
- Feeling paranoid and unsettled
- Difficulty sleeping – nightmares and/or insomnia

While working with the spirit world you will be connecting to energy that is unseen yet very powerful. Imagine the image of a kitchen sponge being dropped into a sink full of water – watch how the sponge absorbs all of the water and becomes heavy and dense. The sponge becomes limp and drips any excess moisture that it can't absorb. If you don't protect yourself psychically, you can become like a human sponge that absorbs the unwanted energy of those around you, and your aura will become heavy and dense like the sponge and your chakras will become unaligned.

What is a psychic vampire?

Psychic vampires can reside here in the physical world as well as the spiritual world. It is important to be aware of when and where these vampires attach to your aura.

A psychic vampire is a person who will burden you with all of their problems, negative thoughts and emotions. They are people who live life with the view of the glass always being half empty rather than half full. They are always unhappy, depressed and can be quite hard to be around due to their lower vibration and heavy energy.

There are also psychic vampires in the spirit world that can attach to your aura when you are not protected. Both of these types of psychic vampires can drain your energy and lower your vibration or frequency, and disengage you from the higher spiritual realms and positivity in your life.

What is a psychic attack and how can it occur?

A psychic attack is when supernatural energies and entities are manipulated and used in a negative way against another. An attack can occur when energies that reside on the lower part of the astral plane are sent or attach to an individual's physical body or place.

Unfortunately, many people do not take the spirit world seriously and dabble with powers they do not understand. Harry Potter is a wonderful movie franchise that explores the spiritual world. However, it has given rise to many young viewers wanting to be like Harry and his friends, and seeking to have experiences with unknown forces in the spirit world. Casting spells and playing with Ouija boards has opened up many young people to the lower spiritual realms and a number of young people have ended up with psychic attachments and negative energies around them.

Would you pick up a hitchhiker on a lonely, deserted road without giving it much thought? I hope your answer to this question would be 'no!' Well, the same can be said about a Ouija board. You don't know who or what you are picking up or what the after-effects of this encounter might be.

These energies can be known as an entity, negative spirit, negative voices, negative emotions and negative thoughts.

Fear is one of the biggest causes of a psychic attack. Fear gives power to negative forces. An attack can bring on depression and isolation and even personality changes within an individual.

It is possible to have a psychic attack occur without being consciously aware of it. You may visit an historical area or home and feel that you are not alone. An attack can occur when a negative energy or entity from the spirit world attaches to your aura.

During your dream state, you can experience an attack by having vivid and frightening nightmares that you feel you cannot awaken from. This experience is commonly called 'sleep paralysis', and it may feel like pressure or a sense of choking. The person may feel that they are unable to speak or are pinned or held down in their bed. Sleep paralysis can be extremely unsettling and can cause the person experiencing it to feel frightened to go to sleep at night for fear of a reoccurrence.

If you experience sleep paralysis, I recommend you go to the clearing section of this book and follow the instructions for how to clear your home. I also suggest, before going to sleep each night, you do a protective white light meditation calling in your guardian angels to help you lift your vibration and ask them to protect and comfort you during the night.

Always remember that the light is always more powerful than the darkness. Fear is what feeds the negative energies around us. By being calm, settled and connected to the angelic realms, you will always be protected and safe.

The spirit world has many different levels of vibrations or what is known as frequencies that different energies reside within. Just as there are good and bad people in the world, there are similar levels of good and bad, light and dark, angelic and demonic in the spirit world.

If you are going to undertake a journey of any kind, it is always important to be prepared. If you were travelling overseas you would pack your bag accordingly and have the right insurance, paperwork and belongings. As you are beginning a journey on a spiritual level, it is also important to be prepared, protected and aware of the positives and negatives you may encounter along the way.

When I was first told I needed to protect myself psychically, I was told to 'white light'. I didn't even know what white light was, let alone know how to do it. I was told that I needed to sit and meditate, working with my chakra points so that I could call in my spirit guides and guardian angels. The thing is I didn't even know what a chakra point was. White light protection is the most common way to protect yourself from any negative energies or entities. It is a form of 'shielding' which protects your aura and surrounds your energy source with protective angelic light.

White light protection is easy to achieve. White light is made up of the seven colours of the spectrum: red, orange, yellow, green, blue, indigo and violet. These are the seven colours that are also present in rainbows and our aura. It is no wonder white light has such a positive effect on the human body.

Ways to protect yourself psychically

Psychic protection is something that can be achieved in a number of different ways. I found initially that what works for some people doesn't necessarily work for everyone.

Take these simple steps before beginning your work each day – breathe in the light, protect your aura, project positive thoughts and raise your vibration and connect to the higher realms. Call in your guides and guardians angels before you make contact with the spirit world.

Here are some examples for you to try out for yourself. The most important thing to remember is that you need to make a connection to your guardian angels and spirit guides to form your protection. As a team it will be up to you and your spirit helpers to decide what is or is not the best way to protect yourself.

Visualise beautiful pure white light showering down upon you from the heavens above. Surround your entire being with pure white light. Visualise any negative or dark energies being cleansed and removed by the light as it surrounds your body with protection.

Visualise your guardian angels surrounding you with their angelic light and enveloping you with their powerful wings to protect you.

Visualise yourself inside a white bubble or white cocoon of protection.

Imagine yourself bathing or swimming in protective light that surrounds you like a forcefield.

Imagine there is an invisible hole where the white light can enter at the top of your head. The invisible hole is located at your crown chakra and it is the colour violet.

Using prayer is one of the strongest connections you can make to the higher realms of spirit to protect yourself in the spirit world.

Using breathing techniques to breathe in the light and exhale any negative energy on the outward breath can enhance your protection from the spirit world.

Staying calm and thinking positive thoughts enhances the positive forces around you and your aura.

By having a shower every morning and every night you can enhance your connection to the spirit world.

There are times in life when you need extra psychic assistance to ensure that you are fully protected from the negativity of others around you, whether they are alive or in spirit. Visualising a mirror between you and the negative person can be an effective way of reflecting the negative energy back to where it came from. You can also imagine a cubed box that is lined with mirrors on each side, imagine the negative person inside the cubed box and close the lid – that way any negativity will not be directed at you.

If I ever feel I need a top-up of white light, or in moments where I may feel fear or danger, I will strengthen my connection to spirit and visualise the white light forcefield expanding around myself, my loved ones, car, home/office or surroundings.

Some people find that they feel more protected psychically by wearing their favourite cross, angel medal, talisman, pendant or crystal. If you have a special piece of jewellery or crystal that helps you to feel protected and connected, wear it. At different times in my life I have been drawn to different jewellery and crystals to wear. As you progress psychically, you will find that your needs change, and you will be drawn to different crystals and talismans or you may find that you don't need any protective items at all. Don't worry if this is the case for you, it is all part of your spiritual evolution. Different crystals have different frequencies and protective abilities. Consult one of the many excellent crystal reference books or internet sites to find out which crystal is best for your own personal protection.

Why drugs &/or alcohol is not a good idea while working with Spirit

Have you ever been out at a party or celebration and the people at the party want to talk about ghosts and spirits? Some people may even suggest it would be fun to play with a Ouija board or ask you to do readings for those at the party.

In many situations like this, people are under the influence of alcohol and/or party or prescription drugs. If this occurs, you need to be strong and tell them the answer is 'no!'. I would strongly advise you do not dabble with the spirit world, especially if you have been drinking.

Yes, I know that you will be more relaxed and will be able to tune in easily to those around you. You will probably pass on amazing messages to those you are reading for. However, have you thought about what levels of the astral plain you are opening up to? You could be connected to your angels and spirit guides, but you could also be opening up the doors to disaster by connecting to lower-level energies who could become attached to you.

People are more emotional when they are using substances, legal or otherwise. You may not be as discerning about what information you pass on if you have been drinking, or on the other hand, the person you are giving the message to may not process the information correctly and take the message the wrong way. The other downside is that you could end up connecting with lower entities that attach to you or the person being read for because of the entities attachment to alcohol and substances.

When a person passes away and becomes a spirit, they don't suddenly become an angel. Some people prefer to stay connected to the earth realm as they miss the life they had on Earth. They may have been addicted to drugs or alcohol and since their passing they realised they can't access either in the spirit realm. The only way they can access these human vices is to connect to a living person who is partaking in the consumption of the substance they love and miss.

So, next time you are asked at a social function to do a reading, play with a Ouija board and you are drinking socially, please stop and think. You don't want to take the energy of an alcoholic or drug user home within your auric field.

Psychic protection meditation

- Find a quiet place to sit and relax. You may wish to enter your sacred space physically or mentally. Gently close your eyes and slowly breathe in. Visualise breathing in positive uplifting energy. As you breathe out imagine that you are exhaling any negative emotions or energies you may have around you.

- Breathe in and out twice more and imagine each time you breathe in and out, you are expanding your connection to the spirit world.

- Visualise a beautiful bright white light surrounding your entire body. Now watch as this light expands to make you glow from its brightness.

- In your mind's eye, see this protective light entering your body via your feet. Watch as the light slowly moves up to your base chakra.

- As the energy reaches your base chakra, it turns a brilliant red. The light then continues to move up through your body and reaches your sacral chakra turning brilliant orange. Watch as the light continues up and reaches your solar plexus turning a brilliant yellow. Feel the energy moving up to your heart chakra as it turns a brilliant green. Allow the energy to progress and move up to your throat chakra turning a brilliant blue. As you feel the energy moving along your body, notice if there are any blockages. If there is any resistance, visualise the light cleansing and clearing the blockage. Watch as the energy now moves up to your third eye, turning a brilliant indigo. Continue to see the energy reach your crown chakra and becoming a brilliant violet.

- Take a few moments to feel the light filling your entire body with its cleansing purity. Feel the energy expanding throughout every part of your being, allowing you to be reconnected with your inner self.

- Visualise your guardian angels showering you with their spiritual light. Watch as the light completely engulfs your entire body in this uplifting and protective, bright spiritual light.

- As the light becomes brighter and brighter, feel your connection to heaven. Feel yourself connecting and ascending into the heavenly realms where you are protected and safe.

- Watch as your fears dissolve and melt away. You are now emanating your spiritual light for the entire world to see. Know that you are now protected and at one with the Divine.

AFFIRMATION

I ask for protection from my guardian angels.
I ask for any negative energies or entities to leave
my environment and return to the light. I am now
safe and protected by the higher realms of the spirit
world, together we are one.

CHAPTER 7:

ENHANCING YOUR CONNECTION TO YOUR GUARDIAN ANGELS

ANGELS HAVE EXISTED ON THE EARTH REALMS from the beginning of time. They have been seen and documented throughout all religions in all shapes and forms, and they are said to be winged beings who are sent from the heavens to protect and guide humans during their time here on Earth.

You just need to look back in time to the ancient records of religion, books and paintings to see what an influence these ethereal beings have had on all of our lives as human beings.

When we decide to incarnate on the earth realms, we are accompanied by our own special guardian angel. This special angel will accompany us throughout our lifetime, and they will leave the earth at the exact time that we do when we return to heaven.

Our guardian angel will never control us or tell us what to do during our time here on Earth. Your angel is here to accompany you with your earthly journey to guide, share knowledge and protect you during your journey. That being said, your angel will always allow you the free will to make your own life choices whether they be good, bad or indifferent.

I have many people tell me that they don't believe in angels as they feel that their own guardian angels have not protected them and guided them in the right direction. I have to say from my own experiences that my own angels have guided me and totally protected me. They have warned me, and if it wasn't for their presence in my life, I would be speaking with you from the other side. To be honest, I have not always heeded their advice only to later realise that I should have listened to them in the first place. I have had many close calls in my life, through my work, with health issues and while driving on the road. Thank goodness, my gorgeous winged messengers have always come through and been my wingman, so to speak, and they have kept me safe and well so I could continue my journey until my use-by date arrives.

Hindsight is such a glorious experience to look back upon. When I look back on some of my judgements, I now understand that what my angels were showing me were different pathways and outcomes of what my future life could be. This gift that they gave me also gave me the challenges and tests that made me the person I am today.

Please do not ever be angry with your angels or blame them for choices that you have made. Always remember that your angels will only give you the challenges or tests that you are capable of handling at that exact time in your life.

I look back now in my life at some of the more challenging things I have experienced only to realise how much stronger and spiritually developed I have become.

I have experienced seven near-death experiences and during these life-threatening events I have been privileged to meet amazing winged beings who have assisted me, given me healing and guidance and returned me

back to the earth realms. To be honest, I was brought up as a Catholic, but as I got older, I never really felt connected to the church.

On the other hand, I have always felt connected to angels and I feel so blessed when I receive an angelic message in the form of finding a feather, seeing angel number sequences, seeing an angelic cloud formation, and sensing and seeing angels surrounding me in my times of need.

I can't even put into words how blessed I feel at the experiences I have had my with my own guardian angels and those in spirit. My angels certainly have saved me from death in many situations. My angels have allowed me to see that they have a higher purpose for me to share their knowledge and gifts with you all.

In traditional religion, there is an angelic hierarchy known as the Nine Choirs of Angels. All angels are typically depicted as winged spiritual beings that do not possess a physical body. Angels have been reported to present themselves to humans in various forms since the beginning of time. Angels can be seen in human form, while others are represented as winged beings and beings of light. They may also appear to us in the form of divine guidance, either visually or through auditory methods, or as humans such as earth angels that appear in our lives exactly when we are in times of need. Each and every one of us has angels in their life even though they may not be aware of them.

Here is a list of the religious representation of the Nine Choirs of Angels.

The first sphere of the angelic realms

Seraphim: Their name means 'the burning ones', and they are said to be at the Throne of God. Seraphim are the highest order of the Nine Choirs of Angels, the defenders of the creator, and their job is to regulate the heavens.

Cherubim: Their name means 'fullness of knowledge'. Cherubim are the second highest angels in the Nine Choirs of Angels, the spiritual leaders in heaven, and they are the keepers of the Celestial records. Cherubim are known for their knowledge and wisdom and are connected to nature as a spiritual power.

Thrones: The third highest angels in the Nine Choirs of Angels, the Thrones are celestial creatures related to the Throne of God. They are considered to be the humble, peaceful authority of God's justice, and they have the ability to channel messages through your guardian angel when they have an assignment for you from God.

The second sphere of the angelic realms

Dominions: The Dominions' primary task is to organise the duties of the lower angels and to create order. Dominions are angels of leadership who mediate power between the Nine Choirs of Angels. Dominions govern over nations and they are the mediators of justice throughout the world and the universe.

Virtues: The Virtues are symbols of divine strength, they are known as the angels of grace. Virtues' primary task is to bring God's blessing to Earth and to assist in creating miracles. Virtues are associated with acts of heroism and bringing courage to those who need it. Virtues are known to be the shining or brilliant ones, they are the overseers of the stars, moon, sun and seasons, and they ensure that the universe remains in order.

Powers: The Powers are the warrior angels who defend against evil throughout the universe. The Powers' task is to prevent 'fallen angels' from taking over the world. Powers are the angelic protectors who assist in protecting mankind and keep the peace throughout the universe and the earth realm. Powers are also known to be the angels of birth and death.

The third sphere of the angelic realms

Principalities: The Principalities are known for their authority. They have command over the lower-level angels in the third sphere. They are known for granting blessings to the earth realm, and they are responsible for ensuring divine guidance from the higher realms are fulfilled. Principalities work closely with rulers and spiritual leaders on the earth. They are known to be the guides of nations, cities and large groups of people.

Archangels: The Archangels are the best-known angels of the angelic realms. Archangels are the conduit in which we, as humans, receive messages from God and the higher orders of the angelic realms. They assist us with knowledge, protection, heavenly guidance and communication. Archangel Michael is the head of the Archangels. There is much debate over just how many Archangels there truly are. In the bible, there are three Archangels in the third sphere: Michael, Gabriel and Raphael. However, in the book of Enoch it is listed that there are seven: Michael, Gabriel, Raphael, Uriel, Raguel, Phanuel and Sariel.

Angels: The Angels are the lowest choir in the hierarchy of the Nine Choirs of Angels. These are the common angels who are celestial beings recognised as the closest angel to us as human beings. They act as our guardian angels and they are with us to be of assistance. They are winged messengers who act as a bridge between heaven and Earth. Many believe that angels have not lived as human beings on the earth realm. An angel is sent by a supreme being for the purpose of delivering messages, to offer spiritual guidance and in some cases heal a physical ailment or to rescue a person from threatening circumstances. Angels are said to be spiritual beings created by a supreme being. There are many types of angels on this level of the hierarchy:

- **Ancestral guardian angels** are connected to you through your family – you may or may not have physically met them during their lifetime on Earth. Our loved ones can choose to act as our ancestral guardian angel after their passing. Some loved ones choose to act as an ancestral guardian angel for a family member even though they have already passed when the family member they guide is born. Many of us are connected to this ancestral guardian angel through having a name that is the same as theirs, such as our first or middle name. Ancestral guardian angels choose to be by our side to guide and inspire us. Even though our ancestral guides are in spirit, they are always watching over us and are a part of our earthly experience. This type of angel is not on tap 24 hours a day as they also have their own karmic journey to embark on. However, the most important thing to remember is that they are only a thought away. When you require their guidance or assistance, it is important to think the question you wish to ask them in your mind and you will be surprised by the answer you receive.

- **Guardian angels** are with us from birth and stay with us our entire life here on Earth. Their assignment to us during our incarnation is similar to how our spirit guides choose to be with us. Our guardian angels are with us to support, inspire and guide us on our life's journey. Our guardian angel cannot interfere with our life's choices, although they will do their utmost to guide us onto the right path. But we all have free will in our life and sometimes we need to make mistakes in order to learn valuable lessons.

- **Guiding angels** are angels who work with us along with our guardian angels. These guiding angels change as we evolve spiritually and have learnt our specific lessons in life. We can have many different guiding angels throughout our life as they evolve as we do.

Other angels can come into your life to assist you with the small and big moments of your life:

- **Parking angels** assist you to find a parking space.
- **Inspiration angels** assist you when you are writing or being creative.
- **Protection angels** assist when you are in a life-threatening situation. An example of this is when you are in a car and you almost have a car accident but somehow the accident was averted. Your angels can step in to save you.
- **Healing angels** assist when you have health issues, or are in need of guidance to heal mind, body and soul. You may encounter these angels when you need to find a new direction with your health

or to undertake a lifestyle change in order to live a healthier and happier existence.

- **Exam angels** can assist you when you are studying; they help you to absorb information to help you pass your exams.

- **Travelling angels** accompany you when you are on a trip to protect you during your travels.

- **Finding angels** assist when you have lost or misplaced something. They guide and show you where the item is and help it be recovered.

There are many different levels of angels in the angelic realm. Some of these angels vibrate at a much higher frequency than we as human beings can access. There are many books on this subject that you can read if you wish to go into this subject further.

Guardian angel meditation

- Enter your sacred space in preparation for your meditation. When you regularly enter this space, your angels will know that this is your meeting point. Also prior to meeting your angels think about what you would like to discuss during your time together.

- You may wish to light a fragrant candle or burn some incense to lift the energy. You may also wish to play some ethereal music that will also lift the vibration of the room.

- Always make sure that you have your journal and pen ready for when you return from your meditation to write down any information that is shared with you during your connection to your angel.

- Once you have entered your sacred space, gently close your eyes and be open to the heavenly connection that you are about to make with your angel. Take in a deep breath and feel your body relaxing and letting go of any stresses or worries.

- Start counting backwards from ten down to one, and as you do so, take a breath in and out. As you do this, focus on your breath. Breathe in slowly through your nose and exhale slowly and mindfully through your mouth.

- Remember that when you exhale, you are exhaling the energies that you no longer need to carry within you or your aura.

  ✎ 10 breathe in then gently breathe out.
  ✎ 9 breathe in then breathe out.
  ✎ 8 breathe in then breathe out.
  ✎ 7 breathe in then breathe out.
  ✎ 6 breathe in then breathe out.
  ✎ 5 breathe in then breathe out.
  ✎ 4 breathe in then breathe out.
  ✎ 3 breathe in then breathe out.
  ✎ 2 breathe in then breathe out.
  ✎ 1 breathe in then breathe out.

- As you finish counting from ten down to one, feel the calmness and peace that now surrounds you. In your mind's eye, visualise heavenly clouds gently floating above you. Watch as they change shape and notice fingers of light forming between the clouds. These gorgeous rays of light draw you towards them and you begin to feel yourself floating up into the clouds before you.

- As you get closer to the rays of light, a stairway appears, beckoning you to start to ascend the stairs up amongst the heavens. As you begin to take the first step, you feel as if you are floating, up and up and up. The light before you becomes brighter and brighter embracing you within its protective light.

- At the top of the stairway a beautiful winged being appears. This is your guardian angel who has powerful strong wings that glisten in the light. Your angel smiles at you and puts out their hand to assist you with your final steps of the ethereal staircase.

- Once you reach the top of the stairs you feel like you have been welcomed home and returned to your loving family that you have known forever. Your angel beckons you to follow them and to sit on a lovely ethereal cloud that looks like a puffy white pillow.

- As you take a seat, look around to see the heavenly images surrounding you. Pay attention and take note if there are any other angelic beings you recognise. Does anyone else feel familiar to you? Do you hear any heavenly sounds such as music or different frequencies? Do you smell any fragrances? What colours are surrounding you? Are the clouds simply white or do they have a colour palette? If they are coloured try to remember the colours for your future connection. Is it daytime or night-time? Are you up amongst the clouds or are you up amongst the stars?

- Now focus on the energy of your guardian angel. Pay attention and be aware of what they feel like, what do they look like, are they male or female? What colour eyes do they have? What colour hair do they have? What is their height? Are they taller or shorter than you? What colours are your angel's robes? Does he or she have any adornments connected to their robes? Are there any special pieces of jewellery or symbols they are wearing? Pay attention to how they communicate with you. Are they speaking to you verbally and if they are, what does your angel's voice sound like? Is it soft, strong, deep, comforting? Are they communicating with you telepathically through thoughts and symbols? Be aware of what you are hearing and seeing. Does your angel show you a special angel sign or talisman that lets you know from what part of the angelic realms they are connected to?

- While you are communicating with your guardian angel you may wish to ask their name. Ask your angel if they have any special messages they wish to share with you. Take this time to have a conversation with your angel and allow whatever is important for you to know right now to flow freely between the two of you.

- After you receive your angelic guidance from your guardian angel, thank them for connecting and protecting you through your spiritual journey.

- Bid your guardian angel farewell and know in your heart this heavenly encounter is one of many more to come. This sacred space is your heavenly place for your future heavenly interactions with one another.

- Your guardian angel now gets up and takes your hand, and you both slowly walk to the top of the heavenly staircase. Your angel ascends with you. Each step down brings you closer to the earth realms from where you came. Your guardian angel comes with you and guides you to your sacred space, and you start to become aware you are back in the location where you began your meditation.

- In your own time, bring your awareness back into your sacred space and feel the love and heavenly connection you have received from your guardian angel. Now, take a few moments to write, draw or record the information you have received in your journal in order for you to remember it for your future journeys.

AFFIRMATION

I am a being of light who is spiritually connected to
the heavens and the angelic realms.
I thank my angel for guiding, protecting and
instilling me with their angelic knowledge.
When I am with you I feel as light as a feather
and my heart soars to new heights.
I now know, I am never alone!

CHAPTER 8:

WHAT ARE SPIRIT GUIDES AND DO YOU HAVE ONE?

BEFORE WE ARE BORN WE ARE ASSIGNED a spirit guide who accompanies us into the earth realm. Your spirit guide will be with you your entire lifetime here on Earth and has accompanied you in past, present and future incarnations.

You may not always be consciously aware of their spiritual guidance, although you may at times get the feeling that you are not alone. Throughout your life you will realise that you are being divinely guided and cared for by your unseen protectors.

Ascended masters are spirit guides that have been gurus, teachers and people that were spiritually enlightened while living on the earth planet. Ascended masters are always available to humans on the earth realm for spiritual guidance and inspiration. They are available to channel evolutionary messages of guidance for the greater good of humanity. Many people have been inspired by the knowledge of the ascended masters.

Our main spirit guide is with us from our birth and others join us as we continue our life's journey from childhood to our final years. Our spirit guides are not here to tell us what to do, however they will step in and give us guidance and assistance when needed.

We all have free will and sometimes part of our spiritual journey is to learn from our mistakes. I am sure there have been times in your life that you made a decision but a little inner/outer voice told you that you were making the wrong choice. You then still went against the guidance and later realised you should have listened in the first place. Hindsight is such a wonderful thing, however what you must take from these types of experiences is that you were meant to learn something from the experience as part of your spiritual growth.

I am often asked the question: 'How many guides do we have?' The answer to this question is as many as you need.

In life your needs are constantly changing and so is the guidance you require. When you are young and have just entered into the physical world, your guidance is suited to the needs of a child. Did you have an imaginary friend? Many children do, and in fact they are not imaginary – they are spirit guides and helpers.

As I have already mentioned our life is supported by several guides who will stay with us throughout this lifetime. Our needs change during the different stages of our life as child, adolescent, adult and parent, and as we enter our elderly years, so some of these guides have already completed what they were assigned to do and there are others who are yet to be invited into our life to help. Sometimes we may need assistance from our guides of a physical nature. For example, we may need to find the right doctor or find the right person to help us on the physical plane. At other times in our lives we may need a specific connection with a spirit guide who will make a connection with us as we are facing a crisis. These types of guides may come and go as the need arises.

Did I know my spirit guides in a previous life?

When you are embarking on a project and you want the best advice possible, you would seek out the help and support of those you can trust completely. Even after being given the advice, you only take on the advice that you feel comfortable with.

When you enter the physical world you know that the clear spiritual vision you had in the spirit world will be obscured. So why would you not enlist the help and support of those spirit guides with whom you can trust your life with, your spiritual life? Now think who in your physical life do you trust so completely that you would entrust them with your life itself?

The love and trust that existed between you and your spirit guides in the spirit realm knows no boundaries between the physical or spiritual realm. Your connection is just as strong and can span many lifetimes shared together. Sometimes the connection you have with them has been established during a time of learning while on the spiritual plane.

Your learning is not restricted to the physical plane – much of your growth has been achieved during your time in the spirit world.

Why do spirit guides appear to us in human form?

Even though our spirit guides are beings of light, they present themselves to us in human form because it is more acceptable to present in this manner and we are more likely to relate to them. Ascended masters and higher beings may present themselves as a colour or light being – this is to indicate their level of spiritual development.

There is a popular myth that a spirit guide will always appear to us a wise guru, for example, or an Indigenous elder, Egyptian goddess, Chinese wise man or American Indian. They have long flowing hair and beards; they wear antique robes with elaborate head dresses or colourful feathers in their hair; they are usually old and always speak with deeply profound words of wisdom.

Without being dismissive, have you ever considered the possibility that a guide could just as easily come from a cattle farm? He could be a happy Australian who enjoys a beer at the local pub. His language might be a little colourful, he might not be particularly wealthy, he might not have a university degree, and he might not understand all about karma and the after-life.

But he enjoys his communication with nature and his friends and family, and that's the extent of his spiritual thoughts. This doesn't make him any less valuable as a source of knowledge and understanding if he possesses the answers to the questions you seek.

Our spirit guides are souls who have lived a variety of lives before. A guide could have been a poor farmer or an all-knowing being. The guidance you receive from your spirit guide does not lie in their physical appearance. What's more important is the individual's soul knowledge and what they can teach you in your present life to smooth your journey while here on Earth.

Many people don't ever see their spirit guides, they may simply feel them. Some people may smell a certain fragrance of a flower or incense; others may feel a wonderful light breeze around them or the feeling of a comforting warmth.

Sometimes people don't feel anything but their minds go into another realm and they are able to access information through thought alone. Your spirit guide's physical appearance isn't really that important, unless it matters to you. If it's important to you, then your guide will understand and they will manifest themselves to you in whatever form they feel you can most easily identify with.

If it is important for you to know their name, you will be told what it is. Your guides have the wisdom of spiritual knowledge and they will draw upon that knowledge when determining your needs.

If you are passionate about Egyptian mythology and feel a deep connection with the Pyramids, your guide will more than likely show themselves to you as an Egyptian god. Your guide will appear to you in that form to make you feel more secure and comfortable. If you are feeling unsure about the whole existence of spirit guides and uncertain whether you can cope with this new discovery, your guides will come to you in the most gentle and subtle way until you feel you are ready to accept their guidance.

What are your guides here to teach you?

The answer to this question is that each lesson your guide teaches is individual to your own spiritual path. Therefore, each person's experience with their guide is a deeply personal one. No two people have the same guides or the same lessons to learn, as we are all unique beings. It is important to remember that you don't need to compare your spiritual progress with anyone else, as this is irrelevant. Different people will progress at different levels according to how well they learn each lesson their guide has to teach them.

The common thing for all of us is that our spiritual journey will be a gentle, loving experience, as our guides are here to protect and guide you. Your guides assist you to open up your mind to new possibilities, allowing you to embrace the energy from a higher source. Your guide is with you offering you true unconditional love that is uplifting and inspiring. They have the infinite wisdom of spiritual infinity and all of the knowledge to draw upon when they determine what best suits your needs. They allow you to receive a reflection of spiritual wisdom.

All of us have protective guides, but many of us never learn how to tune into them. By forming a connection with your spirit guides, you increase their ability to protect you. This is, of course, true for all your guides.

By learning how to acknowledge your spirit guides' presence and work more closely with their energies, you give yourself a greater opportunity to learn and to grow spiritually.

We also have guides that come into our lives for shorter periods and they will have a specific role to play in your spiritual development. When you have learnt what is needed from them, they will then move on to other people and continue their own cycle of assistance. This also allows the guide to continue their own spiritual evolution in the spirit realm.

Why do different people see different guides?

Different mediums may see different guides to what you see, according to the spiritual vibration level they are working on. At times, certain guides may come through to a medium to deliver a specific message to you, if they find it difficult to give you the message directly.

The guide working with you at any moment reflects your own spiritual place and the vibrations you are working with. As you grow, so your spiritual guidance changes. You may have noticed that the energies of your guides have changed during your own period of spiritual development.

We are all energies of light and love on our journey of spiritual growth and learning. Every being has their own spirit path – the more you grow spiritually the more the vibrations of your energy changes. When you meditate to contact your guides, you raise your vibrations to meet your guide's energy.

Does guidance come in any other form?

If you do not take the time to communicate and listen to your guides, they will use other methods to reach you. Your spirit guide may give you messages via a friend's timely advice, a dream, a song that keeps playing in your head. It could be through repetitive symbols or number sequences. Some guides give you messages in the form of birds, animals or insects.

Many indigenous tribes have contact with the spirit world through connecting to their spirit guides as power animals and animal totems. This type of spirit guide provides protection and guidance for shamans and priests during their spiritual journeys.

Mythological creatures and nature spirits such as fairies can also be another way for your guides to get your attention. Each message is unique; it doesn't matter which method your spirit guides use to get your attention to give you the information. What matters the most to them is that they make a connection to give you the guidance and inspiration that you need.

The elemental realm

There are also elemental spirits who work with us during our life. These gentle energies have been part of people's lives since the dawn of time. Many think of them as mythical creatures that are part of folklore. It is only when you begin to take the time and pay attention that you realise that these special little spirits are with us when we are amongst nature.

Our elemental realm is governed by nature. I am sure many of you will have had a connection to nature and the fairy realm as a child. It is only as we grow older that we lose touch with them as we are told that these special spiritual creatures do not exist.

Fairies, elves, gnomes and goblins are earth spirits who are connected to flowers, plants, trees and the earth. For those of you who grew up in Australia the elemental realm also consists of the gumnut and wildflower babies that were written about by May Gibbs. These special spirits will connect with you while you are in nature.

Their ethereal guidance and energy is a blessing to have in your life. The elementals live their life to guide human beings as a species to understand and look after the flora and fauna in their fragile natural surroundings. In ancient times people would connect with nature spirits to heal and ground themselves.

Animal and bird spirits

Animal and bird spirits are very much a part of our human life. Many people do not always appreciate or understand the spiritual guidance a pet alive or in spirit can give to them through the spiritual realms. For those who may not have the opportunity of having a human child in their life, they may be blessed with having a four-legged fur baby or a winged baby who is very much a part of their family. When their animal, bird or other form of pet passes they can also make contact with their loving owner from the spiritual realms.

It is extremely common to receive messages from our loved ones in spirit via the messages from an animal or bird symbol. At other times the guidance can come directly from the animal in spirit. This type of animal spirit can act as your power animal who protects and guides you.

The mythical realm

Mythical creatures such as dragons, unicorns, mermaids and water spirits – just to name a few – are also guides that can connect with you to guide and protect you.

Confusing spirit guides with ghosts

When a person passes away and joins the spirit realm, they do not automatically become a spirit guide or guardian angel. If a person chooses to have negative energy around them when they are alive, they can continue to attract the same energy when they pass away.

This being said, a person who was negative in life can also become enlightened and choose to work in the higher spiritual realms after passing. However, some people can confuse the energy of spirits around them as a spirit guide when in actual fact they have an attachment from a ghost.

A ghost can come in the form of fragmented energy that is confused about their birth force. They may have passed over and don't realise they are in actual fact dead. Or in other cases they choose to stay attached to the earth realm as they really enjoyed being alive and do not wish to continue their spiritual growth and evolution in the spiritual realm. They may be fearful to evolve because of their actions while they were alive on Earth.

In this case, this type of energy can choose to attach to a living person, so they feel they are still alive and connected to the earth realm. If you ever feel that you are in the company of a ghost/spirit, it is important to ask the spirit to go to the light, so they can continue their spiritual journey. It is not positive to have the connection of a ghost/spirit attached to you, as they will make you feel drained and spiritually disconnected. They may give you guidance and messages but these will not be for your highest good. A true spirit guide is with you to give you uplifting spiritual guidance. Any messages your guides give you is for your utmost benefit, whereas an earthbound spirit will selfishly give you messages for their own higher good and not your own.

The way to tell the difference between a spirit guide and a ghost is the energy of a spirit guide is uplifting, light, positive and inspiring. The energy of a ghost is of heaviness, loneliness, sadness, depression and sometimes even anger.

It is important to protect yourself psychically with white light to lift your vibration above the lower spirit realms, as this is where negative spirits and lost souls reside. When you lift your vibration, the negative spirits won't be able to make contact with you.

Preparation meditation to work with your spirit guides

As discussed in earlier chapters, remember to always protect yourself with white light before entering into any work with the spirit world. Prior to undertaking this meditation exercise, clear your sacred space and sit in it mindfully. Think about the questions you may wish to ask your guide when they make their presence known to you. Have your journal and pen ready for when you return from your meditation to write down any information shared with you during your connection to your spirit guide.

Try to do this meditation daily at the same time each day. Before you begin, visualise that you have a regular booking to meet your spirit guides.

- Now, gently close your eyes and be open to the adventure you are about to embark on.
- Take in a deep breath and feel your body relaxing and letting go of any stresses or worries.
- Start counting backwards from ten down to one, and as you do so, take a breath in and out. As you do this, focus on your breath. Breathe in slowly through your nose and exhale slowly and mindfully through your mouth.

- Remember that when you exhale, you are exhaling the energies you no longer need to carry within you or your aura.

  - 10 breathe in then gently breathe out.
  - 9 breathe in then breathe out.
  - 8 breathe in then breathe out.
  - 7 breathe in then breathe out.
  - 6 breathe in then breathe out.
  - 5 breathe in then breathe out.
  - 4 breathe in then breathe out.
  - 3 breathe in then breathe out.
  - 2 breathe in then breathe out.
  - 1 breathe in then breathe out.

- As you finish counting from ten down to one, feel the calmness and peace that now surrounds you. Now focus your eyes on a beautiful glistening path that is situated in a gorgeous green meadow filled with wildflowers blooming before you. The path is made of white pebbles, and as the sun hits the pebbles, they radiate a gorgeous white glow, drawing you along the path on the beginning of your journey.

- Feel the sense of excitement within your solar plexus as you anticipate getting closer to meeting your spirit guide.

- Slowly start to walk along the path and pay attention to your surroundings. What type of flowers do you see? Do you hear any birds singing in the distance? Are there any butterflies or dragonflies flying amongst the flowers? Can you smell the fragrance of the flowers and hear the bees buzzing happily as they collect pollen from each of the flowers in the meadow?

- As you walk a little further along the path, you see a beautiful majestic fig tree with giant roots that are anchoring it to the earth. This tree towers above you and its powerful branches reach up and out to the sky above.

- As you walk closer, you notice that there is a bench seat that is big enough for two to sit on. You walk up to the bench and you take a seat. You are now sitting quietly beneath the magical tree of wisdom. Feel the tree's energy and knowledge surrounding you with protective spiritual light as it towers above you.

- In the distance, a shimmering light starts to appear on the pathway that you have just travelled. As you focus your eyes on the shimmering light, you begin to see the silhouette of a spirit being walking towards you. The spirit being comes closer and appears in front of where you are sitting.

- They are smiling warmly at you. As you smile back at the being, there is a sense of familiarity about them. You have the feeling that you have met this being before and you can feel an overwhelming love emanating towards you. You motion for them to take a seat beside you.

- This intelligent being introduces themselves as your spirit guide and tells you they have been with you for many lifetimes. Your spirit guide informs you they are to accompany you on your current spiritual life journey and they ask you if there is anything you would like to ask them.

- Your spirit guide tells you what their name is and then they begin to give you visual images of your future journey ahead. Pay attention as the information floats before your mind's eye. Are there any symbols, signs, colours, numbers, sounds, fragrances or music that you are being given at this time?

- Pay attention to what your spirit guide is wearing. Do they look like they come from a specific time in history? What colour hair do they have? What colour eyes do they have? What cultural background do they have? Are they male or female? How tall are they? Do they speak with you verbally or through mental thought? Are they wearing any specific type of jewellery or adornments? What type of shoes are they wearing, if they are wearing shoes?

- Pay attention to how you are feeling when you connect with your spirit guide. What is the temperature of the energy around you when you are connecting to your guide? It is hot or cold?

- After you receive your spiritual guidance from your spirit guide, thank them for connecting and protecting you through your spiritual journey.

- Bid your spirit guide farewell and ask them to meet you in this sacred meeting place in future, if you wish to make connection with them again.

- Sit and watch as your guide gets up from the bench and slowly walks back in the direction from which they came.

- Remain on the bench under the tree of knowledge for a few moments and contemplate the information you have just received. When you have gathered your thoughts, walk back along the white pebbled path through the meadow and back to where your journey began. When you arrive at your starting destination, notice the energy shift and become aware you are now back where you began your meditation.

- In your own time bring your awareness back into your sacred space, and notice that you feel energised and spiritually guided by the information you have received from your spirit guide.

- Write, draw or record the information you have received in your journal to remember it for future journeys.

AFFIRMATION

I welcome the presence of my spirit guide into my
life. I am open to your spiritual
guidance and insight. Each time we make contact
our connection strengthens.
Together we are one.

CHAPTER 9:

SIGNS FROM ABOVE

THE SPIRIT WORLD GOES TO GREAT LENGTHS to let us here on the earth plane know that we are not alone. On a daily basis we are bombarded with images, signs, symbols and number sequences from spirit that many of us don't even notice. During this chapter I will discuss what you need to look out for to enhance your connection to the spirit world.

What are the signs from spirit?

Spirit uses many ways to make contact. When those in spirit are trying to get your attention, they will use whatever resource they can find. You have probably already been given signs from above today, but if you don't know what to look for, you may not have noticed.

So, what do you need to do to receive signs from above? 'Believe!'

Once you believe that anything is possible, then so it will become. The next step is for you to be open and aware of what is taking place and pay attention to any subtle changes around you.

The signs we receive from our angels and loved ones will not always be in the form of a lightning bolt coming to you from above, although signs like this have been known to take place. The signs are usually subtle and will involve everyday items, symbols and sounds that we tend to take for granted.

We don't need to live our life hesitantly waiting to make a decision only when we receive a sign from above. It is better to think that the signs we receive are confirmation that we are on or off the right path in life.

Not all signs will be the same for everyone, however there are signs and symbols such as feathers, birds, animals, insects, coins, heavenly messages in the clouds and rainbows of reassurance that tend to be a common message from above to all.

Angelic feathers

Angels are constantly around us – it is only when you start to pay attention that you will see the signs. How many times have you seen a feather floating down before you or found a feather in a place where you know there aren't any birds? I have many clients tell me they believe in angels, although they feel they don't have a guardian angel because their angels never give them signs. It is only when I explain to them what to look for that they realise the signs were there all along.

Feathers, especially white ones, are a common sign that mysteriously appear from nowhere to let you know that your guardian angels, loved ones and spiritual helpers are nearby. These subtle signs give us reassurance that we are on the right path and that we are not alone.

Don't be surprised if you find fluffy white feathers of various shapes and sizes appear when you are in need of angelic help from above. Angels are beings gifted with flight, so it is wonderful to receive a message that they have flown down to be by your side. For those who are sceptical, yes, in reality feathers really come from our bird friends. Questioning where they come from is not what matters most; it is more important to see the signs and feel the joy when you receive your special gift.

From my own personal experience, I have found that when I find white or coloured feathers, I am receiving positive uplifting signs from my angels, loved ones and guardian angels.

However, if I keep finding grey or black feathers, it is a sign that I am being warned that a possible negative experience may be on its way.

It is important for you to distinguish what the different coloured feathers mean to you personally. Depending on the connection to your angels and spirit guides and your belief system, the colours will have different meanings.

For example, if you have a spirit guide who is a Native American Indian, a black feather could mean a positive sign from your guide, as the black crow is a sacred bird to that culture.

When you find a feather, always ask your angels what the feather means. When you ask your angels, pay attention to the first message that pops into your mind. How does the message feel? Does the image of a loved one pop into mind? Is the message confirmation of an answer to a question you have asked your angels or loved one? If you still don't understand why you received the feather continue to ask your angels and loved ones. The message could be as simple as letting you know that you are not alone.

It is also good to communicate with your angels and ask them specifically to give you a sign. You may specify what that sign should be or you could be open to receiving whatever message they choose to give you. The most important thing to remember is to be open-minded to the signs from your beautiful winged messenger. Here are some examples of angelic feathers appearing:

- You are walking in a deserted street and a feather floats down in front of you even though there aren't any birds flying nearby.

- While you are driving in your car, you stop at traffic lights and a feather gently floats down and rests on your car bonnet.

- You arrive home from work to find a feather neatly placed at your front door.

- There have been issues at your workplace and when you arrive at work a little feather is sitting on your desk.

- It is the anniversary or birthdate of a loved one in spirit and you find one or possibly multiple feathers during the day to remind you that you are not alone.

- You or a loved one are undergoing an operation and you find a feather in the hospital room.

- While travelling a long distance in your car, the car is surrounded by feathers. You know that you didn't hit any birds yet there are feathers everywhere. This is a sign that your angels and loved ones are accompanying you on your journey.

- A loved one has passed and you are feeling upset and question if your loved one is OK in spirit. You are surprised by a feather floating down beside you.

Heavenly cloud formations

Our angels, spirit guides and loved ones in spirit utilise cloud formations to give us symbols from above. Have you ever been outside in the garden and laid on your back looking up at the sky? Did you see anything appearing in the clouds above? If you looked long enough and paid enough attention you could be surprised by what you see. There are many signs and symbols that will manifest in the clouds – feathers, wings, angels, religious figures or religious symbols, the face of a lost loved one or pet. You may even see heart-shaped clouds appearing letting you know how much you are loved.

Cloud gazing can be a form of day-dreaming where you ask questions of your current life situations and the answers will be shown to you in the clouds. This type of symbol doesn't always happen instantaneously but if you are patient signs from above will appear.

Cloud gazing is a wonderfully relaxing way to receive confirmation and reassurance that you are being guided by higher beings from above.

Rainbows

Rainbows are magical coloured signs from above. There are legends that have foretold of being able to find a pot of gold at the end of the rainbow. In true essence seeing a rainbow is really the pot of gold. Rainbows can mysteriously appear when you least expect them.

Seeing a rainbow incites happiness, inner peace, joy and leaves you feeling uplifted. The symbol of a rainbow is a sign that all of your cares and worries are being taken care of by your angels and loved ones.

A rainbow is also the bridge between heaven and Earth. It is the gateway for those in spirit to reconnect with the living. Seeing a rainbow is truly a gift from above. What better way for your angels and loved ones to get your attention.

A rainbow doesn't always need to appear in the sky, you may see rainbow lights appearing inside your home reflecting on photographs and pictures. Rainbows may shine through the window reflecting upon the wall. Rainbows can appear within water reflections, puddles and soap bubbles.

A rainbow is made up of seven colours that vibrate on a spiritual level. Rainbows are a big part of our lives as they are a sign of unity, peace and love. The seven chakras contained within the human body and the seven auric layers that surround the body are the colours of the rainbow.

Sunrises and sunsets

Sunrises and sunsets are the artistic canvasses that our angels use to give us peaceful colourful connections to the heavens above. The angels also give you symbols of their connection via rays of light that appear during sunrise and sunset. This type of symbol looks like rays of light from heaven (they are also known as fingers of light) that act as a doorway from above. How many times have you enjoyed the connection to spirit while watching a sunrise or sunset? I am sure there have been many. These beautiful gifts from above take us into another realm, giving us a peaceful reminder that something greater exists outside of ourselves.

Moving pictures

How many times have you passed by pictures on the wall in your home to notice that they are repeatedly crooked when in fact nobody has touched them? This can be a sign from above that can be quite annoying. As we have been discussing, spirit will use whatever means they can to get your attention. So, if you are a little fussy about your pictures hanging straight on the wall then this will be a way for them to get your undivided attention. Next time you notice that your pictures have moved, acknowledge this to your loved ones and let them know you are aware they are close by. You may even wish to ask them what it is they are trying to tell you.

Angel touch

Angel signs can be subtle – at times of great sorrow and distress, our angels can present themselves through sensation and touch. Have you ever been upset about a certain situation in your life and you suddenly felt a beautiful warm feeling surrounding you?

Angel touch can feel like a soft brush on your face, arm, back or neck. It can feel like a tingling sensation on the side of your head, back of the neck or down one arm. Here are some examples of angel touch:

- An invisible kiss is placed on your cheek even though you are alone.
- The feeling of a gentle touch is felt on your face or hand as a sign of reassurance.
- A warm feeling envelopes your entire being, as if you are being hugged.
- While you are asleep, you feel as if someone is lying beside you in bed with their arms around you.
- A warm presence joins you while you are sitting quietly on the lounge.
- A gentle breeze passes by you as if a living person just walked by.
- You may be walking alone in an isolated area when you experience the feeling of being protected by an unseen being.
- While driving in the car, an incident occurs where another car could have collided with your vehicle. An unseen touch guides your hands on the steering wheel to evade the collision.
- You are day-dreaming and not paying attention when a gentle breeze suddenly appears before you to get your attention of imminent danger.

Angel melodies

Angels and loved ones in spirit love to give you concise and clear messages through music and sound. The words contained within many songs are sent to you from above. You may even feel as if the song was written especially for you. You may be questioning if you are on the right path and you will hear a song that contains the answer to what you were looking for.

How many times have you thought about a loved one and their favourite song suddenly begins to play? You may be driving along in the car and your mind gently wanders off into a daydream and a song starts playing on the radio that reminds you of someone you miss very much. What is even more surprising is that the song is not part of the current hits. When this happens, it is a sign that your loved one is close by.

Angels can appear to you through heavenly music or the singing from an angelic choir in your ear or within your mind. Your angels and loved ones are with you more than you think, so don't be surprised to realise that they are aware of your thoughts, hopes, fears, worries and dreams. At times, the answers you seek will appear instantaneously through music. Certain phrases that are special to you will suddenly jump out of a song to get your attention.

Music is such a big part of life on the earth realm, it can raise your vibration and lift your spirits. Significant songs can remind us of significant times in our lives. A song can remind us of our loved ones who have passed. The verses of a song can include angelic messages that feel like they are especially meant for you.

Angels will utilise any item that plays music to get their angelic melodies across. So the next time you are travelling in the car, watching the television, shopping at the supermarket, travelling in the lift at work or hear a random mobile phone ringing, listen to what music is playing. It just might be an angel melody trying to get through to you. Here are some examples of angel melodies:

- You are travelling in the car and a song that reminds you of a loved one keeps playing on the radio.

- You have asked your angels for confirmation that you have made the right decision and songs about angels keep playing on the radio.

- Heavenly choirs suddenly begin to play in your mind.

- You have a decision to make about your career when music with the answer to your dilemma begins to play in the elevator you are in.

- It's the birthday of a deceased loved one, and you wonder if they know you are thinking about them. A song that contains the words 'Happy Birthday' begins to play.

- You are feeling sad and wonder if your angels and loved ones are nearby. Everywhere you go you hear songs with angel meanings within them.

- It is the anniversary of a loved one's passing and their favourite song keeps playing on the radio.

- Songs that were played at a loved one's funeral are often heard to remind you of them.
- The television program you are watching contains music with angelic messages.

Angelic voices

Our angels go to great lengths to protect us. When you are in need of angelic guidance your angel will speak to you either directly or through words that pop into your head. Have you ever been sound asleep and woken to someone calling out your name? When you open your eyes there is nobody around. Hearing angelic, disembodied voices is something that most of us have experienced at one time or another in our lives. Your angels will contact you at times of imminent danger or times of great need.

Angelic voices will appear to you in a loud and clear manner. There will be no mistaking where the message comes from when you hear it – they will be direct warnings or guidance.

Your angel will talk to you to give you warnings about decisions in life. By being open to hearing you will be more in tune with this form of communication. This type of communication is a form of clairaudience.

It is not uncommon for people who have experienced a near-death experience or out-of-body experience to report hearing the voices of their guardian angel or loved ones. Angels are the messages from above and they are known to guide us between worlds. When someone is close to passing, yet it is not their time to die, it is their angel who will tell them that they need to return to the living.

Books, magazines and newspapers

Have you ever felt that your angels and loved ones were trying to get your attention through printed material? You may be questioning a situation in your life or wanting to find the answer to a question. Angels have been known to make books fall off shelves to give you the message you are meant to read. They will also use magazines and newspapers to get their message across.

Next time you are at the local library and a book jumps off and falls at your feet, it is a sign that something important is written inside the book.

If you feel drawn to buy a particular magazine even though it is not something you would normally read, take it as a sign that there is an angelic message within for you to discover.

Coins (pennies) from heaven

Coins from above (also known as 'pennies from heaven') are a sign from our loved ones. Your loved ones will leave coins as a calling card to let you know that you are not forgotten and they are aware of your situation.

This heavenly currency is a sign that your spiritual friends are close at hand. Often coins will appear when you are worrying about your finances. Those in spirit will leave you this sign to tell you to stop worrying about your finances as you will be OK.

Next time you find a coin on the ground remind yourself that it has been sent as a special reminder from heaven. Acknowledge the gift and thank those in spirit for their message.

If your loved one uses this type of symbol to let you know they are around, collect the coins in a special jar. You may be surprised by just how much wealth they shower you with during the year.

One of my clients relayed a beautiful message about coins from above to me. This gentleman came to me for a reading, as his darling wife had recently passed from a long battle with breast cancer. His wife had a cheeky sense of humour. During the reading I kept being shown five cent pieces. Actually, I could see the image of hundreds of five cent pieces being showered down from above.

When I mentioned this to my client, he told me that everywhere he went in his home he would find five cent pieces. When he made the bed, he would find five cent pieces amongst the sheets, and when he did the washing they would appear in the washing machine. If he did the vacuuming, they would appear on the floor. At the end of the reading, his wife told me to tell him that she was giving him a tip in five cent pieces for taking such good care of the housework since she had passed away.

My one fear of this kind of heavenly communication is that, in this day and age, we are starting to phase out the use of coins and cash as our currency. We are more likely to pay for things digitally, and we tend to 'tap and go' with our payments for items. The one positive about our 'pennies from heaven' is the angels are so clever about getting their messages across, I am sure they will find coins in some form to show us they are with us.

Angel fragrances

Fragrances are another way that our loved ones try to get our attention. Have you ever smelt a fragrance, scent or smell that reminded you of a passed loved one? Your loved ones in spirit will use a familiar fragrance you can identify them by. Everyone has their own personal fragrance that identifies them. When loved ones in spirit come to visit you, they will use these fragrances and scents to let you know they are close by.

Common fragrances that you may smell include hairspray, perfume, aftershave, soap, boot polish, hair oil, smoke, cooking smells and deodorant. Pay attention to when these heavenly fragrances appear around you, as they are a sign that your loved ones are coming to be by your side.

It is amazing what memories can be stirred when we receive the fragrances of loved ones past.

Your angels may use the fragrances of common flowers in your garden. Have you ever smelt the strong aroma of roses, gardenias, violets or lavender around you when there aren't any flowers nearby? This is a sign that your angels are trying to get your attention and let you know they are nearby.

Angelic dreams

Your angels, spirit guides and loved ones are inventive when it comes to finding ways of making contact with you. If they can't get your attention during your waking hours, they will most certainly attempt to contact you through your sleep.

Angels, spirit guides and loved ones in spirit will often come to visit while you are sleeping. After all, anything is possible in a dream. When we are sleeping we are more open and relaxed than when we are awake. It's the perfect time for our spiritual friends to make contact. We are not really thinking about what is taking place in the dream as we are too busy being a part of the connection.

How often have you woken up from an amazing dream feeling uplifted and totally alive? The dream felt so life-like that on awakening you questioned whether or not it was really a dream or life experience. During your dreams, it is possible to communicate with your loved ones in spirit. They will appear to you happy, alive and well. They may communicate important messages from the other side. They can also offer you guidance and support in your times of grief.

Your angels and spirit guides may join you while you are sleeping so that they can show you other realms. You may even feel as if you are up amongst the clouds flying through the heavens. Your angels can take you to the 'halls of learning' to teach you spiritual knowledge and offer you guidance.

Next time you are drifting off to sleep, be open to receiving angelic messages and remember what dreams may come, as they are messages from above.

Angel numbers

Angelic messages are often sent to us by our angels through number sequences. These number sequences can be seen on everyday objects that are with us on a daily basis – on clocks, car number plates, receipts, buildings and billboards, as well as in emails, telephone numbers, addresses, birthdays, anniversaries and so on.

When you think about it our entire world is run by numbers, so what better way for your angels to get your attention? The numbers may come to you with repetition of the same number or they may be repetitive sequences that are shown to you in many different forms.

For example, the sequence 11:11 may appear to you. You may be drawn to look at the clock at 11:11 or you may keep waking up at the time of 11:11. The car in front of you has 11:11 in the number plate. This is a sign that your angels are trying to give you a message.

If a loved one is in spirit, they may have passed at 11:11 and are reminding you that they are by your side.

This form of angelic message is one of the more difficult forms to decipher. It is important when you receive this type of message to remember how you feel when you see the numbers. Do the numbers have a significant date that you need to pay attention to? Was it a birthdate or anniversary, or is it a date in the future you need to remember?

If you don't understand the message, ask your angels what they are trying to tell you. If you still have problems understanding the message, there are some wonderful books that go into more depth about angelic numbers.

Here is a list of the most common angel numbers that we are given by the angels:

111 – You're currently in a powerful time where your thoughts are manifesting very quickly. Focus on your desires and release any fears you have to your angels. Focus your energy into what you do want and not what you don't.

222 – This is a time of divine timing. Be patient as everything is unfolding as it should be. Release your worries to your angels and have faith all is well.

333 – The angels and ascended masters are guiding you right now. You are surrounded by their love and guidance, they are assisting you in finding the right path ahead. Anything is possible. Believe!

444 – Angels, angels everywhere. You are fully protected and supported in life by the angels and ascended masters. This is very positive for you – surrender your doubts and fears.

555 – The angels want you to know that there are positive changes coming to you in the not-too-distant future. Stay focused and allow the power of manifesting to take place – your angels will take care of the rest.

666 – The angels want you to stop and refocus your thoughts. Your vibration is not at its highest frequency right now. Surrender any negativity, fear or doubts to the angels. Take time out to meditate and lift your vibration. Ask your angels to assist you with this. You are never alone.

777 – The angels want you to know that you are on the right path. Your connection to the angels and the spiritual realms is expanding and growing at this time. Keep up the good work and stay focused.

888 – This is an abundant time in your life. Financial assistance is on its way. The angels want you to know that you are being taken care of and they are helping your desires come to fruition.

999 – The angels want you to know that this is a time of completion. It is important for you to finalise anything you may have been putting off. Stop procrastinating. For you to move forward, you need to finalise something in order to have a new beginning.

000 – This is the time of new beginnings. Your future journey is about to start. The angels want you to know that your destiny is in your hands. Surrender what has been holding you back and take the first step to your new future. You can do it.

1111 – The angels want you to know that you are in perfect alignment. You can manifest anything you desire and you are on the right path. You are at one with the angels and the universe. Stay in your power.

Angel connections through nature

Insects such as butterflies, dragonflies and ladybirds are a way that our angels and loved ones make contact with us while we are amongst nature. Insects are also connected to the fairy realm. If you are more connected to the fairy folk, it can be a sign they are around.

Butterflies and dragonflies are symbols of great spiritual significance. Both of these insects symbolise the message of rebirth and transition of the soul. Butterflies are often used as symbols for femininity, luck, death, rebirth and immortality. A butterfly is also the symbol of metamorphosis, freedom and transformation.

Our life journey can be compared in some ways to that of a butterfly. A butterfly's journey begins as an egg, then it turns into a caterpillar, next it forms a chrysalis, then it evolves and emerges as a butterfly.

Our life as a human being goes through similar stages of evolutionary growth. We enter this world as a young innocent being that goes through many steps of spiritual growth becoming an adult. At the end of our physical life, we then pass into the spirit world when our time here on Earth is over. We then continue on with a spiritual journey on the other side. So it seems relevant that a symbol from the spirit world would be a butterfly. This is a sign when a soul has gone through its spiritual journey and has reached its next stage of life.

Dragonflies are symbolic of transformation, adaptation, change, activity, whirlwinds and swiftness. The symbol of a dragonfly is similar to that of a butterfly as they also symbolise rebirth and immortality. When dragonflies mate they make the shape of a heart which also symbolises love.

A dragonfly is a symbol of transformation through spiritual awakening. If you see a dragonfly while you are out in the garden, take it as a sign that good luck is on its way. It can also mean that you are going to experience transformation through a spiritual awakening.

The ladybug is connected to the energy of regeneration and renewal. The name ladybug originated in the middle ages when the beetle was dedicated to the Virgin Mary. It was called the 'Beetle of our Lady'. The name has links to religious devotion and spiritual beliefs. Ladybugs also have a link to mothers.

Many people receive messages from their mothers or matriarchal females in spirit with the visitation or symbol of a ladybug. A ladybug is a messenger of change that connects the living to those in spirit. It helps us to release fear and grief, allowing us to return to a sense of love and hope.

When you see a ladybug it is telling you that spirit is trying to connect with you and provide guidance from above.

Exercise – Signs-from-above speed journalling

This is a fun little exercise I want you to try. Grab your journal, pen and something to use as a timer, such as your watch or phone. Don't spend too much time on the exercise – just write the first thing that pops into your head. This exercise is designed to help you work with spirit and to find what symbols the spirits want you to recognise when they give you a message. Don't worry if what you receive from spirit is different to some of the descriptions above – this is about *your* direct connection to spirit, not anybody else's. Once you start to determine what your specific messages are, it is much easier to understand what your spirit team is sharing with you.

To begin, set your timer to five minutes. If you can't think of anything when you get to a specific word in the list below, skip it and go onto the next one. If you have time, go back to it; if you don't, that's fine too. Write as fast as you can and don't worry about the spelling or what you get, just write it down.

When the five minutes is up, go back to what you wrote for each symbol and elaborate on the meaning and how that symbol applies to it.

For example, the juggler. Is the juggler a male or a female? How many things are they juggling? What items are they juggling? Are they balls or physical household items such as eggs, a clock, a book or crockery? Are they dropping any of the things they are trying juggle? This symbol could be telling you that, when you see this item, it means that the person is trying to do too many things and they need to balance and prioritise their life.

Once you have found out what the following symbols mean to you, focus on other symbols that you see repeatedly. Once you pick out what those symbols are, write them down and repeat the exercise.

Here is a list of example symbols you can focus on:

- baby
- eagle
- speed hump
- jewellery
- flower
- ocean
- tunnel
- keys
- person
- sunset
- mountain
- perfume
- car
- holiday
- tight rope
- tools
- snake
- colour
- scales of justice
- ghost

- dream
- bridge
- musical note
- health issue
- country
- money
- phoenix
- past life
- spirit guide
- fox
- dead end
- spider
- juggler
- loved one
- car
- ostrich
- clock
- tree
- book
- television screen

Signs-from-above meditation

- As discussed in earlier chapters remember to always protect yourself with white light before entering into any work with the spirit world. Keep your journal and pen at the ready for when you return from your meditation to write down any signs and symbols that you see.

- Enter your sacred space by either physically or mentally sitting or lying down in a comfortable position. Now, let's begin by gently closing your eyes and focusing on your breathing.

- 🖊 10 breathe in then breathe out.
- 🖊 9 breathe in then breathe out.
- 🖊 8 breathe in then breathe out.
- 🖊 7 breathe in then breathe out.
- 🖊 6 breathe in then breathe out.
- 🖊 5 breathe in then breathe out.
- 🖊 4 breathe in then breathe out.
- 🖊 3 breathe in then breathe out.
- 🖊 2 breathe in then breathe out.
- 🖊 1 breathe in then breathe out.

- Once you finish counting feel the calmness and peace that now surrounds you.

- Visualise light moving up from the earth beneath your feet. Watch as brilliant light enters through the soles of your feet and watch as the white light moves up through your body; see the white light moving along your legs up to your thighs and watch as it ignites the white light throughout your entire body.

- The white light is so bright you can feel it making its way to your crown chakra. Feel the warmth and comfort this beautiful white light is circulating within every cell of your body.

- Call in your angels, spirit guides and loved ones in spirit and ask them to show you any signs from above during this time together.

Ask them to make their presence known to you by surrounding you with beautiful golden energy.

- Visualise the golden light appearing above your head flowing through to your crown chakra. You now feel the connection of light flowing freely throughout your body, primarily focusing in your mind's eye. Contained within this golden energy is knowledge from above. It contains signs, symbology and numbers that have been shown to beings such as you since the beginning of time. There may be symbols you are already aware of or they may be new ones to assist you with your spiritual growth and spiritual journey ahead.

- These symbols come from the pages of the Akashic records; they may appear as words, drawings, numbers, images of animals, people, places.

- You may be given the messages through small snippets of information in the form of a movie clip that plays out before you or they may give you information in the form of signs, symbols and colours.

- Look at what you are being shown and take in the feelings they are sharing with you while you are connected to the golden light of knowledge.

- Take your time to really absorb all of the information they are sharing with you. What feelings do these symbols instil within you? Do the symbols make sense to you?

- Is there a being with you sharing the information with you? Is the being a guardian angel, spirit guide or loved one in spirit? If you don't understand the symbols, ask the being with you what the meaning is.

- If you don't know who the being is, ask them who they are. This will assist you in understanding what type of symbol you are being given.

- Once you understand the symbol you have been shown, ask the being if there are any other important symbols they wish to share with you at this time.

- Take a few moments to focus on any other symbols or messages they may wish to share with you.

- Do you wish to ask them any questions? Is there anything you need to do with these symbols?

- Take a few moments for the answers to come. Pay attention to them so that you can write them down in your spiritual journal when you finish your connection.

- Once the images cease to be shown to you by your angel, spirit guide or loved one in spirit, thank them for sharing the information with you and bid them farewell.

- Feel your awareness returning back into your sacred space. Be settled with the knowledge that, whenever you need to reconnect with your angel, spirit guide or loved one in spirit to receive more signs from above, you have the spiritual awareness to do so.

- Now, please write or draw any signs, symbols, numbers or visions in your spiritual journal.

AFFIRMATION

I am open to receiving signs from above to guide
and enhance my spiritual growth and evolution.
I thank you for the knowledge you share and
instil within me.

CHAPTER 10:

WHAT IS A PSYCHIC CIRCLE?

WHEN I FIRST BEGAN MY SPIRITUAL JOURNEY, I really had no idea of what I was doing or where I could turn to for assistance and guidance. To be honest it was quite a frightening time, as I was suddenly thrust into a world of daily nightmares and voices that would not leave me alone. I was frightened to go to sleep each night, as I would see visions of women being murdered and see the events taking place either through the victim's eyes or that of the murderer.

Over 30 years ago, to speak of spirit and ghosts was not a common thing to do. Thankfully, I was told on more than one occasion about a woman I should contact named Patricia. Finding Patricia was the beginning of my spiritual journey, and it was the way to find out how to work with spirit and be at one with my guides and angels.

Sitting in circle is the key to opening up mediumship

Patricia ran a psychic development circle, and I was grateful she asked me to be a participant to develop my abilities. The circle had five to six members who would sit regularly once a week at a lady named Faye's house in the suburb I lived in.

Each week we would sit in Faye's loungeroom and begin the circle with a prayer and dedication to spirit. We would then do a meditation and discuss what each of us had experienced during our meditation. I was in awe at what each person relayed about their meditation. Some of the people in the circle would channel messages from higher beings and angels, while others would talk of incredible meditation experiences. Time permitting one or two of us were chosen to hold an item of jewellery that belonged to one of the other members in the group to be read.

Towards the end of the evening, Patricia would have a list of names that were on a healing list. We would all concentrate and call in spirit and ask for each person on the list to be given healing and a quick recovery from their illnesses.

We would then finish with a closing prayer or a message from White Eagle, who is a spiritual teacher in spirit.

During the reading part of the evening, I used to get stressed as I felt like I was back in school and would be asked a question that I wouldn't know the answer to.

The first few times I was asked to read an item, I told Patricia I wasn't picking up anything and I asked if she could choose someone else in the group to give a message. Patricia gently smiled at me and encouraged me to try and tune in. She told me that it wasn't a test – I should think of it as a learning exercise to help me connect with spirit.

One particular night, I was given Faye's watch. I sat and closed my eyes and little by little images, thoughts, words and feelings began to pop into my mind.

The image I received was of Faye in the backyard underneath her clothesline. I saw a little frog pond; I could hear frogs croaking and I could see fairies in the garden. I saw Faye dancing and singing in the yard, and I felt that she was happy in this space. I could see that she could also see the fairies, then suddenly everything stopped, and I was back in the room sitting in the circle with everybody.

Patricia asked me to relay what I saw. I told her that I didn't want to say what I saw as I thought it was too ridiculous to say. Patricia then reminded me that what I saw and the messages I received were not for me. Spirit had shared this message with me to give to Faye, so it was not for me to judge what I saw.

Shyly I began to relay the images. I told Faye I saw her in the backyard under the clothesline, dancing and singing with the fairies. I pointed out that I could see a frog pond and I could see how this space made her feel happy.

After I finished, I gave Faye her watch back, and I looked at her, waiting for her to tell me that what I had just told her was complete and utter rubbish. To my surprise Faye was staring at me with a huge smile on her face. She then began to tell us all how she had just built the frog pond for the frogs and fairies. She also confirmed that she did dance and sing under the clothesline as it made her happy.

You wouldn't believe the relief I felt at this confirmation. I finally knew I was on the right track and I was actually tuning in correctly.

Little did I know that this was going to form the foundation of my future work using psychometry to further develop my mediumship abilities.

When I first joined the circle I would sit amongst the gifted others and feel way out of my depth. When I relayed the visions I received during my meditation I would say to them that I saw this, felt that, smelt this, heard that. At first I thought that this was how everyone else in the group received their messages. It wasn't until I felt more comfortable with the group that I asked how each of them picked up their information. To my disbelief each person told me that they experienced the messages from spirit in different ways.

Some people experienced all that I did, while others only heard things but did not see, or they felt things but did not hear. This was a huge awakening for me, as I had thought we all just received information in the same manner. This was when I realised that the psychic senses are very different to the five senses we are familiar with and use on a daily basis.

The fact that other circle members did not see the same way I did does not take anything away from how each of the members in the circle received their information. Each of them was incredibly gifted and picked up amazing information from the spirit realms.

This realisation showed me how we can all work with spirit in our own way and that there is no right or wrong way to receive information from our spiritual teachers. What is most important is the message that is shared and not how we receive it.

I sat in the circle on and off for a few years from this point on. As my children were quite young during this time of my life, I could only go when it fitted in with the family. I look back on this time now and I am very grateful for the experience. Sitting in a circle was an extremely powerful learning time for me in helping me understand my mediumship abilities. It was so wonderful to realise that there were others like me who were also on their own spiritual path of discovery and exploration. This was the time that I realised that not being like everybody else was something to be proud of and not something to be ashamed of.

To develop your psychic abilities and mediumship skills I strongly recommend that you join a psychic development circle to strengthen and develop your gifts.

Sitting in a circle is a great way to connect with other like-minded souls as well as sending out positive healing energy into the world. At this point in time on the earthly realms we need as much positivity and light as we can muster.

What is most important is that we connect with spirit in any way shape or form, receive information, share it with others, heal and teach as many souls as we can while we are here on Earth. Sharing is the way forward for us all.

What is a psychic development circle?

A psychic development circle is a group of spiritually minded people who sit regularly (usually one night a week) to connect with spirit and to develop their psychic and mediumship abilities. It is important that the circle has a focus such as development and/or spiritual healing. To be honest, if you are sitting in a circle and connecting with higher beings and angels, it is important to use this powerful energy to help others and make a difference to the world we live in.

Many development circles are run through Spiritualist churches. Circles are run in different ways. An open circle is a circle where different people can attend each week.

A closed circle is where a dedicated group of people choose to sit weekly, sometimes for years on end, to make contact to higher consciousness. This type of group doesn't change participants often, whereas an open circle has people who will come and go within the group.

A closed circle is usually held at one of the group member's homes. Usually there is a leader of the circle who is an experienced medium who will run the circle. Circle members usually sit in the same seat each week in order to keep up the continuity and vibration of the circle's connection to spirit.

Personally, I find that a closed circle is far better for me, as it is important to keep the energy levels balanced and connected to spirit on a constant frequency. If you have people coming and going in the circle, it is harder to achieve your required connection. Your intention and frequency is of utmost importance. If you are on a higher vibration or frequency, the higher the beings and knowledge you will access during your time in the circle.

What is the benefit of sitting in a circle?

Sitting in a circle is highly beneficial for your spiritual progression. It is also a great way to connect with like-minded spiritual people who have similar interests to yourself. However, the best part of being in a circle is the strengthening of your connection to the higher beings in the spiritual realms.

By being part of a circle, you can expand your gifts and do different exercises each week that will allow you to develop. It is always beneficial to work with others who are also spiritually enlightened to gain knowledge of their personal experiences and to give you a greater understanding of how spirit works with each and every individual.

Sitting in a circle doesn't have to always be a totally serious affair. One of the most memorable circle experiences I had was when we all did an 'om' meditation to raise our vibration. The leader of the circle played a guided 'om' meditation of Buddhist monks that we all repeated. We did our 'om-ing' for about five minutes, and as we did this, the vibration in the room quickly rose and we all started to get louder and louder. One of the group burst into laughter as she felt so happy with the experience. The laughter was infectious and we all went into hysterical giggles. After we finished the meditation, the messages that spirit shared with us that evening were some of the most insightful and uplifting that I had ever experienced.

It is good to change up the learning exercises each week and do different meditations to help the people in the circle to explore their strengths and weaknesses.

To assist you with your own spiritual development, you may decide to join a psychic development circle or you may even decide to begin your own circle. Looking up your local Spiritualist church is always a great place to start, or you could join a meditation group.

Starting your own circle

If you decide to start your own psychic circle to work with like-minded people, there are a few things to keep in mind.

Find a sacred space to hold the circle that is available at the same time and day each week. It is important, when you hold your circle, to remember you are making a date with spirit to connect with you. It is best for the circle to be held at one of the circle member's homes if possible as the space can be more controlled. You can rent the same room each week, however, maintaining the vibration may be more difficult.

Invite people who you feel will have similar energy and interest in being part of the circle. You will need at least four to six people in the circle but not more than twelve. I find it is important to have an even number so that the group can have a partner to do exercises with. I also find that if there are too many people in the circle, it is harder to manage with the space as well as the personalities.

Set up the circle with comfortable straight-backed chairs, so that the members can sit comfortably but not fall asleep during the meditation.

Find appropriate spiritual music to assist with the spiritual vibration.

Decide who will be the leader/head of the circle to conduct the circle each week.

Hold the circle at the same time each week.

Hold the circle for one to two hours. I find that less than an hour is not long enough, but after two hours everyone becomes tired and loses their focus.

Discuss with the circle if members are open to using incense or aromatherapy oils before using them.

Ensure that everyone is punctual as you do not want people to interrupt the opening meditation.

Ask members of the group not to drink any alcohol or use any substances if they are going to attend, as this can drop the vibration and unwanted spirits may attach to the group.

Food or drinks (except water) are not to be consumed during the circle. After the circle is finished, the group may wish to have light refreshments.

Once the circle participants are chosen, be mindful of inviting new members as this could interfere with the connection between the group.

Be respectful of the person running the circle and be respectful of the information that spirit shares with the group. Sometimes the information that comes through is of a very personal nature.

Decide your purpose for the circle. Is it going to be purely for the development of the group? Is it going to be to explore psychic phenomena?

Or is it to be held for healing purposes for the participants and the world around them? Perhaps it could be for all of the above.

Have a format for the circle members to follow. This will help the group as well as the spirit members who connect with the group each week. For example:

7.00 pm – Circle members arrive. Settle your things near your seat, use the bathroom if necessary. Group members take their seat and be ready to begin the relaxation process.

7.10 pm – The group all sit and hold hands and the leader of the circle invites spirit to join the group in the space with a prayer or affirmation.

7.15 pm – Circle members do a meditation that allows them to sit in the power of spirit. This allows the individual group member's energies to blend with spirit. The meditation will usually last from 15 to 30 minutes.

7.45 pm – Circle members then each discuss the experiences they had during the meditation with the rest of the group.

8.00 pm – The circle now embarks on a specific development exercise that the leader of the circle had chosen for the group to do. Such as participants being chosen to do a small reading via psychometry for members in the group.

8.45 pm – The leader reads out names from a healing list for those in need of healing from spirit and the group. The circle is then closed with a prayer of gratitude by the leader.

8.50 pm – Members of the group may participate in light refreshments and help to clean up the room before ending the evening.

Of course, the above information is only a guide for your circle. I am sure that once you begin your group, spirit and circle members will find what works best for all to connect.

CHAPTER 11:

CLAIRVOYANCE – HOW TO SEE INTO THE SPIRIT WORLD

What is clairvoyance?

The word 'clairvoyance' comes from the French words *clair* and *voyance*, meaning clear seeing. Clairvoyance is the ability to see via your normal senses and connecting to your sixth sense. When you see clairvoyantly you access this ability by activating your third eye. Your third eye is the chakra point that is located in the centre of your forehead between both of your eyes.

Individuals who have the gift of clairvoyance can pick up psychic impressions through their mind's eye, and some people will actually see with their physical eyes. It is possible for people with the gift of clairvoyance to see both ways, however it is more common to see via your mind's eye (third eye). The information will be relayed through sight, visions, dreams, movie-scenes and symbols from the spirit world.

Those who see clairvoyantly with their physical eyes may also be able to see spirits as clearly as if they were still alive. Generally, people who have this gift will have other psychic gifts working hand in hand with this ability. Many gifted clairvoyants are also clairaudient and clairsentient. With these other gifts functioning at the same time, it assists the clairvoyant to hear, see and feel what those in spirit are trying to communicate.

People who are highly visual have a greater connection to clairvoyance. People who are creative, imaginative and artistic are already connecting to this gift via the right side of their brain for inspiration. It can be more difficult for those who are constantly working on the left side of the brain, as they are more rational and find it harder to trust what they see.

Some clairvoyant individuals may have the ability to see colours around people, animals and plants. They may also be able to see spirit beings such as angels, spirit guides, ascended masters, loved ones in spirit, other worldly beings, ghosts or apparitions.

As a child, this ability is very normal and commonplace. It is only when children get older and are told that their spirit friends are figments of their imagination that they can close down this wonderful gift.

I had strong clairvoyance as a child and I could see spirit every night when I went to bed. As none of my family could see what I could see, I found it hard to cope with. It was an extremely frightening time for me because nobody else believed me. I wish that I had a book like this one to give me the guidance and direction I needed to access and assist me with my gifts when I was a child.

In the early stages of learning to use the gift of clairvoyance, you may discover that your clairvoyance can be intermittent and hard to understand. When my clairvoyance began to open up, I could only access it through meditation or during my dream state. Through perseverance and practice, I have been able to turn the ability on and off at will. I no longer need to be in a dream state to access my visions. If you are someone who finds it easy to visualise things or daydream, then this gift should be easy for you to open up.

Many clairvoyant individuals have the abilities to see into the past (postcognition), the present (the most common side of clairvoyance) or the future (precognition).

Signs of being clairvoyant

- You have visions about the future that come true.
- You have vivid dreams that feel as if they actually happened.
- You have the ability to know if someone is nasty or nice upon first meeting them.
- You can tell if someone is healthy or not by looking at them.
- You can read other people's minds.
- You can visualise what a person looks like while communicating with them via the internet or phone even though you haven't met them before.
- You find it easy to imagine and visualise things.
- You can relate to things you see rather than what you hear or feel.
- You can memorise things that you see.
- You can envisage things before they happen.

How do you see clairvoyantly?

To see clairvoyantly, you can access your clairvoyance via your third-eye chakra or physically see with your eyes. Some people will access both areas at once to see spirit. It is more common to see via your third eye or inner mind's eye instead of using your physical eyes. While accessing the spirit world this way, you can have images shown to you in the form of mini-movie clips and symbolic messages. It is as though you are watching images projected onto a theatre movie screen. These images can be a quick flash or may last a few seconds.

Initially, it is easier to shut your eyes and focus on the images; with time and patience you will be able to see the messages with your eyes open.

When I am doing a reading for a client, I will be given messages on a blank screen. I find it easier to look off to the right-hand side of my client's head, as this is where my psychic projector is playing out before me. I can be shown images of the past, present or future on the screen. For instance, a significant time in the person's life may be played out before me that I am asked to relay to them. I can be given symbols, words and numbers relating to the person being read. If I am receiving the messages in symbols, words or numbers, these images float across in front of the person I am reading. I find when I am receiving messages this way, if I don't decipher the message, it will be replayed to me until I work out the message.

If I am making contact with a person in spirit, they will stand on different sides of the client, so that I know which side of the family they come from. If the person is from the client's mother's side, they will stand on the right-hand side of the client. If they are from the client's father's side, they will stand on the left-hand side. If the person has a partner and they are female, their partner's side of the family will stand on the left-hand side. If the person I am reading is a male, their partner's side will stand on the right-hand side. At times I must admit that this is not always the case, as sometimes a spirit for the person I am reading for may be strong and they will take over the reading, and they will stand on whatever side of the person will get them the most attention. I find it really interesting that if someone is strong and pushy in life, they can remain the same once they have passed over.

The spirits also come through on different levels. Sometimes I can be shown the symbol of a family tree. For instance, a younger person will stand in front of someone who is older in age; if a person is older they will stand behind someone who is younger than they are. If a person in spirit wants me to tell the client that they look like them, they will superimpose their face over the top of the client's face so that I can see the similarities between them. For instance, the client might have the same-shaped eyes as their mother, but a different colour.

When I first tune into a person to do a reading, I will get a sense of a spirit person being with them trying to make contact. They will start off being more of a vague impression, and as I tune in further, they can become solid and lifelike as if I was actually seeing someone who is alive.

On one occasion, I was shown teeth floating before my eyes and the front tooth was gold. Then a man appeared with a big wide grin showing me his gold tooth. When I asked the client about this, they said that their father had a front gold tooth and he was very proud of this. This was shown to me to give confirmation to the client that I was indeed picking up her deceased father. I find that at times working clairvoyantly is like playing a game of charades, as you need to decipher the information you are receiving. You may see a symbol, number or word that makes a lot of sense to the client, but to you – the psychic – the message seems insignificant. As my gift has expanded over the years, I have learnt not to judge what I receive. Always remember that the message is not for you. You are only the messenger. Relay the information verbatim to the client, so that none of the message is lost in translation. You will surprise yourself at how accurate you will be when you trust in your own ability. Remember you are working with an unseen spiritual team that connects with your energy to give you the messages.

When accessing your clairvoyance at a historical location, it is possible to see the location as it was at a certain time in history. If you are in a historical home you may see what the furniture used to look like in a room or even see the past owners of the location appear before you. Many spirits like to stay in their home even though they may have passed many years before. Seeing a spirit clairvoyantly can feel like you are actually seeing the person when they were alive. It can be quite hard to tell the difference at times because their energy can be very clear. At other times, you may only see the essence of the person, and they may appear to be a bluish/white haze you can see through.

Signs and information that you may access while doing a clairvoyant reading

You may be shown mini-movie clips of the person you are reading for. This information could be about their personal life. You will find that whatever is the most important issue in the person's life at that particular point in time will be the first information you receive. It is very important that you *always* pass this information on first then the other information will begin to flow.

It is imperative that you tune into the person you are reading for before they give you any information. It is much better to work blind (without prior knowledge) as you will find that the information comes through to you more clearly and without any preconception of what they are expecting you to see for them.

Once you have passed on the important issues that the person needs to know or be aware of, you can then allow them to ask you whatever issues they are still concerned with.

You may receive messages in symbolic form from the spirit world for the person being read for. For example: The person may be making the decision to move to a new house or to renovate the current property.

If the person is going to move house you may be shown a For Sale sign at the front of a house and this can indicate they will be moving. If however they are going to renovate their house, you may be shown through the person's current property and shown where and what they will be changing. If there are any foreseeable problems, these will also be brought to your attention, such as their house having any water problems they need to look at. This vision may be a leaking shower or you may be shown the property flooding.

If I am doing a reading on a location, then my clairvoyance will work in a different way. I could go to a location that is historical, and I need to tune into the prior occupants of the location. The location could be that of a rundown period home or it may be the location where a new home has been built on the location of the old home.

This type of clairvoyance is interesting. I can see things that are layered in time. I can be shown what the property looked like when it was first built, and I can be shown what the original owners and prior occupants looked like and what their life was like. If the location has had more than one use during it's time, the layers of the past will present themselves. The spirits from each generation can also be seen.

There are so many different ways people can perceive their gift of clairvoyance. Initially, when I began to work with spirit, I would only see spirit during my dream or meditative state. I would experience a number of different 'triggers' that would indicate to me that I was having a clairvoyant experience.

When I was drifting off to sleep, I would start to feel like I was lifting out of the room, and it felt like I was floating. I would then feel that I was being enveloped in a black velvet-like vortex that would rotate around me. The vortex would then open up and begin to swirl, and the colours would change to hues of purples, blues and green with the black fading into the background.

I would then experience a popping-type sound and I would feel like I was transported into whatever location I was to receive the message about. I found that if I consciously tried to make a connection, I would become frustrated as the connection was unpredictable. I would have to be relaxed and calm for anything to come through. The angrier and more frustrated I became, or if I tried too hard, the less I would see.

There could be days and even weeks at a time when I would not see anything clairvoyantly. I would feel like the initial messages I received were my imagination as I couldn't make a connection on demand.

As I worked more on clairvoyance, my ability progressed in different stages. The way the images came through to me changed from only being able to make contact through dream and meditative states to being awake and fully conscious.

This was a step forward but also still quite an unstable way to make contact. I found that certain things would suddenly open me up to visions.

In particular, I found that while I was in contact with water I would instantly have a vision. The visions could happen while I was washing up the dishes, while I was swimming, paddleboarding at the beach or while I was having a shower. The images and visions I received were visual and prophetic. The clarity was becoming more and more clear and easy to understand.

Once I left the water the visions would stop just as quickly as they began. I realised I couldn't just stand in the shower or float in the water all day. I found that if I kept a notepad close by and if I wrote the information down immediately, the image would progress to a new vision. If I didn't understand the information then I would be shown the same vision over and over again, as though I was watching a movie that would be rewound and replayed until I made sense of what I was being shown.

Clairvoyant symbols

Meditating is the best way to open your clairvoyance. There are many visualisation tracks that you can purchase to enhance your gift. Open-eyed meditations can be beneficial for you to open up and enhance your abilities.

Next time you decide to go for a walk, leave your phone/device at home. I find that we are all so connected to our devices these days the spirit world has to work even harder to get our attention, as we are always looking at our screens. Why not take some time out and go for a walk and really look at your surroundings, be aware of the clouds above you, look at the birds in the sky, pay attention to what type of vegetation is around you. Look at the flowers that are in bloom as you walk. Pay attention to the types of living beings that you pass, whether they are human, animal, bird or insect. Pay attention to any angelic symbols you may pass by as you walk.

Do you see any feathers along your path... do you see any butterflies or dragonflies? Are there any symbols you see in the clouds above you? When you return home from your walk, make note of any specific signs or symbols you may have noticed along the way. Next time you go for a walk, look at the world through different eyes and be surprised by what messages you receive from above.

Clairvoyance meditation

- Find a quiet place to sit and relax. You may wish to enter your sacred space physically or mentally. Gently close your eyes and slowly breathe in. Visualise breathing in positive uplifting energy while you surround yourself with white light from above.
- Breathe in positivity and light.
- Exhale any negativity you may have around. Imagine that you are ridding yourself of any emotion that does not belong to you.

- Breathe in the light.

- Exhale any residual energy you may feel is still attached to you.

- Visualise a beautiful bright white light surrounding your entire body. Now watch as this light expands to make you glow from its brightness.

- In your mind's eye, look down at and see this protective light entering your body via the soles of your feet. Watch as the light slowly moves up to your base chakra.

- As the energy reaches your base chakra, it turns a brilliant red. The light continues to move and reaches your sacral chakra turning a brilliant orange. The light continues up and reaches your solar plexus turning a brilliant yellow. Feel the energy filling your body and continuing to move up to your heart chakra turning a brilliant green. Allow the energy to progress and move up to your throat chakra turning a brilliant blue. As you feel the energy moving along your body, notice if there are any blockages you may need to spend more time on. If there is any resistance, visualise the light cleansing and clearing the blockage. Watch as the energy now moves up to your third eye turning a brilliant indigo.

- Take a moment to focus all of your energy onto your third eye, feeling the energy expanding. You are now entering your special sacred space of sight. Watch as the colours of green, blue, violet and indigo swirl before your eyes, mixing and melting before your eyes.

- Look at the pinhole of light that opens before you. Feel yourself moving towards the light as this opening expands. The light becomes brighter and brighter until you are engulfed within it.

- Take a moment for your eyes to adjust to your surroundings and the light around you.

- Take note of what you are seeing. Are you seeing anyone familiar to you? Are the beings you are seeing your spirit guides, guardian angels or deceased loved ones you dearly miss? Does this person have any message they wish to share with you?

- If you are not seeing any beings, look to see if there are any significant symbols or colours in this place. What do these symbols indicate to you? How do you feel when you see these symbols? Question what these symbols are connected with.

- Take your time and pay attention to everything you see in this place and remember how you feel when the signs or symbols come into view.

- Thank your spirit team for connecting with you today and know in your heart that you may return to this place in the future to reconnect.

- In your own time bring your awareness back into the room, and when you are ready, gently open your eyes.

- Now, take some time to sit quietly and write as much information as you can remember about this clairvoyant experience. Draw any symbols, signs, colours or pictures you saw during the meditation. Write down any messages you received from your spirit guides, guardian angels and loved ones in spirit.

AFFIRMATION

(to be said daily)

*I allow the gift of clairvoyance to come to me
through the opening of my third eye.
I accept the positive visions and images that my
spirit guides and guardian angels
share with me to guide my spiritual path.*

CHAPTER 12:

CLAIRAUDIENCE – TUNING INTO SPIRIT

What is clairaudience?

The word 'clairaudience' comes from the French words *clair* and *audience* meaning clear hearing. Clairaudience is the ability to hear via your normal senses and connecting to your sixth sense. Some would say that it is the ability to connect to the *third ear*.

Clairaudients are people who can receive psychic information through either inner or outer hearing. The information is transmitted via the person's spirit guides, guardian angels and deceased loved ones. Individuals who have this gift can pick up the sounds of voices, names, dates, words, sayings, phrases, music, vibrations and frequencies of the spirit world.

There are different ways of hearing clairaudiently. You may hear via your own mind in your own voice. This form of clairaudience can be confusing, as you may wonder if the thoughts are your own; you may question if you are imagining things or question whether the messages are actually psychic in origin. As you practice, you will be able to distinguish the difference of whether it is your own thoughts or a psychic message. This form of clairaudience is called subjective hearing.

You may also hear clairaudiently via sounds and voices that are heard externally. With this form of clairaudience, you may hear your name called out; you could hear music, words, names and even warnings if you are in danger. The voice may be male, female, young or old; sometimes the voice can even have an accent. This form of clairaudience is called objective hearing.

You may be able to hear via this form of clairaudience when your loved one reaches out from spirit to let you know they are OK. You may be just thinking about them and you suddenly hear their voice talking to you as if they were still alive.

I find with this form of clairaudience you will know that it is not your imagination, as the words and phrases used are those of your loved one and not your own. It is not uncommon to think a question in your mind and the answer to your question is instantly answered by your guide or loved one.

Many mediums and psychics have the gift of clairaudience, which enables them to communicate directly with beings in the spirit world. When the spirit world communicates with you using clairaudience, they do so via a frequency. It can be likened to tuning into the correct radio station.

The frequency in your radio tunes into the same frequency as the radio waves that have been broadcast from the station you have chosen, thus making a connection and picking up the signal and hearing the sound.

The connection with spirit happens in the same manner only you are the radio receiver and the spirit world is the radio station broadcasting directly to you via your ear. With practice, you will be able to simply think about making a connection and you will plug in directly to the spirit world. (We will do some tuning-in exercises later in this chapter.)

In the early stages of working with spirit clairaudiently, the connection can be intermittent and quite frustrating to sustain. The more you practice connecting to spirit the stronger your connection to the spirit world will become.

Clairaudience is one of the less common psychic senses and is probably one of the hardest ones to deal with. It can be quite off-putting in the beginning, as hearing voices when you don't see a person can be a little frightening if you don't understand what is going on. Don't worry, it is perfectly natural to feel a little confused. When I began my journey I was not at all open to hearing the voices and the guidance I was offered. It took some time before I was open and accepting of this gift.

Signs of being clairaudient

There are many signs that indicate you have clairaudient abilities. Listed below are the more common indicators of clairaudient hearing:

- You are very sensitive to sounds around you.
- You hear sounds that those around you don't hear.
- You discern the differences between different people's voices.
- You remember things better by hearing them than seeing or reading them.
- You prefer listening to music rather than watching television.
- You have mental conversations in your head and hear the other side of the conversation.
- You hear other frequencies or noises outside of the normal range (this can be known as tinnitus).
- You experience these frequencies in one ear more than the other.
- You receive messages or ideas in your head as though you are being spoken to by an external/internal source.

How do you hear voices through clairaudience?

Many people hear voices but do not realise the significance of them. Some may think that these voices are their own inner voice or guidance, while other people may find it difficult to cope with.

Some people who hear voices have been diagnosed as having a mental illness. Don't worry, not everyone who hears voices has a mental illness; it is just a matter of being aware of who is communicating with you and what the voices are telling you to do. If the voices are telling you to self-harm or to harm others, or if the messages are negative, derogatory, abusive, then you may need to seek medical advice.

Many people live perfectly healthy and happy lives and consider the voices to be a positive guiding part of their lives. Hearing voices via clairaudience can be a little hard to explain, especially if you haven't heard the voices for yourself. However, the phenomenon of hearing voices is not as rare as many would think.

Hearing voices via clairaudience can be the same as hearing a human voice in the normal way we hear via our ears. The only difference is that there is no physical source. You may think that you have not experienced hearing with clairaudience. Then have a think about this, are you sure that you haven't heard voices? It is not uncommon to hear someone calling your name, only to find that there is nobody physically near you.

Research shows that people who have recently lost a loved one often hear the voice of their dearly departed loved one. You may hear them speaking to you even though in reality you know that they are no longer alive. There is no need to worry if you are having this type of experience. It is a message from your loved one who is in the spirit world. They are trying to make contact with you, to let you know they are OK. They may even be trying to give you guidance and comfort from the other side.

It is not your imagination or wishful thinking. In fact, it can be a gift from the other side.

Many people don't like to speak about their clairaudience experiences for fear of being thought of as different or even ridiculed. You may need to review this thought about yourself as you are actually gifted and hearing guidance outside of the usual human realms of hearing.

When I began to hear clairaudiently via objective hearing, I did not want anything to do with the voice I was hearing. I would do everything possible to not listen to what I was 'told' to do. I am a stubborn person and the more that I was 'told' to do something, the more I would do the exact opposite.

When I began to hear the voice, I questioned my sanity. As I did more research about this phenomenon, I discovered that there can be a misconception that people who hear voices have a mental illness and are often diagnosed as schizophrenic.

I didn't feel that I was schizophrenic, although I could hear things outside of the normal realm. It was only when I began to realise I was having unpleasant experiences due to *not* listening to the voice that I decided I should challenge it to confirm who it was, where it came from, and what was the reason I was hearing it. I was given confirmation about who the voice was – that's when my spirit guide Running Horse introduced himself.

He explained to me that he had chosen to be with me to guide, teach and protect me. At first I found this a bit challenging, as to be perfectly honest, listening to a person who you can't see and listening to their advice does seem a bit crazy.

It was only when I worked with my gut feelings (solar plexus chakra) and was given proof that Running Horse had my best interests at heart that I accepted his assistance.

As you progress with your own journey, you may have to go through a similar experience yourself to be able to accept your gift of clairaudience fully before you can acknowledge when you hear voices objectively.

I have to admit that the experience is quite challenging at first. Once you make a strong connection, you will also find it fulfilling when you finally understand that there are other beings in the spirit world who have chosen to work with you for the greater good.

I feel so blessed to be part of an amazing spirit team that has so much more knowledge and understanding of the universe than I have myself.

Most of us have heard voices throughout our life. Whether it be our own inner voice giving us encouragement to keep on trying, or it may be a voice that tells us we didn't do something well enough or encourages us to try harder.

The voices you hear can come in the form of your own voice, and it may come as words that pop into your head. It could be your inner voice. It could be that of someone who you love dearly that has passed who spontaneously pops into your head when you think of them.

All of these descriptions are ways we hear independently of using our own outer ears and is more of a way of using our inner ear and inner hearing.

You may discover that you receive messages from spirit in all of the ways I have described or only some of them. Don't worry, there isn't a right or wrong way to hear clairaudiently. The most important thing is for you to discern the best way for you to work with the spirit world.

You too can have the same connection as I do with my guide by listening and connecting to your guides and angels via clairaudience. We will go through a meditation exercise later in this chapter to help you to connect and hear your guides, angels and loved ones.

The most important thing to remember is to not block your gift of clairaudience through being fearful or having negative thoughts. If you work with your spirit guides and angels on the higher spiritual realms, you shouldn't have any negative experiences.

Whenever you are working with the spirit world, no matter what your psychic gift is, you should always work with the light and protect yourself before beginning the contact.

Why do some mediums have tinnitus?

Many people who have the gift of clairaudience also experience tinnitus. Many well-known mediums report noticing the presence of tinnitus, and it is the frequency spirit makes contact with them on.

Tinnitus is a condition that occurs in one or both ears or in the head. It is described as a ringing noise and can take the form of a high-pitched whining or buzzing sound. I personally have tinnitus and would describe the sound I hear as the sound of crickets, bees or cicadas constantly buzzing in my ear.

I wasn't born with tinnitus. I was a scuba diver, and I had a diving accident which burst the oval window in my inner ear. From that time onwards, I have suffered with tinnitus.

In the beginning, the constant buzzing sound I experienced was quite debilitating, and it disturbed my life significantly as I never felt that I ever had any quiet or peace. Over time, I have learnt to live with what the doctor told me was called 'head noises'. I was quite surprised as my psychic gifts developed that the ear with the tinnitus was the ear I randomly began to hear voices, music and sounds in clairaudiently (my right ear). I believe that tinnitus works in a similar way to the way white noise does.

Many people will be familiar with temporary tinnitus when they go to a rock concert or experience an event with loud sounds such as fireworks with their explosions and bangs. This type of tinnitus is usually temporary.

It is interesting to note that a lot of musicians have tinnitus due to the loud amplifiers and sounds they work with on a daily basis. Many composers have heard and dreamt of musical melodies and riffs playing in their head during their dream state. They have then composed beautiful masterpieces that were inspired from the spirit realm.

What is white noise?

Many believe that white noise is not really a noise as such – it is more of a sound frequency – and it is also known as white sound. The signal that a person hears when they are hearing white noise can be similar to the sound of a gentle hiss, radio, wind rustling through trees, a waterfall or the sound of the ocean.

Have you ever picked up a shell and put it to your ear? The sound you pick up sounds like the ocean inside the shell when in fact you are picking up another form of white noise.

White noise is a frequency that spirits use to make contact with the living from the spirit world. I find that when you are not concentrating and there is a background noise, it is easier to access spirit via white noise.

Clairaudience meditation

Go into your sacred space to begin the exercise. When you are starting out, it is advisable if you speak to your spirit guides and let them know if they want to make contact with you they should only do so while you are in this space. This will ensure that you are protected and surrounded with positive energies and vibrations.

As discussed in chapter 6 on psychic protection, it is always important to work only with those energies that resonate on the higher realms of the spirit world. As you progress you will be able to have your spirit guides work with you regularly. The most important thing to remember is that you need to be patient!

- Before you start to make a connection, be prepared by having your spiritual journal and pen with you.
- Sit quietly and relax. Gently close your eyes and slowly breathe in through your nose and exhale through your mouth. Visualise breathing in positive uplifting energy. As you breathe out imagine that you are exhaling any negativity or stress that you may be experiencing.

- Once again, breathe in positivity and light.

- Exhale.

- Breathe in the light.

- As you exhale this time, focus on any energy that no longer feels a part of you. Remember, it is time to let it go!

- Visualise a beautiful bright white light surrounding your entire body. Now watch as this light expands to make you glow from its spiritual brightness.

- In your mind's eye, visualise yourself walking along a beautiful sandy beach. As you walk along the beach, you see that you are not the only person in this peaceful place.

- A being appears in the distance and they look like a shimmering light. As you walk towards this being, you notice the many beautiful shells that have washed up on the shore.

- The being keeps walking towards you and you finally meet. The being meets you with a welcoming smile, and you realise this ethereal being is part of your spirit team, and you recognise them as your spirit guide or guardian angel.

- In their hand, they have the most amazing colourful shell you have ever seen. The shell glistens in the sun with every colour of the rainbow.

- They hold out their hand to you and give you the shell. As you touch the shell, a brilliant golden light appears before you. The energy around you begins to change. Your spirit being beckons you to hold the shell up to your ear and listen to the sound within. They want you to pay attention to any sounds you may hear.

- Hold the shell up to your right ear to listen to the sounds and then swap over and hold the shell up to your left ear and do the same thing.

- The sounds you hear may be as simple as hearing your name, a letter, a word, a sentence or even just the feeling of someone blowing into your ear. Do you hear the sound of the ocean from within the shell?

- Notice if there is a change in the frequency in your ear – is there a temperature change surrounding you?

- Pay attention to whether the messages are received in your left or right ear, or you may receive guidance in both ears at once. Do you hear the message inside your own mind or is it as though someone is whispering in your ear externally?

- If you have any questions that you wish to ask the being, patiently wait to hear the answer they have for you. If you don't understand the answer to the question, ask them to explain it to you.

- Sometimes the answer may come to you as a sound or it may be the words of a song. It can be quite surprising in what form your answer may come.

- Take your time and pay attention to everything you hear from your ethereal being.

- Don't worry if you don't receive any messages at all. Make note of any feelings you may experience at this time and record them later in your spiritual journal.

- Thank them for coming to work with you and sharing their knowledge with you.

- When you are ready, gently bring your awareness back into the room and open your eyes.

- Sit quietly and write down as much information as you can remember about your clairaudient experience.

AFFIRMATION

(to be said daily)

I welcome the gift of clairaudience into my life.
I am open to receiving guidance and positive
inspiration from my spirit guides and guardian
angels through the gift of sound.
Together we will work as one.

CHAPTER 13

CLAIRSENTIENCE – LISTEN TO YOUR FEELINGS

What is clairsentience?

The word 'clairsentience' comes from the French words *clair* meaning clear and *sentience* meaning to feel. Clairsentience or 'clear feeling' is an ability that relies on the use of your sixth sense to allow you to pick up impressions about people and places that are not picked up by your conscious mind. Clairsentience gives you the ability to pick up on the feelings, emotions and health of others.

Clairsentience is one of the most common forms of psychic senses. This gift is usually one of the first psychic gifts we develop as a child. Most of us use this ability on a daily basis without even being aware of it. Clairsentience is closely linked to clairempathy. Most people who are clairsentient are also an empath.

People who have the gift of clairsentience are more sensitive than someone who is merely an empath. The most important thing to remember when understanding the differences between these two clairs is a clairsentient will physically feel the emotion in their own body, whereas a clairempath will sense the emotion but will not feel it.

If a person has both the gifts of clairsentience and clairempathy, they will sense and feel the emotions of others and/or the location around them.

Through using the ability of clairsentience, clairvoyance and clairaudience are also often triggered at the same time. The gift of (clairtangency) psychometry is also linked closely to clairsentience, as both of these abilities connect to other people's auric fields, allowing the reader to empathise with the feelings and emotions of the person being read for.

A clairsentient person can receive their information by physical and mental impressions that assist them in explaining the emotions they experience. Clairsentients can pick up information through visual flashes that show them events connected to what have caused a person's feelings and emotions. The flashes may appear as mini-movies that pop into the mind's eye. People who have clairsentient abilities tend to work as mediums, psychics, healers, nurses, kinesiologists, naturopaths and massage therapists.

Clairsentience guidance

Clairsentience guidance usually falls into three main categories: gut feelings; physical sensations; and spirit and clairsentience.
I will discuss the difference between each category in depth below.

Gut feelings

The most common form of clairsentience, gut feelings are a strong physical response to your emotions. When you are picking up messages using gut feelings, you may get a feeling of excitement or a feeling of dread.

Clairsentience is picked up via your solar plexus chakra (see chapter 5 for more on chakras), located in the abdomen/stomach area. That is why it is also referred to as your 'gut feeling' because that is where the feeling is picked up – the gut.

Your gut feeling is something I am sure you have experienced throughout your life. It feels like a heaviness in the stomach/abdomen area. It could be a sinking feeling or nauseousness in your stomach that makes you feel like you want to vomit. The negative side of your gut feeling has the feeling of warning you of impending danger, doom or despair.

On the other hand, the positive side of your gut feeling is the exact opposite. The feeling is usually light and uplifting. You may feel excited and extremely happy; you may experience the feeling of 'butterflies' or 'bubbles' in your stomach. You may even experience a euphoric sense within you that you can't explain. This once again is your in-built spiritual GPS warning system confirming that you are to experience a positive outcome or that you are on the right track.

As you begin to pay close attention to your gut feelings, you will be able to instantly recognise what the right or wrong thing is for you to follow in your life. It is something that will become second nature and you won't even need to think about it as it will just happen. As you progress, you will see with hindsight things you experienced in your past that you may have not had a good feeling about, but you proceeded anyway and discovered it wasn't a good choice after all.

Here are some examples of gut feelings:

Have you ever gone for a job interview only to feel that your future boss is going to be a nightmare to work with? The money was great but something deep down in the pit of your stomach made you feel sick. This is a very strong warning not to take the job. You may be offered an excellent wage, but your work life is going to be difficult and unpleasant.

Have you ever met a person and for some unknown reason you have taken an instant dislike to them? The person hasn't been rude or unpleasant but for some reason you just didn't like their personality (energy). This is when your gut feeling is reacting to the other person's vibration. The reason you feel this way is because you and the other person's vibration resonates on different frequencies. Your gut feelings will always allow you to sense immediately whether or not you should or should not trust or like someone.

Have you ever been walking in a location at night where you suddenly felt that you were being watched or followed? You didn't see anybody but something within you was warning you to be careful. Suddenly, a person appears from nowhere and comes towards you. Your senses tell you to get away as quickly as possible.

You are looking at buying a new property, and when you arrive at the property, something just doesn't feel right. The home looks nice but on entering the house you feel there are rooms that are cold and uncomfortable. You feel like the house has an overwhelming heaviness to it and you can't wait to leave. This is a sign that this is not the home for you.

You walk into a room crowded with people. For some reason you just can't stand being in close proximity to a person who you don't even know. There is a feeling of darkness about them that your gut is warning you to keep away from.

You are driving to your local shopping centre and you have a strong feeling you should drive to a certain area of the car park. The car park is full of cars and there aren't any free car spaces, although you are still being drawn to a certain area. When you arrive, there is a car space waiting for you.

You go to an event and meet someone for the first time and you feel as if you have known them for ages. You feel relaxed and talk for hours and discover that you have lots of things in common. This is because your frequency is resonating on the same vibration as the other person.

When you have an inspirational idea and your senses start to go 'off', you get tingles up your spine and feel like you are being buzzed from an external source. This is a sign that the idea will be successful.

You may go out on a date for the first time and feel 'butterflies' in your stomach. The person you meet is fun and uplifting and you have an instant attraction to them. The person ends up being your partner.

Physical sensations and feelings

Clairsentience is something that can speak to you via physical sensations throughout different parts of your body.

Have you ever had the experience of feeling like something was touching you on your face, head, arm, skin or other parts of the body?

Have you experienced the hairs on the back of your neck standing up on end? Sometimes it can feel like a spider or bug is crawling on you, or like a tingling or buzzing feeling.

These physical sensations are hard to deny – how many times have you felt a tingle up your spine? I am sure you have had it many times in your life, as this is a common form of physical clairsentience. These types of feelings can occur when you are having a visitation from the spirit world, or it may be to give you confirmation that what you were thinking is correct. It can also be a warning of impending danger, from a living person or from a spirit from the other side.

Physical sensations can be accessed when you visit locations. You may enter a home and notice a particular room feels angry or uninviting. It could also feel cold when the rest of the house feels warm. If you experience this kind of feeling, it may be because the room is the location where arguments or disagreements have taken place in the past. It could also be a room where someone has passed away.

Over the years of seeing clients, it has been interesting to note that if a client has bought a home that has been sold because of an unpleasant divorce, when the new family moves into the property they begin to have marriage problems and may even divorce. This is because the vibration of the property has absorbed all the negativity of the previous owners within its walls.

You may also visit a location or home where someone has suffered or died from an illness. It is also not uncommon for people who live in these types of properties to begin to experience their own health issues. Sometimes the new residents may dream of the prior owners or see or feel them moving about the house.

I would always suggest, when you go to a location, be guided by your first impression, as it will always be correct. If you are looking at buying a new home, take a notepad and write down what you feel in every room. It would be good to draw a house plan of each room and identify the feelings that you and your partner feel in each room. If you don't feel comfortable in the house, then this is a warning that maybe the home you are thinking of purchasing may not be right for you.

Usually when you experience physical clairsentience, the feeling is positive. Have you ever visited a relative's home where one of the occupants has passed away? You are well aware that the person is now in the spirit world, yet feel as though they are alive and well in the room with you.

You may even experience an overwhelming sense of peace when you sit in their favourite chair and suddenly feel their touch along your brow. This type of feeling is common and most of us have had this type of experience during our life.

I find that usually the first twelve months after someone passes is when the deceased person's energy is the strongest. As time passes, their energy will fade, and you may not notice their presence as strongly. It is not to say that they don't still reside in their home or around their family. It is more the fact that we become accustomed to our loved ones energy and probably take it for granted that they are always with us.

Clairsentience is a unique gift that can connect you to others in ways that you can only imagine. The love you have for another human being can keep you linked together via clairsentience. Your loved one may be in a different state or even another country, yet you can pick up their energy. You may have the image of that person constantly in your head or the feeling of them in your heart. The feeling may be that the person is homesick and missing you. It could be that you worry about their safety or health. You may feel whatever they are feeling, whether it is sad or happy, without even thinking about it. Many family members have this type of connection to each other. It is very common for mothers to feel the connection to their children and just 'know' if their children are OK. I feel it is part of our natural instinct. There are many reports of twins being separated at birth and still feeling the connection to each other even though they have grown up in different households, sometimes not even knowing that the other twin exists.

Over the years I have worked on many police investigations. The parents of many victims have reported to me that at the time their loved one went missing or the time something happened to them, they had a feeling or knowing that something was wrong

It would be truly wonderful if we could take our feelings one step further and use them to look after our loved ones to warn them of impending danger.

Spirit and clairsentience

The easiest way for spirit to make contact with us on the earth realm is through clairsentience. I have discussed some of these forms in prior paragraphs.

Spirits don't have a physical body so they find it hard to make contact with those who are not spiritually aware. If you are tuned in and aware of your psychic gifts, it can be much easier to pick up the subtle energy shifts those in spirit use to make contact.

The energy shifts spirits use can be felt physically by the human body. Yet many of us will ignore or dismiss them. I also find that those in spirit prefer to make contact with us when we are alone. They seem to be a bit sneaky like that.

This is because we are not focused on something else that could hinder us from noticing their presence.

You may be sitting quietly in a room reading a book when you feel a subtle breeze or coolness enter the room, even though there aren't any windows or doors open.

On the other hand, you may experience a physical sensation of heaviness in your body or a crawling sensation that people would call the 'heebie-jeebies' (this is a term my dad used a lot when I was a child), which gives you the creeps and makes you feel really uncomfortable. If you experience this type of sensation, I strongly recommend you smudge your home to get rid of the energy, as this type of feeling is usually connected to a negative spirit or entity.

You may be thinking of an idea when you receive a buzz or tingle up your arm or the side of your face. This feeling is yet again confirmation what you are thinking about is a good idea. This type of feeling is a positive confirmation from spirit.

You may be lying in bed having thoughts about how much you miss a loved one in spirit, when you feel a reassuring touch to your arm or face even though you are the only one in the room.

After a family member has passed over, the living members of the family may sense their relatives in spirit at significant times such as birthdays, Christmas and anniversaries. The feeling is usually of a warm loving sense of calm experienced by multiple family members. Don't be frightened by any of the above scenarios, as this is just confirmation you are not alone.

When I have any experiences such as the ones described, I simply thank my guides, angels or loved ones for making their presence known.

Sometimes when you receive subtle feelings from those in spirit, it will be followed by a physical event occurring, such as the television, radio or light suddenly turning itself on. You may question yourself as to how this actually happened, even though you had a subtle sign from spirit just prior to it happening. Believe!

Haunted locations

Haunted and historical locations are well known for clairsentience and physical happenings. I have visited many historical sites to be met with the smells and emotions of the past.

Have you ever visited the ruins of a historic location and felt uneasy, like you were being watched or followed? Have you picked up the feeling of sadness, illness, dehydration, despair or even hunger that isn't connected to yourself? Have you felt frightened or distressed for no apparent reason while visiting a historic location?

All of these feelings can be connected to the location and relate to the history of the site and are not necessarily connected to you. You may go on holiday and visit an area where the native owners of the land no longer reside. Yet you get a sense of what those people looked like, dressed like, what they ate and how they lived. You may be drawn to certain rock formations or ruins others around you may not even know exist, as you feel drawn by something you can't explain.

Have you ever visited a location and had a sense of being there before? You may return from the historic site or home only to begin dreaming about its prior occupants. You may even see yourself as being a part of the location in a previous life. This could be because you may in fact have lived or been a part of that location in a previous lifetime, and revisiting the site has awoken your memories of the past.

These types of feelings and memories are occurring because the spirits of the past are making contact with you.

It is always a good idea if you are visiting a historic location to white light yourself prior to visiting. I also recommend before leaving a location, you ask any spirits there to not follow you home and white light yourself again just prior to departing your location. That way, when you leave, you won't bring any spirits home with you.

If I am going on a ghost tour or working at a historic site, when I return home, I always have a physical shower to wash off any residual energy that may have become attached to my auric field. That way I know I am well and truly rid of any unwanted guests.

I have had clients who tell me they have willingly invited spirits to come home with them after doing a ghost tour as they wanted to have a ghostly experience. After they have done this there was no end of problems that began to happen at their home. One lady came to me for assistance as her children began to have horrible nightmares and had trouble sleeping. The children became quite unwell after this experience.

You must always be very careful with the spirit world, as there are energies and forces that we do not totally understand. Children are open from the moment they are born. Children will have clairsentient experiences without even being aware of them. So always be careful what you wish for. If you are going to invite ghosts into your home, you are only asking for trouble. Not to mention that the trouble won't just stop at you, it can affect your entire family.

It is a bit different however if your darling nanna has passed away. If you ask your nanna to help protect you or your children, for instance, this isn't going to be an issue. When people die, they are not around you 24/7, as they also have their own spiritual journey to undertake in the spirit world. They are, however, only a thought away, so it is totally fine to ask someone who you know and love to be of assistance to you or your family from the other side.

Being in control of your clairsentience

It is wonderful to be empathetic to others, but you also want to have control of your own feelings and life. When you are too open, you will be on an emotional rollercoaster ride of your and other people's feelings. It is hard to be completely shut off, but it is possible to be protected. The pictures below show what a protected energy field (aura) and an unprotected energy field look like. When the person is not centred and protected your aura or forcefield will appear with gaps or breaks within it.

The unprotected aura

When you are stressed, your energy field is weaker than normal which can then lead to you being more open and vulnerable to other's feelings and emotions. Use the exercises below to help protect yourself.

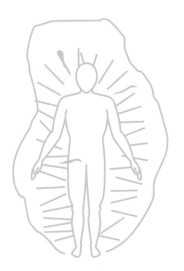

The protected aura

When we are protected, our aura is round and unbroken around our body.

Quick ways to help you be protected

Here are some suggestions to assist you with centring and protecting yourself. In everyday life, it would be wonderful if, when we feel we need to reconnect with ourselves, we could just sit and meditate. This is impossible, as we are all busy people and don't always have the time and place to just stop and meditate for an hour.

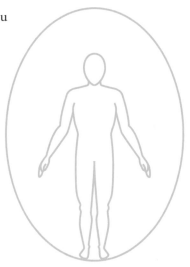

Personally, I found it hard to make time to meditate on a daily basis and was constantly told that this was not good for my spiritual growth. At the time I had three small children and having five minutes to myself was impossible. I believe it is important to find what works best for you. We are all individuals and have different demands on our time. So, I have some suggestions that you may find helpful as a quick fix to protect you when you are out and about in your daily life.

Whenever you feel that things are becoming overwhelming. Stop, slow down and focus on your breathing. With each breath imagine breathing in white light. When you exhale, visualise breathing out what it is that is causing you concern.

Drink lots of water as this helps you to keep the energy flowing through your body and keeps you hydrated.

Imagine your guardian angel by your side. Visualise your angel surrounding you with their wings shielding you with their heavenly protection.

If you are in a situation where a person is draining your energy and making you feel uncomfortable, visualise yourself surrounded in a bubble of white light. The light can be your protective forcefield that repels any unwanted energy or attention.

If a person is being unpleasant to you, visualise surrounding them in their own bubble of light. I always use pink light as I am sending them love and light from my heart chakra. I ask my guides or guardian angel to protect me from their negativity.

Being in a crowd can be quite confronting for clairsentients. I visualise a bubble surrounding me, glowing with brilliant white light. I expand the bubble around myself, so that it is like a forcefield that repels others' energy. When you do this, people around you tend to give you more space and don't bump into you.

You may even like to imagine you are like Harry Potter, with a cloak of invisibility surrounding you when you are in crowded places. You can visualise you can see others but they can't see you.

Visualise your chakra points shutting down like lotus flowers. Start at your base chakra. See a beautiful lotus flower that is red and see the petals closing up nice and tight. Then move to your sacral chakra and visualise an orange lotus and see its petals closing up tightly. Next move to your solar plexus chakra and visualise the lotus flower is now yellow and the petals are closing up tightly. Continue up to your heart chakra and visualise the lotus flower is a brilliant emerald green. Visualise the petals closing tightly. Continue up to your throat chakra and visualise the lotus flower is a brilliant blue. Watch as the petals tightly close. Now move up to your third-eye chakra and see a violet-coloured lotus flower – watch as the petals close tightly. Now move up to your crown chakra and visualise an indigo-coloured lotus flower. See the petals close tightly shut. Now surround yourself with a brilliant white light that surrounds your auric field.

Another way to do this exercise is to place your hand on each of your chakra points and imagine that there is an invisible switch only seen by you. As you place your hand over each chakra point, visualise the colour that corresponds with each chakra and imagine that the switch is turned off.

Imagine that you are in your home taking a shower. The shower is surrounding you with spiritual protection. When the water droplets fall onto your body, they wash away any negative energy. As the water flows, the negative energy is washed away down the drain.

In Chapter 14, I have included a meditation that will help you to work with both your clairsentience and clairempathy abilities. This will assist you to clear any unwanted energies and help you to find your natural state of being.

CLAIREMPATHY – FEEL YOUR EMOTIONS

What is clairempathy?

The word 'clairempathy' comes from the French word *clair* meaning clear and the Greek word *empatheia* meaning emotional feeling. Clairempathy, or clear feeling, is the ability to sense others' thoughts, emotions, feelings and symptoms. The difference between clairempathy and clairsentience is that clairempaths will sense emotions and clairsentients will physically experience all of the emotions within themselves.

Clairempaths sense and know things, relying on the psychic senses to pick up impressions about people and places that are not picked up by the conscious mind. Clairempathy enables them to sense the energy of others.

Clairempaths are extremely sensitive to the vibrations and energies that surround them. This can be both a good and bad experience as constantly picking up the emotions of anger, fear and happiness, as well as feeling the physical ailments of people, animals, places and things can become quite draining if you are not protected.

When a clairempath is too open to their environment, they can find it hard to know whether what they are feeling is their own or the feelings and emotions of those around them. It is important for a clairempath to protect themselves spiritually, as they can become bombarded by everyday life and go into spiritual overload. Clairempaths need to be able to protect themselves, maintain a healthy balance and ensure they don't have negative energy attached to their auric field.

Empathy

The gifts of clairempathy and clairsentience are closely connected and work hand in hand. A clairempath tunes into the heart chakra while a clairsentient tunes in through the solar plexus chakra.

Empathy is the ability to tap into or read the feelings of another person. You can empathise with the emotions of another and see things from their perspective.

Being an empath means that you have the ability to connect to another person's aura, allowing you to feel and experience what is going on in their life on a personal level. When you are not psychically aware of this ability, it can happen unconsciously. On the positive side, it helps you to relate to others and have an understanding of others around you. However, empathy can be a challenging ability to deal with, as it allows you to become emotionally involved when you may not wish to be.

Being empathetic is part of human nature and it is a necessary part of our life. However, if you don't learn how to control or shut yourself down from being a constant empath, you will become like a human sponge and absorb the emotions and feelings of everyone around you.

It is OK to be empathetic to your friends and loved ones, as that is part of what a friendship or relationship is about. Being supportive and taking the time to listen to others' needs is fine, but if a relationship is only one sided and the person is not a good support to you, then maybe you need to have a chat to your friend/partner and explain how you feel about this situation.

If the person doesn't understand, then it may be time to disconnect from the friendship/relationship. People who constantly do this to others are called 'psychic vampires'. Sometimes they are not aware of their actions, while some actively feed off the positive energy of others, as it makes them feel stronger and more powerful.

To be able to work with the spirit world and those in the living world, it is important to be able to be empathetic to both sides. However, it is also important to shut yourself down when you have finished your work because otherwise you will become very drained and depleted, which can result in health and emotional issues.

I always make a point of white lighting myself if I am going to be in a situation where there are lots of people around me (see chapter 6 on psychic protection). This doesn't mean that I am shut off from the world, as it still allows me to pick up the information I need, but it stops me from being constantly bombarded by the emotions and feelings of others.

It has only been through experience and lots of practice that I have been able to achieve this. The most important thing to remember is to practice and be patient.

Are you an empath?

Do you ever feel like you are different and don't always feel like you belong?

Do you watch the news and see tragic events that affect you on a personal level and you feel as though the event is personally happening to you? You may feel the pain of those affected.

Do you find it hard to say 'no' to others even though deep down you do not want to do what is being asked of you?

Are you the person that everybody comes to with their problems? Your friends come over feeling depressed and upset. When they arrive you are happy and positive, when your friends leave after dumping all of their problems onto you, you feel drained, tired and depressed yourself.

You are a person who always puts others needs before yourself as you feel responsible for them even at detriment to yourself.

You have a tendency to like your own space because you tend to get caught up with others' problems and emotions.

You feel distracted when you are speaking with people because you start to pick up on the problems of the person you are with.

Have you ever met someone and shaken their hand or given them a hug to later feel that you suddenly have picked up the other person's ailments? For example, you may shake the hand of someone who is suffering with back issues. After making contact with the person, you suddenly feel that your back is hurting, when prior to meeting them you felt fine.

Empaths can use their gift to be able to diagnose or feel illnesses and ailments in other people's bodies. Many gifted healers, reiki practitioners, naturopaths and psychics have the ability of empathy. The important thing to remember is you will need to have control of how and when you connect to others' pain.

Do you forget to take time out for yourself to have fun?

Are you invited to events where everybody wants you to give them advice, or does your phone constantly ring with people seeking your advice?

You may find it hard to be amongst crowds, as when people hustle and bustle past you, the emotional baggage of others may be picked up and absorbed into your own energy field (aura) which is your spiritual body.

Meditation can help you stay centred

It is important to be able to turn your clairempathy and clairsentience on and off and to remain centred. Being centred is when you shut down your auric field, so that you can protect your energy field from others. It is like imagining that any chinks in your armour are closed off from the outside world.

Being centred will help you to reconnect with your inner self and own emotions. In this state, you are connected to your own wants and needs and not those of others.

The meditation below will assist you with clearing any emotional baggage you have surrounding you and it will allow you to feel more centred. As you have already practised and visualised working with chakras (see chapter 5), you can now reconnect and go within to become more centred and balanced.

Clairempathy and clairsentience meditation

- Find a quiet place to sit and relax. Gently close your eyes and slowly breathe in.

- With each breath in, focus on what thoughts and emotions are part of you, and with each breath out, release what you feel no longer belongs to you.

- Breathe in positivity and light.

- Exhale any residual energies and emotions still lingering around you.

- Breathe in the light.

- As you exhale, visualise all the unwanted emotions disappearing and being evaporated by a beautiful protective white light.

- In your mind's eye, imagine that you are standing outside in the garden. You can feel beautiful soft green grass beneath your feet.

- Look down at your feet and feel protective healing light coming from beneath the earth slowly moving up into your body, entering through the soles of your feet.

- As you take each new breath, the light becomes stronger and brighter moving up through your body, reaching your root chakra.

- As the energy reaches your root chakra, it turns a brilliant red. The light continues to move and reaches your sacral chakra, turning a brilliant orange. The light continues up and reaches your solar plexus, turning a brilliant yellow. Feel the energy filling your body and continuing to move up to your heart chakra, turning a brilliant green. Allow the energy to progress and move up to your throat chakra, turning a brilliant blue. As you feel the energy moving along your body, notice if there are any blockages you may need to spend more time on. Pay extra attention to the areas around your solar plexus and heart chakra. If there is any resistance in these areas, visualise the light cleansing and clearing the blockage. Watch as the energy now moves up to your third eye, turning a brilliant violet. Continue to see the energy reach your crown chakra and turning bright indigo.

- Take a few moments to feel the light filling your entire body with its cleansing purity. Feel the energy expanding throughout every part of your body, allowing you to be reconnected with your inner self.

- Call in your angels and ask them to help you release any feelings and emotions that do not belong to you. As you do this visualise the emotions floating away from you as if they are butterflies flying off into the distance.

- Ask your angels to help you to be centred and back in control of your own body and life. Recognise the feeling of releasing the burdens of others' emotions.

- This is an important feeling to remember, as each time you feel you are absorbing others' emotions you need to centre yourself and become connected to this place of peace and tranquillity.

- Now, ask your angels to strengthen the connection. Visualise them surrounding you with their wings of light and showering you with their love. As you do this, watch the light repair any cracks, fractures or openings within your auric field. Notice the difference when your aura is restored to its natural state.

- Thank your angels for their assistance and know in the future you can always return to this place.

- In your own time, gently bring your awareness back to the here and now and slowly open your eyes.

AFFIRMATION

I allow the gifts of clairempathy and clairsentience
to flow through me with love and guidance.
I ask for protection from my
angels when I use this gift.

CHAPTER 15

CLAIRTANGENCY – TUNING INTO OBJECTS (PSYCHOMETRY)

What is clairtangency?

The word 'clairtangency' comes from the French words *clair* meaning clear and the Latin word *tangibilis* meaning to touch. Clairtangency, or clear touch, is more commonly known as 'psychometry', and it is an ability that psychics and mediums use to tune into and see the history of an object they are holding. A person who has the ability of clairtangency/psychometry is called a psychometrist. Using this gift, a psychometrist can see, sense and feel through their hands. From this point forward throughout this chapter, I will refer to clairtangency as psychometry, as this is the more common name for this ability.

Psychometry is a combination of normal psychic awareness and the ability to read the psychic impressions that are stored in objects around us. Psychometry is closely linked to the psychic gift of clairsentience. Both of these gifts often work concurrently. Many of us use this gift on a daily basis without even being aware it.

Have you ever held an item and begun to notice strong feelings about the item or the owner? If the answer is 'yes', then you have already had a glimpse of psychometry.

When you shake hands with a person, it is also possible to receive strong psychic impressions via psychometry about that person without consciously doing so. Have you ever had someone touch you and you felt an instant like or dislike for them? This is because you are tuning into the other person's energy field or aura.

We as living beings all have our own energy field and when we wear an object or live at a certain location, our energy can become imprinted within our surroundings or within an object.

By practising psychometry, you will discover that other psychic gifts will open up to you. Many who work with psychometry discover they also have the gift of mediumship.

How does psychometry work?

We touch objects on a daily basis, and every time we do this, part of our energy is imprinted into an object. The longer we own the object, the more our energy is absorbed into the item. Psychics who practise psychometry are able to read a person's energy by tuning into their magnetic energy field. A perfect example is to think storing the image of a photograph onto an SD memory card. You can't see how the image is transferred onto the card, but you hope and believe that it is there when you wish to access the photographs.

It's exciting when you plug your SD memory card into your computer and print your photographs out or take the card to the photographic shop to have the image printed out and have proof that the moment took place.

When you have a reading done by psychometry, the item being read must be something important to the owner and regularly worn by them. Otherwise, it will be difficult to make contact with the energy.

One thing to remember while handling an object is, if the object had multiple owners, the energy of each will be imprinted on the object. This can make the reading quite difficult unless the owner is aware of the history of the previous owners of the item.

Psychometry is a great tool to use to open you up to the spirit world. Through using your gift of psychometry, you can enhance your gift of mediumship as well.

The practice of psychometry involves using both the right (intuitive) and left (rational) parts of your brain to work together.

When doing any psychic work, the left-brain is too rational and sometimes interferes with the messages. However, with psychometry, we need to feed our right-brain intuitive processing with some of the left-brain facts about what we feel, see, smell or hear.

When working with psychometry, it is possible to sense a person's moods, and the psychometrist can actually feel the same way themselves. It is not uncommon to feel any health issues within the body while doing a reading with psychometry.

The most important thing to remember when doing a psychometry reading is to stay calm, relaxed and open-minded.

Psychometry is an ability that takes time to develop. When you try too hard, you tend to block off the information you are trying to pick up.

The other thing to remember is that no matter what information you pick up, even if it seems silly or insignificant, please take note of it. Remember, the messages are not for you – they are for the person being read and the smallest detail to you could be something that is extremely important to them.

Some people get amazing results immediately, while others can take months or even years to develop their abilities. It takes time and practise to be a good psychometrist, so allow yourself to be patient and you may be surprised by what you uncover.

Part of working with psychometry is trusting yourself and allowing the information to flow freely. Taking notes while tuning in can also assist you when you first begin, as once the information begins to flow, it can come very quickly and makes it hard to remember everything at once.

When I do a reading while using psychometry as the main psychic tool a number of things will take place. Firstly, I will start to see symbols that are connected to the person I am reading for (the sitter). I will also start to hear voices (clairaudience) that are usually the spirit guide or loved one in spirit of the sitter. Those in spirit who wish to make their presence known will start to appear before me in a psychical form.

Information about the sitter's mother's side will usually appear on the sitter's right-hand side and their father's side will appear on the left. If the person is married or has a partner, the left-hand side is where their loved ones will appear.

I see little mini-movie-like visions about the person's life and information that is important to the sitter at the current time.

For example, the person may be thinking about buying a new car. I will receive the vision of an old car driving away and a new one appearing in its place. If the client is in early pregnancy or thinking of falling pregnant, I suddenly see my own stomach rising as if I am pregnant. I also see the image of a baby wrapped in a blue or pink bunny rug depending on what sex the baby is.

It is interesting to note, when I am doing a reading for a person who has family members in spirit that didn't speak English, when they communicate with me I can understand what they are saying. Some spirits work telepathically when making contact.

It's important to pay special attention to what the energy feels like when you are tuning into an item. If you are doing a reading for someone who wants to make contact with a loved one in spirit take note of the different feelings you pick up. The energy of a person who is alive feels much lighter and they literally feel alive. With someone who is deceased, the energy feels heavier, and they may appear in front of you which indicates they are deceased.

Different types of psychometry

There are a range of different types of psychometry – object psychometry, energy and hand reading, photograph reading, flower reading and location psychometry. I will discuss these below.

Object psychometry

When doing object psychometry, it is best to work with an item made of metal. Preferably the item is jewellery and worn or held by the sitter. Items that are best to use include watches, necklaces, bracelets, rings, reading glasses or house/car keys. I find that earrings or material items don't absorb as well. This is not to say they don't work; they just don't have the storing properties that the other items do and it is more difficult to work with them.

You will find that most males don't wear as much jewellery as females do, so choosing glasses or keys is usually the best choice when reading a male. A watch is always my first choice to tune into, as they are worn more often than any other type of jewellery.

I do not recommend using a mobile phone as mobiles emit electro-magnetic energy and this can cause interference. Clothing such as a hat, shoes, shirt or dress can also be used, however you must be careful that the item has been well worn and loved by the owner. Any item being read must be more than three to six months old to have absorbed enough of the owner's energy.

When an item is being read, usually the information imprinted within the object pertains to memories or glimpses of the life of the person the object belongs to. If the object is an antique it will contain the information of the multiple owners who owned it. This can cause confusion for the psychometrist as the object will have what I call 'layering' imprinted within it.

When you are new to object psychometry, try to only read items that have had one owner. This will help you to hone your skills and strengthen your gift. If there is 'layering' connected to a piece you will find it difficult to understand the messages you are receiving. Messages will come through from different eras and lives that may make you doubt the information you are picking up. In time, as you strengthen your gift and gain more confidence, proceed with an antique item to challenge yourself.

The information contained within an object can relay very personal details about the owner such as: whether the person is male or female, their personality, emotional state, any health issues, their opinion of a particular situation or person, even their current location for example. While doing this type of psychometry it is very important to be careful of how you relay information that you are receiving.

For instance, if you see the sitter has health issues, it is advised you suggest they may need to visit a doctor instead of giving medical advice. You may be picking up messages incorrectly and you don't want to alarm them.

If you read an item or object that has been touched less often, it can still be read, however the information may not be as strongly imprinted. Unusual objects such as a TV remote, chair or garden trowel can also be read. In the case of large objects such as a motor vehicle, a door or piece of furniture, the psychometrist will travel to the site to receive psychic impressions about those who have touched the item. Usually with such objects, the information will pertain to those who have touched or owned the item. For example, if the object being read is a cupboard, the information may provide details about what happened in the room it has been kept in, or it could tell you what type of objects were stored in it. For example, there may have been a precious dinner set or jewellery contained in it, or important family paperwork such as a will that was once stored within.

Energy and hand reading

Reading a person's energy can be achieved by holding the person's hand to tune in to them psychically. It is easiest to do this by sitting down at a table with the person sitting opposite you and holding their hand. By holding the person's hand you tap right into their source energy, however it can be a little confronting.

The most important thing to remember when doing this type of reading is to break connection at the end of the session. As you have been in close proximity to the other person's aura, you need to disconnect, so that you are not still connected to them after the reading has ended. I always wash my hands at the end of every reading to disconnect the psychic connection between clients. If you are doing multiple readings and don't have the opportunity to go to the bathroom or have access to a sink, I suggest you have a bottle of hand sanitiser with you for cleansing and disconnecting.

The other thing to remember is that once you open up to this type of psychometry reading, you need to be aware of how open you are when you are in crowds. If you open up through human touch when people are in close proximity to you, it will enable you to read them readily, even if you don't wish to tune in. So if you are in a crowded environment always

protect yourself by using white light and shutting your aura down
(see chapter 6 on psychic protection).

Photograph reading

Reading a photograph using psychometry can be a useful tool to
assist you in making a connection to someone in spirit. It can also be used
to read a person who is alive and can relay significant information.

When you are choosing a photograph to be read, it should be a front-on
view of the person you wish to tune into showing a clear view of their face and
especially their eyes. If they are wearing sunglasses, a hat or hooded jacket this
can make it more difficult to make a connection. The eyes are the window
to the soul, so it is vital that the eyes are easy to see to tune in properly.

By reading a photograph, it is possible to gain valuable information
about the person. Many glimpses of the individual's life can be captured
via psychometry. Photo reading can help ascertain the emotional state
of the subject, whether or not they are alive or deceased and other
vital information pertaining to the person. This makes photograph
psychometry a valuable tool that can assist in police cases of a missing or
murdered person.

If the photograph is of a location – for example, a house, a piece of land
or a gravestone – the information the psychometrist may receive could
include information about the people who live at the location. It can also
provide information about any previous owners, such as spirits that may
reside at the location. Photograph psychometry can assist with the history
of the location and whether or not there are negative entities or ghosts still
residing at the location.

A photograph of a house or gravesite of a deceased person can also be
used to attempt to make contact with the spirits of the deceased, especially
when there are no photographs of the actual deceased person provided at
the time of the reading.

Some psychometrists require the photograph they are reading to be an
original copy, and they will not work with an electronically produced or
emailed copy of the original. This is because they prefer to read the energy
of the original photograph, which may have been handled by the person
in the photograph or people connected to that person.

I personally don't have a problem if the photograph is digitally captured and emailed or whether I work from an original photograph.

I find that when I tune into the photograph, I read the person's face and their energy as to whether it feels like they are dead or alive. I question as to whether they were happy, depressed, active, shy, loud and other traits. Through doing this, I can usually begin to hear the person talking to me or see visual images in mini-movie clips that can give me more information about the person.

While doing photographic psychometry, I will access the photograph with many visual symbols. Over the years of working with spirit, I have been given a collection of symbols that my guides use while I am doing readings. These symbols have become my psychic encyclopaedia for the spirit world. Whenever I see a specific symbol, I instantly know what they are referring to and the message they are giving me.

Through your own practice with photographic psychometry, you will be able to judge what works best for you. You may find that it is better for you to hold an original photograph or it may not bother you if it's a copy or an emailed image. As you progress, your guides will be able to set up a set of signs or symbols that will give you the best access to information. Always remember there are no specific wrongs or rights when working with the spirit world. The only thing that matters is what works best for you.

Flower reading

Flower readings are very common at Spiritualist churches. As flowers are a living thing, they can easily absorb a person's energy and record their psychic impressions. To conduct a flower reading, the person requiring the reading must have picked the flower themselves and nobody else touched it. The person needs to sit and hold the flower imprinting their energy and thoughts onto the flower. Meditating while holding the flower makes the connection stronger.

Once the person has finished imprinting their energy into the flower, they should then place the flower into a brown paper bag to keep the energy stored within it. If there is a group of people being read for, all of the flowers, enclosed in their brown paper bags, should be placed in a container. This stops the energy from the other flowers from imprinting

onto others. It also gives the
psychometrist the chance to pick
which flower they are drawn to.

The person reading should
remove the flower from the bag and
then sit quietly and tune into the flower.
Whatever first impression comes through
when the person is initially holding the flower
is always correct.

Personally, I find the flower needs to be something
that has soft petals and leaves. Carnations, gerberas,
frangipanis, hibiscus and roses (thorns removed) are usually good at picking
up the energy of the person being read for.

This type of reading can be challenging for some people, as the more
you hold the flower, the more the energy of the flower dissipates, and
the flower tends to wilt and die. This type of reading is not something
everyone is good at doing.

Location reading

Location psychometry is best conducted at an historical site. Every living
being has their own energy and emotions. When we are alive, our emotions
are left behind at locations just as much as they are imprinted on our
personal items. The strongest impressions from location psychometry are
left at locations where there were dramatic or significant historical events.
This is because the memories of those who went before are stored in the
surroundings. For example, a battlefield, gaol or even a mental institution
will have stored strong memories of the prior occupants. Through this
type of psychometry, it is possible to retrace the history and sometimes
contact spirits that are still connected to the location.

If you are conducting a reading at a location using psychometry,
there are a few simple things I would recommend to assist you. Firstly,
pick a location that you know has some history. If you decide to pick a
friend's place, and it has been newly built, you probably won't be very
successful unless it has been built on the site of a previous home that
has historical significance.

Usually locations such as old hospitals, battle-grounds, mental asylums, orphanages or historical homes are the best choice. You may wish to look up the history of the site to find out about the prior occupants of the location and to find out what area of the property has had reports of the most psychic activity.

When you choose your site it is always a good idea to walk around the site quietly by yourself. Spirits don't always show themselves when you are in a crowd; they tend to make their presence known when you least expect it. Always remember the saying: 'Careful what you wish for, you just might get it!' Always be respectful of the prior occupants as you don't want them to get angry with you, and don't ever, ever, invite them to come home with you, as you might get *much* more than you wish for: a psychic attachment.

When you do your investigation of the site, be armed and ready with a camera, notepad and/or your mobile phone. These days our phones come with voice recorders, digital notepads, and built-in video and cameras.

My iPhone is an amazing tool to assist when I am doing an investigation of a site, as it can photograph and video spirits easily; the golden rule is to always video or take a photo with the flash turned on. I am sure that other android phones will also be of assistance for your psychometry investigation, however whatever phone you use, you will need to use the flash, as the spirits reflect off the light and their energy will show up in your photographs.

If you don't have an iPhone or android handset, a digital camera will suffice to capture any spirit activity on film. Taking photographic evidence always gives you confirmation of what you are picking up via psychometry (see chapter 24 for more on spirit photography).

Another thing to remember if you wish to tune into a location is that spirits of the past are creatures of habit. The spirits will still do things at a set time, so if, for example, they would congregate at a location on the property at lunch time and you are visiting at that time, sit quietly at that place and see what you pick up. I have visited many locations and have noticed that keeping to the routine of the location is when you will receive your best communication via psychometry.

Many people think that ghosts or spirits only come out at night. Location psychometry can happen any time of the day, depending on what the people who once lived at the location would do at any specific time.

For example, if you have chosen a hospital site to visit, be observant. If the nurse did her rounds at a certain time at the hospital you are visiting then there would be a lot of activity at that time of the day. Here's what to tune into at a historical site:

- Sit quietly and really tune into the location.
- Do you sense any emotions or feelings?
- Do you smell anything significant?
- Do you hear anything?
- Can you taste anything?
- Do you pick up any spirits at the location?
- What do they look like?
- Are they male or female?
- Do they communicate with you?
- Do they have an accent or do they speak the same language as you?
- Ask the spirit why they are at the location?
- Ask what the spirit's name is?
- Ask what era did the spirit come from?

After finishing your investigation, write down all of the information you have received. Check to see if you have captured any images at the site. Do some investigating to check if there is any information confirming what you received at the site. You will be surprised by how much information you have actually picked up about the location that is correct.

Always remember to clear yourself prior to leaving a historical site, as you don't want any spirits from the past to come home with you. Spirits don't usually try to attach to you – however, they may follow you home or attach to you because they are stuck in a period of time and they get excited that you can see and feel them when others who visit the location cannot.

To clear yourself run your hand along both of your arms, legs and body, brush your hands through your hair and imagine flicking off the energy that has attached to your aura. Then imagine a white bubble of light surrounding you. I always have a shower when I arrive home from a historical site to ensure that any unwanted energy has been removed.

What to do when you see negative images

When tuning into an item, you have to be prepared for what you might see. When you have a person to read and you don't know their background, you may not always be prepared for the information that filters through.

The most important thing to remember is that what you say can affect the person's life dramatically. People come for a reading for guidance, and it is important that you pass on messages to them in a positive light.

For instance, if you see someone crossing a road and being hit by a car, you wouldn't say, 'Don't cross the road or you will die'. This will make the person panic every time they cross a road. If you worry about something negative happening to you constantly, you can literally draw what you fear to you and it can manifest into reality.

What you could say is that your guides are giving you the message that the person should always be aware of their surroundings when they are crossing the road. Remind them to take their time before stepping off the kerb. You may be picking up an image of something that could happen, but always remember when you do a reading that nothing is set in concrete. What you are picking up is a glimpse in time that could be changed by the person taking different actions. The other thing to remember is that we all have karma with the spirit world and it is between spirit and the soul of the living where things are pre-destined. You, as the reader, don't have total control over anything that takes place – always remember, you are only the messenger.

I always believe in worrying about what you can change and not worrying about what you can't. Getting your client to focus on the positives in their life is so much more important than focusing in on the negatives. There are enough negatives on the television every day. Endeavour to shine the light on the good things people have to look forward to, as well as giving them gentle guidance in the challenging times.

If, for instance, you do a reading for someone and get the feeling that they may have a health issue, instead of giving them a diagnosis (as you are not a doctor), tell them where you may be picking up the discomfort in your body, and ask them if they have any issues that are similar to what you are picking up. If they agree they have had symptoms similar to what you are picking up, ask them to see their doctor and have it checked out as soon as possible.

When you see this type of information, it is important to open up the conversation to the person you are reading for and give them the relevant information. Once you have passed the information onto them, it is up to them to make their own decision about what they want to do. You cannot take responsibility if they do not decide to heed your warnings, however hard that may be for you to accept.

Are there haunted antiques in your home?

Do you spend time with your antiques before you purchase them? I mean, do you really tune into antique, vintage or second-hand items and let your sixth sense explore any negative energy present before bringing any potentially haunted items into your home?

Have you bought something second-hand only to begin experiencing ghostly incidences in your home after the item's arrival? Always remember that everything has its own energy. Always pay attention to how an item, antique or piece of furniture feels to you before you buy it. It is extremely important to get a sense of any new objects that will be joining your family, especially if they are antique or second-hand items.

If you don't know the history of second-hand items, then you don't know what type of energy the item will have connected to it until you get it home. Spirits can be attached to material items, so you may buy more than you bargained for.

Before making your decision about the object, if it is a piece of furniture, if possible, sit on it, lie on it or place your hand on it and see what feeling the furniture gives you. The first impression that pops into your head will be the correct one. If you feel sick, angry or distressed when you do this, the message is not to purchase the object. If you feel happy, excited or connected to the item, then this is a sign that your new addition is the right choice for your home.

If the item is a piece of jewellery, hold it in your hand and tune into it. Feel the item in your hand – are you getting a warm comforting feeling from the piece or are you feeling sad or angry? Do you get any visions of the previous owner? In your mind, talk to the piece and ask it why it was sold. For instance, the piece may have been sold due to a marriage break-up; if this is the case the piece will not have positive energy connected to it. The piece may have been sold due to someone not needing it anymore. Ask the piece if it is happy to be yours – if you feel happy and at peace with the decision to buy it, then go ahead and make the purchase.

Psychometry meditation

- Find a quiet place to sit and relax. Gently close your eyes, slowly breathe in through your nose and out through your mouth. As you do this, visualise breathing in positive uplifting energy. As you breathe out imagine that you are exhaling any stress or worries that you may have around you.

- Once again breathe in positivity and light, and as you do so, feel beautiful protective energy around you.

- This time when you breathe in, visualise you are drawing white light towards you.

- Exhale and expel any stagnant energy you wish to let go of.

- Now, visualise a beautiful bright white light surrounding your entire body. In your mind's eye, watch as this light expands to make you glow from its brightness.

- Look down at your feet and see this protective light entering your body via the soles of your feet. Watch as the light slowly moves up to your base chakra.

- As the energy reaches your base chakra, it turns a brilliant red. The light continues to move up through your body and reaches your sacral chakra turning a brilliant orange. The light now continues up and reaches your solar plexus turning a brilliant yellow. Feel the energy filling your body and continuing to move up to your heart chakra turning a brilliant green. Allow the energy to progress and move up to your throat chakra turning a brilliant blue. As you feel the energy moving along your body, notice if there are any blockages you may need to spend more time on. If there is any resistance, visualise the light cleansing and clearing the blockage. Watch as the energy now moves up to your third eye turning a brilliant indigo. Continue to see the energy reach your crown chakra and turning a brilliant violet.

• Take a few moments to feel the light filling your entire body with its cleansing purity. Feel the energy expanding throughout every part of your body, allowing you to be reconnected with your inner self.

• Focus on this beautiful bright energy moving through your body and visualise it flowing down along your arms and reaching your hands. Feel the energy flowing through your palms and watch as your palms radiate with the flow of this energy.

• Visualise yourself placing your two palms together, then gently pull your palms apart and see a ball of energy forming between your hands.

• Feel the glistening ball of light move between your hands and feel the warmth that it radiates. Watch as the energy between your palms grows bigger and bigger, so that the ball of light grows and moulds as if it is putty in your hands.

• Visualise lightning bolts of energy coming from within the ball of light. The ball gives you the knowledge that your palms are charged and ready to begin your psychometry work. Be settled in the knowledge that you have what it takes to be connected.

• Now watch the ball of light, feeling the connection growing within you to the spirit world. You are given confirmation from above that whenever you need to make a connection via psychometry, the ball of light will appear in your mind's eye.

• Remember what the ball of light looks like. Focus on what colour it radiates to you. Remember what it feels like to have the energy flowing through your hands and palms. Record this vision and feeling within your mind's eye for future connections.

- Sit quietly and feel the difference within you.
- In your own time gently bring your awareness back to the room you are sitting in; you now have the awareness to feel and tune in via your hands. Now slowly open your eyes.
- You are ready to begin your psychometry work.

AFFIRMATION

I allow the energy of light to flow through me.
I feel uplifted and guided by source energy. I utilise
the guidance and assistance from my guides in the
spirit world to enhance my gift of psychometry.
All messages I receive will be utilised to be of
assistance to others.

Getting started with psychometry: basic exercises

Pick a token object, so that you can tune in your mind and begin psychometry. You may start by seeing the briefest of flashes, however by practising the following exercises, your ability will build and your understanding of what you are seeing will increase. As you practise these exercises, your gift will grow and you will see more and more of an item's history.

Just think of the exercises as if they are your training regime. If you were a weightlifter, you would exercise your muscles daily. As you are working with the psychic realm, you are exercising the same way with your mind.

The following exercises are basic, however they will help you to learn and develop your psychometry abilities individually and in a group. Everyone has the ability of psychometry to some degree, but most of us don't consciously focus on it. With practise, you will become proficient and discover that psychometry can be a useful tool. It is always important to remember to only use your gifts for the highest good and not to invade someone else's privacy unsolicited.

Which hand to use

Before you begin to use psychometry as a psychic tool, it is important to determine which is your dominant hand.

For most right-handed people, the left hand is the receptive hand. For left-handed people, the right is likely to be the receptive hand. If you are in doubt, or were changed from a left-hander to a right-hander as a child, the following test will help to determine which is your receptive hand.

Hold your hands at chest level with your fingers pointing up and your palms facing one another, in a prayer position.

Next, rub your hands together slowly, making sure that you activate your palms and stimulate the energy to flow throughout your hands.

Move your hands together and apart to make the energy flow more efficiently. You should be able to feel which hand is emitting the stronger psychic energy by the heat that is building up in your palm area.

The hand that is feeling the warmest is your receptive hand. You are now ready to begin the following psychometry exercises.

The hand you use to receive psychic impressions from objects is important. Your dominant hand relays information while your non-dominant or receptive hand receives the information.

When you are beginning your work in psychometry, always pick up or touch an object with your receptive hand. Try to make a habit of using your receptive hand to take things from others. This will be a challenge to begin with, as you are probably used to picking things up and holding things with your dominant hand, but with practise, it will help you to remember to use your receptive hand for psychometric work.

Exercise 1: Energy reading

This is a fun exercise that can be used to help you to read the energy of others around you. This exercise is best undertaken in a group situation such as a workshop or psychic circle. It is best to do this exercise at the beginning of the gathering, so any personal information has not yet been shared amongst the group.

Split the group into pairs, preferably with someone they don't know.

Ask each pair in the group to sit opposite each other, close enough for them to be able to reach and hold the hands of the person opposite them.

Each partner in the pair should then hold the other's hand.

Both partners should shut their eyes and take it in turns trying to feel the other's energy.

Each person should try and tune into how their partner is feeling. Feel if the person you are reading is relaxed or tense. Are they happy or sad? Does the person feel hot or cold? Does the person have any areas that you are drawn to in their body? Do you feel that they have a headache or a nervous stomach for example? Are there any parts of their body that feels tired or sore? Do you feel that area in your own body? Take your time and get used to reading each other's energy.

The most important thing to do is trust whatever you are feeling. The first impression is always right. If you don't feel anything, take note of what, if any, symbols or impressions pop into your mind. This will help you strengthen your connection to psychometry in the future.

Share the information you received about your partner and take note of the amount of correct '*hits*' (correct information you received about the person) you received during this exercise.

Feedback is one of the most important ways to confirm you are tuning in correctly. It also helps you to understand the information you receive and to develop your gift with clarity and confidence.

At the end of the exercise, make sure you thoroughly wash your hands to make sure you break contact with the person you have been reading. It is important to shut down your auric field when you finish doing a reading.

Exercise 2: Reading an object

Before beginning psychometry, find an object that you wish to 'psychometrise' (read). Start with something small that is easy to hold in your hand. I recommend using an item that is metal, preferably jewellery such as a watch, ring, bracelet, glasses or keys. Also have a notepad and pen handy, to make notes about any information you receive.

Don't pick an item that is relatively new or something that the owner has not worn frequently. Pick something that has some history with the owner. Try using an item that is loaned to you by a friend, so that you are able to receive feedback about the item.

Initially, it is best to read an item that is not an antique, as you will find it confusing if there is information that comes through about multiple owners.

Now, find a comfortable chair, sit and relax in a room where you won't be disturbed.

Place your hands in your lap with your palms facing up. Now, sit calmly and clear your mind so that you are in a receptive state to begin your psychometry work.

Pick up the item with your receptive hand and then hold it in both hands. Feel the item and move it slowly between your hands.

- Gently close your eyes as this will make it easier for you to concentrate. Breathe in and out slowly three times. With each breath out, clear your mind of any thoughts or worries you have. Try not to think too much, just imagine you are part of the object.
- Think about what the object feels like.
- What is it made from?
- How do you feel while you are holding it?
- Do you pick up any feelings or emotions?
- Does the object feel happy or sad?
- Does it feel hot or cold?
- Do you pick up any sensations from the object?
- Do you smell or taste anything while holding the object?
- Do you see a person connected to the item or do you see a location?
- What does the person or location look like?
- If you are seeing a person connected to the item, does the person feel like they are alive or passed over?
- Are you picking up any symbols or images connected to the object?
- Do you hear anything connected to the item?

- Are there any sounds, voices or music popping into your head?
- Is anyone talking to you about the item?
- Are they male or female, young or old?
- Do they speak English?
- When you have finished tuning in, try to remember as much information as possible. Write down everything you can remember. You may find it easier if you draw any symbols or pictures that are significant to the item.

If the owner of the item is in the room with you, relay everything you have picked up about the item and ask them what, if anything, makes sense to them. I find that once I begin to relay the information to the owner, I receive more information that will add to the reading.

It is always good to get feedback, as this will help strengthen your connection in the future while doing this type of work.

The most important thing to remember is not to rush and to stay relaxed. Don't try to interpret or analyse these psychic impressions – the messages are for the owner, not necessarily for you. No matter how silly the impressions may seem, just take note of what the message is. Don't try too hard – if you try and force the information, you will find that you won't pick up anything and you will become frustrated with yourself.

If you aren't picking up anything don't be too hard on yourself either, as some days you are more open to receiving messages than others. Also, remember that some items will speak to you better than others.

If I am not getting anything from an item, I will ask for a different object to work with. Sometimes the reason you are not picking up anything is because the owner of the item is nervous and closed down. They inadvertently could be blocking you without consciously doing so.

Psychometry is a personal psychic tool and sometimes people are shocked by the intimate information you can pick up from an item. So, if you are getting too close to personal information, the owner may also shut down.

The more you practise psychometry, the more detailed the information you will receive. The important thing to remember is to be respectful of the information you are picking up and be careful how you pass that information onto the owner of the item.

At the end of the exercise, make sure you thoroughly wash your hands to make sure you break contact with the item you have been reading. It is important to shut down your auric field when you finish doing a reading.

Exercise 3: Group exercise

The following exercise is for a group of people who are developing their gifts.

Firstly, I recommend that the group position themselves so you are all sitting in a circle facing each other, preferably on chairs.

An opaque bowl is required for the group to place personal items into to be read. Preferably the item will be a piece of jewellery to start with – for example, a watch, bracelet, ring or necklace.

Each person should have a notepad and pen to take notes while they are tuning into the item.

Ask the group to discretely place the personal item into a bowl without speaking to the rest of the group about what the item is. This is important, so you don't know who the item belongs to.

As discreetly as possible, everyone puts a piece of their jewellery in the bowl.

Each member of the group then reaches in and takes out an object that does not belong to them.

Sit and hold the object in your receptive hand and tune into the item. You may wish to swap the item from one to the other to see which hand gives you the strongest impression.

Allow 20-30 minutes for the members of the group to psychometrise the object.

While the members of the group are tuning into the object they should write down any impressions, feelings, visions, signs or symbols they receive from the item.

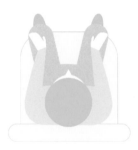

After 20-30 minutes is up, ask everyone to stop writing. Each member will then give their feed back to the respective owners of the object. Feedback is extremely important for the group to develop their abilities.

In a development group setting such as this, try not to say anything that might make someone in the group feel uncomfortable. Be as tactful and diplomatic as possible while you are describing your thoughts, feelings or the symbols you are picking up while giving feedback to the owner of the object.

When the exercise has finished make sure each member of the group washes their hands thoroughly to break the connection with the person being read for. This is important to remember as some people get attachments from the items they are reading because they have opened up their auric field to make the connection. Just as you open a door, you need to remember to shut it behind you.

Even the smallest of visions will help both yourself and the rest of the group in terms of psychometric skills.

Remind the group that they can't make a mistake and to believe in their own abilities.

When I tune into an object, I take notice of the feelings I get. I also notice what images pop into my mind. Symbology is a big part of psychometry – I often see the image of a house like on a Monopoly board. This usually indicates that the person is thinking of moving or buying a new property. Other times I see the image of a car driving away from me, which indicates that the person is thinking of buying a new car, or they should take notice of their car for some reason. If the car needs to be repaired, that part of the car will flash strongly in my mind – for example, a tyre or the engine.

When it comes to a female being pregnant, I can actually experience the feeling of being pregnant myself, or I may be shown a small baby wrapped in a pink or blue bunny rug, depending on the sex of the child.

As you practise your ability, you will develop your own personal symbology to assist you in understanding your messages from spirit.

CHAPTER 16

CLAIRCOGNISANCE – TUNING INTO YOUR INNER KNOWING

What is claircognisance?

The word 'claircognisance' comes from the French word *clair* and the Latin word *cognitio,* meaning clear knowing. Claircognisance is the ability to know things about something or someone without any prior knowledge or logical reason.

The primary 'clair' senses are clairvoyance, clairaudience and clairsentience. These three primary senses are connected to sight, sound and psychic touch/sensations. However, the gift of claircognisance isn't connected directly to any of our physical senses such as hearing, seeing or feeling. It is something that is connected to your inner self. It is a knowing that you may not even fully understand as to how or where the knowledge comes from.

This gift can be something that is so profound – you hear yourself saying something so accurate you wonder where on Earth it comes from. It is as though your inner self is aware of what is going on before you as a human being has any inclination.

Since discovering my claircognisance gifts, I have discovered that the best thing to do in life is to embrace whatever messages or information come to you. It is important to take notice and store the information received, although you may not always act on it. If you do not use the information at the initial time of receiving the messages, take note and put that message aside for future reference.

Examples of claircognisance

- You are compelled to work for a higher purpose in life and want to make a difference to others.
- You are with a friend and you know exactly what they are going to say before they say it.
- You have received inspirational ideas and guidance about your life's purpose from an early age.
- You know whether or not you like someone, from the moment you meet them.
- You are offered an amazing opportunity, yet you know that it is not a positive thing for you to do, but you don't know why.
- You feel drawn to sit and write down inspirational guidance from above.
- You just *know* things beyond any reasonable doubt.

Many of us access this gift daily but if we thought about where the knowledge came from logically we would dismiss the information. Have you ever had a moment in your life where you suddenly felt like you have awakened and a light bulb moment took place where you have the clearest view of what you should or should not do in a certain situation?

Have you ever met someone and, without even thinking about it, accessed knowledge about the person or a situation concerning them without any prior knowledge? To be honest this experience can be quite confronting when you first discover you have the gift of claircognisance.

You will find, when you begin to tune into this gift, you will be enlightened with many 'light bulb moments' or what is also known as an epiphany. These feelings seem to come from somewhere outside of yourself, when in fact, if you look further, you will realise you need to look within, for this information comes from deep within you.

Where does the information come from?

Claircognisance can come from your higher self and your spirit guides. Claircognisance is accessed through your crown chakra. It is your internal guidance system, similar to your own built-in GPS. If you can accept this knowledge and use it to give you spiritual direction and guidance, you will be surprised by how things become calmer and more settled in your life.

People who are highly analytical can find it quite hard to accept when claircognisance information just pops into their head. They will question how, why, when and where the information comes from. Sometimes it is better to not think about things so much and easier to feel things.

The most important thing to remember is that you are not imagining the information – it is divine guidance given to you for a higher purpose.

Of course, we all have free will, so there will be times in your life you have been given information from your spirit guides warning you not to proceed with something, yet you go against your better judgement and the result is not what you would have liked.

Sometimes in life we need to have this type of experience so that we can differentiate what is the right or wrong thing to do. If we didn't make mistakes in life, we wouldn't grow and expand our spiritual awareness.

My motto in life is that we learn from our mistakes. So next time you wish to kick yourself for not paying attention to your claircognisance when it was 'right' and you were 'wrong', sit back and take a minute to think about what you have learnt from the experience. The most important thing to remember is that next time you *will* listen to your inner guidance!

Ways to enhance your claircognisance

Meditation is a wonderful way to open your mind up to your spiritual gifts. With any of the 'clair' gifts, stilling your mind and shutting it off from the everyday chatter of life is always beneficial.

Exercise is also another wonderful way to open your mind to claircognisance. When you go for a walk, run, swim or even bike ride, your mind has access to the higher realms. It is also another form of active meditation. When we don't try to receive the answer we are looking for, it suddenly pops into our head unannounced.

Another way to access your claircognisance gift, and one of the best ways, is through automatic writing.

Your solar plexus is the psychic muscle connected to claircognisance, so practising and strengthening this psychic area will open up and enhance this ability.

Trust in yourself and the information you are receiving, as it is given to you to enhance your life and not to hinder it.

Ask your guides to share their guidance with you through claircognisance.

Be open and aware when you experience an epiphany. Take notice of which part of your body you experience the feeling in – is it your solar plexus, or do you feel a buzz or tingle on your arm or the side of your head?

How do you feel when you are receiving the information – does it feel positive or negative? Once you learn the difference between the sensations you will realise that your claircognisance has become stronger.

What is automatic writing?

According to the *Oxford Dictionary*, automatic writing is produced by a spiritual, occult or subconscious agency rather than the conscious intuition of the writer.

You may find this a scary thought, accessing the spirit world this way, but it's not really the case if you work with the light. Your spirit guides and guardian angels will protect you, so there is nothing to be afraid of. Always remember when undertaking any spiritual work, you need to be prepared by protecting yourself with white light to access the higher realms of the spirit world.

There are probably many times in your life you have tapped into your claircognisance to write an inspiring letter, poem, song or even just an inspirational affirmation. Now is the time to take that ability to the next step and tune into your hidden gift of automatic writing.

There are different ways that you can undertake automatic writing. By experimenting and practising, you will be able to determine which way works best for you. These different ways are discussed further, later in this chapter.

Some people choose to go into a trance-like state and channel information through automatic writing. I don't recommend this type of writing until you are more competent, as you are opening yourself up to the spirit world, and you need to be sure you are in contact with the higher realms of the spirit world and not lower entities.

Why do automatic writing?

When you start doing any type of automatic writing, I suggest setting aside 30 minutes a day to practice. Setting a timer can help, as it allows you to focus your mind on the answers you are seeking and can keep your energy focused for that period of time.

You may find when you first begin this type of psychic work that nothing happens at all. You may even feel frustration and feel that it is a waste of time. Do not despair, with patience and practise, you will be able to exercise your automatic writing skills. If you feel frustrated, take a break, go for a walk, even have a shower or a bath to get your focus back. I find the more relaxed I am the better the flow of information will be. The more you try to force this kind of information, the harder it may be to connect.

Here are some examples of questions you can ask your spirit guides and higher self:

- What is the guidance you wish to share with me today?
- Am I on the right spiritual path?
- Are there any signs I should be looking for from you – my spirit guides or guardian angels?
- How can I make the connection to you stronger?
- What am I meant to be doing with my: life, career, spiritual work etc?
- How will I know if it is you (my spirit guides/guardian angels) that is giving me this information?

Ask them to give you a sign, feeling or symbol when they are working with you as confirmation.

You may even ask your spiritual helpers to guide you with inspiration on a specific subject or answer a question that is burning inside of you. Or your question may be as simple as asking daily, are your guides happy with your achievements for the day.

If you are not comfortable with pre-writing questions or you just want to see what information you receive, then do so. Part of doing automatic writing is getting into the flow of writing. Just write about what pops into your head the same way as you would if you were writing a letter, journal or a story. Don't worry about what the information is or if it makes sense – just write.

Try not to let the rational left side of your brain overrule the information you are receiving. You may question where the information is coming from or wonder if what you are receiving is correct. Just keep writing everything down and when you have finished read through it.

The feeling you should have when conducting automatic writing should be of clear guiding messages that make you feel light, uplifted and inspired. If, for any reason, you feel the opposite to these feelings, then stop immediately as you have not protected yourself enough before beginning the exercise.

When you are receiving information from the spirit world, the messages are usually phrased in different words to what you would normally use if writing things down yourself. There is also a feeling of guidance and authority about the information that is received. Many times the messages will come to you in metaphors, which may take you time to decipher. Remember you are connecting to ancient and higher knowledge with insight into all things.

After you have finished your writing session, thank your guides and higher self for giving you spiritual inspiration.

When I first began to work this way with spirit the information was quite out there, and it didn't make any sense. It was only when the information was expanded on in future sessions that I came to fully understand what my guides were trying to tell me.

Hindsight is a wonderful thing – sometimes we feel we are receiving information that doesn't seem to make any sense at the time. It is only when we allow all of the pieces of the puzzle to fall into place that we can then see the whole picture. Your spirit guides have certain messages and lessons they wish to share with you at specific times in your life. Sometimes you have to go through particular experiences and lessons before they will allow you to progress to the next step of your spiritual growth.

The following methods of automatic writing are quite similar and the information received will be the same with either method. It is more a matter of working with the method that is the most efficient process for you to use.

Hand-written automatic writing

Before beginning hand-written automatic writing, you will need your spiritual journal and a pen or pencil. Find a comfortable place to sit and try to be as relaxed as possible. You may find that sitting in your sacred space will enhance the connection.

If you have any questions you wish to ask your higher self or spirit guide, write them down in your spiritual journal. It is best to write them down in bullet point form, so that when you make a connection, you can refer to them. It is also important to write the date and time you begin your writing, as you can then refer back at a later date. It also assists you to see how you have advanced with your spiritual work.

Sit with the pen/pencil comfortably positioned in your hand, clear your mind of your everyday worries or concerns. Focus your thoughts onto your questions and read over them quietly in your mind. Allow any thoughts that pop into your head to flow through your hand. Place your hand over a page in your spiritual journal.

Do not think about what you are hearing or experiencing, just allow the information to flow through your hand. Some people may begin to feel a shaking or tingling sensation pulsing through their body, arm or hand. If this happens to you, don't worry, as this is a sign that your guides have arrived and are ready to work with you.

When the information begins to flow through you, don't worry about the spelling, grammar or what your hand-writing looks like. It is more important that you write the information down as quickly as possible in your spiritual journal. Sometimes when the flow begins, it can be quite challenging to keep up with the information. If this is the case, still your mind and ask your guides to slow down the information, so you don't miss any important messages they wish to share with you.

Finish your session by thanking your spirit guides and higher self for sharing the information they deem important to share with you at this time.

Automatic writing with your computer

I personally prefer this form of automatic writing as it is the quickest and easiest way to work with my claircognisance. I can type much quicker than I can hand write, and I can also correct any spelling errors when I am finished. If you use Microsoft Word to do your automatic writing, the program will pick up any spelling or grammatical errors for you.

Ask your spirit guide/higher self what spiritual guidance you are meant to receive. You may wish to set yourself a list of questions that you pre-write in a Microsoft Word document, for example. Again, make sure you add the date and time of your writing. The good thing about computers is that they record the date and time automatically when you create a document.

If you have a laptop, you may wish to take it and sit in your sacred space to do this exercise. Sit at your computer, read each question to yourself, and ask your spirit guide or higher self to give you the answers you are seeking. You may hear the answer to your questions in your own mind. The messages could be in your own voice, that of your spirit guide, or it could just be the words and sentences popping into your mind. You may find that your fingers just take over and start to rapidly write the answers without you even thinking about what information you are receiving.

Don't worry about how the information appears, just type it as quickly as possible and allow the flow to begin. Once you have received the answers to the questions, save the file and read back through the information. Take note of any guidance you have received and act upon it prior to making contact in your next session of automatic writing. Thank your spirit guides and higher self for information you have received.

Candle contact – automatic writing

It is also possible to use this form of automatic writing to make contact with your lost loved ones in spirit. By doing a candle contact meditation, it is possible for you to receive messages from those in your life who have transitioned to the spirit world.

Our loved ones in spirit are only a thought away. Many times in life we have regrets about what we wished we had said to those who have now transitioned to the spirit world. Sometimes these feelings can hold you back from being amongst the living. You may constantly reminisce about what you wished you should have or could have done while your loved one was alive. This is a wonderful way of assisting you with contact.

For this type of automatic writing, you will need a candle. You may prefer an aromatherapy candle to help you relax and lift your vibration to make contact with your loved one while doing this exercise. Your spiritual journal and a pencil/pen are also required.

Go to your sacred space where you know you will feel uplifted and connected to the spirit world. You may wish to have a photograph or belonging of your loved one you can hold or look at while doing this exercise. Light the candle and have your journal ready to begin your connection.

Think about all of the wonderful loving experiences you had while your loved one was alive. Take your mind back to your most vivid experience you can remember having with them. Begin by writing how much you love and miss them as this will begin the process of making contact.

Pause for a moment and think about all of the things you wished you had said to them before they passed. If you feel that you don't need to do this, begin by telling them about the experiences you and the family have had since they passed.

Now stare at the candle flame. Watch as it jumps and flickers before your eyes. You may begin to see pictures or symbols within the flame. Your loved one may even appear before your eyes within the light of the flickering flame. If this happens, don't worry, you are not imagining things, you have made contact. Spirit uses many methods to make contact and this is another doorway for them to connect with you.

Below are some examples of what you may wish to communicate with your loved one in spirit while doing this exercise:

- Ask your loved one about their experiences since they have passed and joined the spirit realm.
- Ask them what messages if any they have for you or other family members.
- Ask them if they are now healed since they passed over.
- Ask them if they are aware of family events that have taken place since they passed – for example, the arrival of a new family member.
- Tell them how much they mean to you and how much you miss their presence.
- Ask them who they met during their journey to the other side, and are they with those people now.
- Ask them is there anything they would like you to do for them here on the earth realm.
- Ask them are they happy now they have transitioned.
- Ask them to give you any signs or symbols you should look for when they come to visit you.

When you receive answers to your questions from your loved one, make sure you write them down. This will give you the reassurance you need to know that your loved one is alive and well in the spirit world. It is possible to use this method of contact whenever you wish to communicate with your loved one. Sometimes it may take a few attempts before this form of communication works for you. Don't worry, if this is the case – with practise and persistence it will work. You must always remember to be patient, calm and relaxed, so that you are open-minded and ready to connect with spirit.

Claircognisance meditation

As discussed in earlier chapters remember to always protect yourself with white light before entering into any work with the spirit world. Prior to undertaking this meditation exercise, you are advised to enter into your sacred space. This can be achieved by first doing the sacred space meditation or it may be more of a physical undertaking of sitting in your devoted sacred space. Make sure you have your spiritual journal and pen close by.

- Sit or lie down in a comfortable position.
- Gently close your eyes and focus on your breathing.
- Now, inhale slowly and as you do this imagine you are breathing in pure white spiritual light.
- As you exhale imagine breathing out any negative energy you may have been holding onto.
- Breathe in positivity and light.
- Exhale any negativity you may have around. Imagine you are ridding yourself of any emotion that does not belong to you.
- Breathe in the light.
- Exhale any residual energy that is still attached to you.

- Call in your spirit guide/guardian angel and ask them to protect you during this meditation. Feel their presence behind you protecting you.

- Visualise that you are connected to the earth and watch as your feet start to sprout like tree roots grounding and centring you to the earth.

- Visualise light moving up from the earth beneath your feet. Watch as the light enters through the soles of your feet, and watch as the light moves up through your body. See the light moving along your legs up to your thighs and watch as it ignites the light of your base chakra and turns a brilliant red.

- The light now continues to move up to your sacral chakra – watch as it glows brighter and brighter and turns a brilliant orange.

- Now visualise the light moving up to your solar plexus as it turns a brilliant yellow.

- Watch as the light moves up to your heart chakra and turns a brilliant green.

- The energy now moves up to your throat chakra and turns a brilliant blue.

- The energy continues to move up to your third eye, turning a brilliant indigo.

- Visualise the energy reaching your crown chakra, turning a brilliant violet.

- Pause here for a moment and visualise the energy continuing to come up from your feet and moving through your entire body. Watch as all of the colours of the rainbow expand and flow throughout your body. The colours move and circulate throughout each and every space within your being.

- Visualise beautiful golden energy appearing above your head connecting to your crown chakra. This energy intertwines with the energy flowing throughout your body. Contained within this golden energy is knowledge that comes from the higher realms. The information contained within this energy is connected to everything you have ever said, experienced or seen. It is also connected to everything that is around you at present and what you will experience in the future.

- This energy is warm, comforting and guiding; it is part of your higher self and is your direct line to your future experiences. Trust this knowledge is there for you to tap into at will. Imagine this energy of knowledge turning into a giant light bulb above your crown chakra. Every time you wish to access this knowledge, visualise the light bulb glowing brightly above your head, giving you the information you are seeking at that time. Give this energy the permission to be able to light up in times of need, if you are in danger or in need of inspiration.

- Hold the vision of the light bulb shining brightly and remember whenever you need to access the energy of knowledge and your higher self that it is only a thought away.

- Be settled with the knowledge that whenever you need to reconnect with this energy that you have the spiritual awareness to do so.

AFFIRMATION

(to be said daily)

I acknowledge that I am open to the gift of claircognisance. I allow my guides to assist me with the inner knowing I know that I possess. I trust and believe that I will be guided in the most positive and enlightened way possible.

CHAPTER 17

CLAIRGUSTANCE – CONNECTING TO SPIRIT VIA TASTE

What is clairgustance?

The word 'clairgustance' comes from the French words *clair* and *gustance* meaning clear taste. Clairgustance is the ability to receive a message from spirit intuitively through the sense of taste. This gift is not often spoken about, but it is a common ability when you start to think about it.

In our physical world we use the gift of taste every day. When we eat or drink things, we may or may not like the taste. Food or drinks can be sweet, sour, spicy, salty, smoky, bitter or bubbly. Recognising these differences is all part of developing our palate to what we do and don't like.

Clairgustance is closely linked to clairalience (see chapter 18) and claircognisance (see chapter 16), and it is connected to our throat chakra. As you will find while working through this book, many of the psychic clairs are interconnected and work together to provide you with psychic information or clues.

Sometimes when I do a reading for a client, I will receive the taste of a favourite food that the deceased person loved, or it may be the taste of a popular type of dinner or dessert that they cooked for their family. Other times, if the person in spirit liked a certain type of beverage, whether it be a special coffee or cocktail, they will give me that taste in my mouth, so that I can relay it to the person I am reading for.

I do also notice that when I pick up a taste this way, I will also receive the smell of the item, as if it is actually physically in the room with me. For example, Grandma was known for her famous apple pie. I will receive the taste of the pastry with the sugar and the cinnamon on top and the green apples she baked in the pie. I will smell the pie as it cooks and may even get the taste or smell of custard and ice cream, if that is how she served her pie.

These smells do not stay with me for a long time; they are quite fleeting smells that stay with me just long enough for me to share the message with the loved one who is having the reading.

When I am working on a murder investigation, I can pick up the taste of blood in my mouth, the taste of cigarettes or the taste of alcohol or a poisonous substance, for example, if that is how a person has died. This information is provided by the person in spirit so that I can give it to the investigating officers.

Spirits use many ways to get their message across to you. They will share information with you in ways that you are familiar with. As human beings, we relate to many memories in our life through taste and smell. This is why spirit will share these tastes with us, to remind us of things we have shared or experienced with our family.

When I was a child, I used to stay at my nanna's house and she would always have lollies – butterscotch drops, chocolate-coated crystalised ginger and barley sugar. At times when I do a reading, I will pick up one of the tastes that remind me of my childhood and visits to Nanna's house. The taste is usually shared with me by a person in spirit from her era in time and with a similar taste in sweets.

When you do a reading for someone, always pay attention to the tastes you receive when you are tuning in, as this will be another way to strengthen your connection to those in spirit. You may feel the taste of licorice in your mouth is your imagination, when in fact the sitter's father or grandfather is trying to make a connection with them.

CHAPTER 18

CLAIRALIENCE – CONNECTING TO SPIRIT VIA SMELL

What is clairalience?

The word 'clairalience' comes from the French words *clair* and *alience,* meaning clear smelling. In the same way our normal sense of taste and smell are connected, so are clairalience and clairgustance. Both of these psychic clairs are also connected to clairsentience and to our throat chakra.

The gift of clairalience is an important sense that is not always noticed. It is something we take for granted and at times can be ignored. It is an underrated clair as is clairgustance.

This clair is also strongly connected to memory and it's a powerful tool when used in a reading. How many times in your life have you smelt a fragrance of some sort that has transported you to a happy time in your life? The fragrance could be of a perfume your grandmother wore, the hairspray she used, the frangipani blossoms you smelt when you were on holiday, the smell of aftershave of your father, the smell of Mum cooking her special dish, the smell of your grandfather's boot polish. These fragrances are just some of the smells that loved ones in spirit share when they are making contact with us.

I will never forget when I tuned into the energy of a gorgeous young man who had taken his own life. His mother had come for a reading and all I could smell was dirty wet socks. He then showed me a football and held the smelly socks even closer to my nose. At first I worried if I passed this information onto his mother, she would be offended by me.

As her son persistently held the socks in my face, I finally told her what I could smell. To my relief her son then removed the socks from my nose and his mother's face lit up and tears began streaming down her face.

She confirmed I did really have her son there in spirit, as this smell was how she knew he was in the house paying her a visit from the spirit world. The woman confirmed her son was an avid football player and he was known to leave his smelly socks in his room, which she would have to retrieve and put into the wash.

Before my nanna died, she would always say that no matter what happened in her life she was going to make sure that she would come to my wedding to see me get married. Unfortunately, my nanna died when I was only 21 and I didn't get married until three years after her death.

What I found to be one of the most comforting things I have ever experienced was that on the day before and on the day of my wedding I could smell my nanna around me. Everywhere I went for those two days, I knew she was with me and I could smell her by my side. It wasn't until after the wedding was over the smell disappeared. I knew in my heart that she was there for my special day and she kept her promise. I am so grateful for that gift.

Human beings and animals alike all give off pheromones. All of us have our own odour, mixed with the smell of perfume, aftershave, hand cream fragrance, hair spray, shampoo, washing powder fragrance or cooking smells.

Many males in spirit have come to me with the smell of cigarettes, alcohol, the smell of wood, motor oil, foot odour, the smell of freshly cut grass or the smell of gumtrees.

When I have worked on police investigations the victim in spirit has given me clues as to what the vegetation smelt like, the smell of fire, the smell of the sea or the smell of wet rotting leaves, which have proven to be important to the case.

When you tune in during a reading, spend some time focusing on all of the sensations being given to you from the spirit world. The smell of the lavender or roses you are picking up on is not always a real physical smell; it may be a smell that someone from spirit wants you to pick up to relay to a loved one that they are by their side.

CHAPTER 19

DIVINING WITH PENDULUMS AND DOWSING RODS

WHEN CHOOSING WHICH PSYCHIC TOOL is best for you, there are a number of things you need to consider. Firstly, you need to think about what you wish to use your tool for. There are many different types of psychic tools that can be used to enhance your psychic abilities. Some tools are used to divine information, while others are used to connect to spirit or provide personal guidance.

Dowsing or divining (as it is sometimes called) is another way that we can divine and interpret information. The tool itself doesn't have any power or ability; it is merely a tool that can be used as a communication device. It is believed that dowsing rods and pendulums can be used to connect the diviner (the person using the dowsing tool) to higher celestial consciousness to divine information. Others believe that dowsing equipment can be used to connect to your higher self to receive the information.

We will briefly look at some of the more commonly used tools in this chapter.

Dowsing using divining rods

Dowsing is an ancient art that is also known as water witching. Dowsing rods have been used since ancient times to find underground water, buried minerals, metals, oil veins, lost objects and ley lines.

Traditionally, dowsing rods were made from a forked (Y-shaped) branch most commonly made from hazel, witch-hazel, peach or willow-tree branches. The two ends of the forked side are held in either hand, and the stem of the Y-shape is pointed straight ahead. The diviner walks over an area where they are trying to locate an object, and when the dowsing rod dips down to the ground, it is an indication that the rod has located what it was looking for.

Dowsing rods can also be made from two pieces of metal that are bent into an L-shape. L-rods are usually made out of brass or copper at a size ratio of 3:1. They can have plastic or copper sleeves placed over the short ends to allow the rods to turn easily.

It is possible to make the rods with the 3:1 ratio by cutting down a pair of metal coathangers. Two plastic pen barrels can be placed over the shorter ends to act as sleeve handles.

It isn't important what the rods are made out of, as it is you and your intuition tapping into the spiritual realm that allows the rods to function properly.

L-rods can be used to dowse messages of 'yes', 'no' or 'maybe' responses like a pendulum (as discussed later in this chapter). However, they are better used for finding things or to measure an individual's auric field.

When you first begin to work with divining rods, it is important you hold them in the balanced 'ready' position. When you hold the rods, it is good to hold them firmly but not too tightly, so that you don't choke the handles. Ensure that your index finger is approximately 1 cm (.4 inch) down from the top of the handles.

If you are using the rods without a sleeve, it is even more important not to hold them too tightly or the rods will not be able to move freely when they are scanning. While you are holding the rods, you need to ensure that your arms are bent at approximately a 90-degree angle. Hold the rods pointing away from your body and make sure that they are parallel to the ground.

When you first begin using divining rods, you may find it easier if you hold your arms close to your body, tucking your elbows tight against your waist, as this will help you to stabilise the rods.

When you are divining, always be aware of who is around you, as once your divining rods are working and tuning in, they can move rapidly and you don't want to poke anyone's eyes out – including your own.

Tuning your rods in

As with a pendulum, you need to tune your divining rods in. Before using the rods, you need to determine which position will indicate to you when the rods have found an item. There are two positions for *'found'*. The L-rods can either cross over when they have found what you are looking for or they may both open up, with the left rod pointing left and the right rod pointing right.

Dowsing Rod Positions

Ready   Found Positions

Personally, I prefer the rods to cross when I have found what I am searching for. I like to think that X marks the spot. Play around with your rods to determine what works best for you.

Once your rods are tuned in, it is time to ask them to look for something. You may wish to test your rods to see if they are actually tuned in properly. For example, ask a friend to place your keys in a location without telling you where they are. Next ask the rods to scan and search for your keys. Take your time to focus and tune into the keys. Think about how many keys you are looking for – visualise the keys in your mind. Watch as the rods suddenly spring to life. They may begin to vibrate in your hands; they may even begin to move rapidly from side to side as they scan and tune into the keys you are looking for.

Walking with divining rods

When you are beginning to look for something, you will need to hold both of the rods parallel and facing forward in the *'ready'* position. When you begin to walk with your rods, you need to walk slowly and calmly keeping an eye on where you are walking. Try not to stare directly at the rod as you may walk into something. Always focus on just slightly ahead of where you are walking.

How to focus while using your divining rods

When you first begin to use your divining rods, it is important to focus on the outcome of what you are looking for. Be as relaxed as possible and try not to let your ego become involved. Focus your attention on the direction your rods point to and adjust your direction as your rods scan and move in the direction they are pointing to.

Also focus on what you are looking for, telling the divining rods what you wish to find. For example, you may wish to find a particular headstone in a cemetery. The name you are looking for is John William Smith. You will need to say either in your head or aloud that you are looking specifically for John William Smith. As this name could be common you need to ensure that you tell the rods that you want to find John William Smith and not just John Smith.

Stand for a moment and visualise the name in your mind – you may even wish to say the name aloud. I recommend speaking to the rods. As you walk with the rods, keep asking that you be guided in the direction of where John William Smith is. You will know when your rods are scanning and trying to find the location as they will move back and forth in unison. When they have decided on a direction, they will both point in a particular direction. Stop and turn your body in that direction and continue walking. Repeat this exercise until you find what you are searching for.

Don't worry if it takes time for you and your divining rods to make a connection. The key is to relax and have faith in your connection to the rods and spirit. While working with the spirit world, it is important to remember that everything happens in its own time. Famous painters didn't learn to paint overnight, nor did great inventors have success with their first invention. If you can remember this and practise, practise, practise, you and your rods will make a connection to your higher self. Be patient!

Exercise: How to measure the aura with divining rods

This exercise is one I do regularly when I run an in-person workshop with students. If you wish to conduct this exercise at home, this is also possible. As we have discussed earlier in chapter 4, some people have the ability to see the auric field while others can only feel the aura. This exercise will show you how you can expand and compress your aura at will, as well as showing you how to measure the aura with divining rods.

The requirement for this exercise is a set of divining rods and a willing participant. If you are in a group situation, please pick someone who would like to participate. If you are at home with a friend, ask them to be your test subject.

To determine when you have reached a connection to the participant's aura, predetermine with spirit and the rods whether or not when you touch the aura the rods will cross in a closed position or whether or not they will face backwards in an open position. I find when I do this exercise, the rods will both face outwards in an open position, as if the person's aura is repelling the rods and protecting the person's energy field.

This is something you will need to experiment with to decide how you and your rods work.

To begin, ask your willing test subject to stand in front of you, facing you with their eyes closed. The person needs to be at least 2 metres (6.5 ft) away from you space permitting.

Ask the person to shut their eyes and focus on their breath. Ask the person to think of themselves as a dolphin with a blowhole located on top of their head where their crown chakra is located. For the first part of this exercise, ask the person to breathe in through their nose and out through their mouth. Ask them to project their energy up into their crown chakra and expand their energy out around themselves like a giant forcefield. With each breath, ask them to keep expanding their energy/aura so that it flows through the top of their head and then surrounds their entire body with protection.

Allow them a few minutes to focus on building their energy and expanding it wider and wider into their current environment. It is important for the participant to keep their eyes closed during the entire time of them expanding their aura, so they are not aware of how far you are away from them.

Now, ready yourself with your divining rods and have them in the scanning position. Ask spirit and the rods to let you move forward and measure the participant's aura.

Ask the participant to keep expanding their aura throughout each and every breath, and as you walk closer to them, ask spirit to let you know when you have connected to their aura.

Take small steps towards the person, allowing your rods to scan the area. An indication that the rods are scanning is when you hold them close to your side, and they start to rotate back and forth voluntarily without your interference.

When you reach the person's aura, your rods will either cross in front of the person, or they may both rotate outwardly as if they are repelled by something.

When the rods give you a reaction, ask the volunteer to open their eyes and pay attention to how far you are from them when the rods gave you the measurement. This will give you a measurement of how big the person's aura was at the time of the exercise.

Exercise: How to reduce the aura

This exercise is similar to the one above, only this time it's about reducing your aura and focusing on how much to reduce it.

How many times have you been on a plane or in a public place where you felt that you were being bombarded with other people's energy? To be honest, I am a private person and I really hate it when I am on a plane and the person next to me is in my space and takes both their own and my armrest, and they sit in my energy. Some people have absolutely no idea about another person's personal space.

Have you ever been in a supermarket queue and the person in front of you is stressed? They may even be in a bad mood and are feeling angry, or they may have their children with them, and they are fighting while standing in the queue. You, on the other hand, were in a great mood when you went shopping and you were happy and just waiting to get through the checkout and go home.

Due to the blending of your auras and energy, by the time you leave the supermarket, you are in a really bad mood and angry with the world around you. It isn't your fault, and you don't even know why you are feeling this way.

The reason is that you have blended with the energy of the other people in the queue and you have picked up their negative thoughts and energy.

People who are not spiritually aware have no idea how much their energy can affect and overlap with others' energy. Being in someone else's space can be annoying and off-putting for a sensitive person.

With this exercise, we are focusing on reducing the aura instead of expanding it. The requirement for this exercise is the same as before. You will need a set of divining rods and a willing participant. If you are in a group situation, please pick someone who would like to participate. If you are at home with a friend, ask them to be your test subject.

Repeat the question with spirit about what the reaction will be when you connect with the participant's aura. Ask your willing test subject to stand in front of you, facing you with their eyes closed. The person needs to be at least 2 metres (6.5 ft) away from you, space permitting.

Once again, ask the person to shut their eyes and focus on their breath. This time, ask the person to keep all of their energy close to their body. Ask them to focus on each breath and to reduce their aura by pulling it closer and closer to their body. Give them a few minutes to focus and reduce their energy field as close as they can to their body, shrinking it as much as they can.

Once again, ensure they have their eyes closed throughout this entire process.

Now, ready yourself with your divining rods and have them in the scanning position. Ask spirit and the rods to let you move forward and measure the participant's aura.

Ask the participant to keep reducing their aura throughout each breath, and as you walk closer to them, ask spirit to let you know when you have connected to their aura.

Take small steps towards the person, allowing your rods to scan the area. An indication that the rods are scanning is when you hold them close to your side, and they start to rotate back and forth involuntarily without your interference.

When you reach the person's aura your rods will either cross in front of the person or they may both rotate outwardly as if they are repelled by something.

When the rods give you a reaction, ask the volunteer to open their eyes and pay attention to how far you are from them when the rods gave you the measurement. This time you will be surprised by how much closer you actually are to the person's aura.

These exercises will give you physical reference as to how to expand and reduce the aura. In the future, when you need to expand or reduce your energy focus on the exercise above.

Dowsing using a pendulum

Dowsing can also be conducted using a pendulum. A pendulum is a weighted object that is suspended by a cord or chain from a fixed point. A pendulum can be made from crystal, metal (such as silver, brass, copper) or wood.

A pendulum is a tool that we can use to enhance our intuition, as it gives us access to information that exists within our subconscious mind. The more you practise working with a pendulum, the more you will enhance your connection to the spiritual realms. A pendulum can give you guidance from your spirit guide, guardian angel and subconscious self.

With practise and patience, anyone can learn to use dowsing equipment. The more you practise the more accurate you will become.

Choosing a pendulum

Pendulums come in many shapes and sizes, and can be made from metal and/or various types of crystals. The most important thing to remember when choosing a pendulum is to choose the one that feels right for you. It doesn't matter what it looks like – it is more about how it resonates with your energy. Choose the pendulum that feels most comfortable when you hold it suspended between your finger and thumb. Take a few moments to feel how it swings back and forth. Does it swing perfectly balanced or does it feel lop-sided. If it isn't balanced, then this means it is not the right choice of pendulum.

Different crystals also possess different energy within them, so if you choose a crystal pendulum, choose one that amplifies your energy when using it. It is best to choose a pendulum that is symmetrical in shape as it will move better.

How to use a pendulum

Everyone can learn to use a pendulum; however there are a few important steps you need to undertake to train your pendulum before you use it.

After you have chosen your pendulum, before using it for the first time it is important to determine in which direction you will receive your 'yes' and 'no' responses.

Hold the pendulum between your thumb, index and middle finger, or you may choose to rest the cord or chain over your index finger, using your other fingers to hold the top of the chain or cord. It is important to ensure, whatever hold you use for your pendulum, your hand is held steady and doesn't move while using it.

Now, ask your pendulum – either by asking the question aloud or by thinking the question within your mind – to indicate in which direction the 'yes' response is. Watch as the pendulum swings in a particular direction. Now repeat the exercise, notice if the pendulum behaves in the same manner. If it doesn't, it is important to stop and begin the exercise again. It is always important to let the pendulum know that you are in charge, as you are using it to tap into your higher consciousness. Once the pendulum begins to behave in the same way each time you have asked for the 'yes' response, you can move on to ask it to show you the 'no' response.

Repeat the exercise, only this time asking the pendulum to show you which direction the 'no' response is. There is a chart on the next page with an example of how your pendulum may behave. If your pendulum uses different directions to what is written on the chart, that's fine; you can draw up your own chart using the directions your pendulum works with and simply use the illustration provided as a format example.

By training your pendulum you will be able to ask it the answers to various questions by asking it for a 'yes' or 'no' response. The next response you will need to train the pendulum to reply with is 'I don't know'. Once you have ascertained the direction for this response, you will need to set up the movement for the pendulum to let you know if you need to 'ask the question again'. When training your pendulum, you will need to ask it questions that will give you a definite 'yes' or 'no' answer.

Once you have determined all four responses from your pendulum, you can start to practise your technique further. Ask your pendulum to move to the 'yes' position, then ask it to stop and then move to the 'no' position. By doing this you will establish a strong connection with the pendulum that will help to provide you with clear and concise answers to your questions.

The centre point on the diagram is where you begin working with your pendulum. Hold the pendulum still above this point before asking your question. When you ask the question clearly, ask your pendulum to 'search' and to give you the answer by either swinging in the direction of 'yes' or 'no'. If the question has been asked clearly, the pendulum will begin to swing in whichever direction the relevant answer is. If the pendulum doesn't swing at all or it swings in either the direction of 'ask the question again' or 'I don't know' then you will need to rephrase the question more clearly.

What can a pendulum be used for?

A pendulum is a useful divining tool that can assist you in finding the answers to universal knowledge. It can assist you with making decisions about a wide range of subjects. When asking your pendulum a question, you need to ask about things that you have a right to make a choice about.

Here are some issues you may wish to ask your pendulum about:

- Whether you should change your current employment
- Whether or not you can trust a particular person in your life
- To help you find a lost object – for example, asking, 'Have I lost my ring?'
- Whether you should buy a particular house. (In this instance, it's a good idea to have a map of the property to tune your pendulum into. You may wish to ask if the property has any problems with the neighbours, for example. Or you may wish to ask if there are any water issues in or around the property.)
- Whether your current partner is the right one for you
- If you should go on a holiday or save your money

- To help you with information on any health concerns you may have
- To help you locate something on a map – for example, find a missing person or pet
- To help you find water, ley lines, minerals
- To predict the sex of unborn children.

Before you begin asking your pendulum any questions it is best to undergo some preparation. Firstly, I would advise you sit and really think about what questions you wish to ask your pendulum. Next, you should write the questions down on a piece of paper. Number the questions in order of priority. The most important thing to remember is to make sure that the answers can be answered by a 'yes' or 'no' response.

Pendulum etiquette

Don't let others use your pendulum once you have tuned it into your vibration. It is best to keep it aligned with your vibration. However, the worst thing that can happen is that you will need to realign it with the 'yes' or 'no' response.

Keep your pendulum in a safe place. Ideally, keep it in a protective bag or cloth to help maintain your vibration on it.

When consulting your pendulum for answers always keep your mind clear from distraction. Try and be as calm and centred as possible as this will allow you to connect with the spiritual world more easily.

If the pendulum is not giving you an accurate reading, it is because you are not phrasing the question properly.

Try not to overuse your pendulum. Consulting your pendulum too frequently to make decisions is not healthy. It is a wonderful tool for guidance, but it should not be used as a spiritual or emotional crutch. (If you find you are relying on it too much, it is time to put it away for a while and re-centre yourself.)

Don't be impatient. The spiritual world works with divine timing, so if the answer you seek has not happened as quickly as you would like, it is because the timing is not yet right.

Don't consult the pendulum when you are over-emotional and angry. You will find that you will not receive the best response during this time. Wait until you are calm and centred to receive your guidance.

If you are not receiving clear responses it could be because you are tired, or it may be that the time is not right. Another reason may be that you need to make the decision for yourself and not rely on the pendulum's answer. Put the pendulum away and consult it the following day.

If you receive an answer by using your pendulum, always use your common sense. If the message goes against your intuition or gut feeling, then ask yourself why is this so?

The pendulum is a tool to assist you to connect to your higher consciousness, it is not a tool to be used to manipulate and give you the answers that you *want* to receive. If you use your pendulum like this, you will be disappointed by what you seek not coming to fruition.

A pendulum is a tool that can act as a bridge between you and the spirit world; used correctly and with patience, it can be a wonderful tool to provide you with hidden guidance from above.

PENDULUM DEDICATION

(Hold your pendulum over your heart chakra and
recite this dedication either in your mind or out loud.)

I wish to make a connection to the spirit realm
through my connection to you. Together we shall work
as one to divine knowledge, guidance and information
from my higher self, spirit guides and angels. The
information we channel together will only be used for
my highest good. Together we will work as one!

CHAPTER 20

NUMEROLOGY – DIVINING BY NUMBERS

NUMEROLOGY IS AN ANCIENT FORM OF DIVINING by using numbers. Numerology has been used throughout many cultures and times. Mathematicians throughout history have discovered that numbers are the key to unlocking the vibration within all things.

The beginnings of numerology can be traced back to around 10,000 years ago to Babylonia and Egypt. However, it is the Greek mathematician Pythagoras who developed many of the basic theorems that form the foundations of modern-day mathematics and also those used with numerology. Pythagoras was a mathematician, philosopher and theorist. He was known as a numerical master and it is his strong influence that has been credited with the widespread use of numbers. He was arguably one of the greatest Greek philosophers who had the wisdom and understanding of metaphysics and its energetic force.

What is numerology?

Numbers are a big part of our life, when you think about it they are everywhere we look. Our birthdate is broken down into numbers. Our name can also be translated into numbers. We live in homes that are numbered, our motor vehicles have registration plates that contain numbers in them. We have phone numbers, pin numbers, identification numbers just to name a few instances. When you begin to look at your life you will realise that numbers rule your world. Did you know that all of these numbers have a very big influence on your life?

What can numerology be used for?

Did you know that your destiny is connected to the energy of numbers? Numbers will show you how to understand yourself and to tune into and understand your loved ones. You can use numerology for the following purposes:

- To determine an individual's personality
- To discover your talents
- To highlight your strengths and weaknesses
- To show you what obstacles are ahead of you
- To tell you what cycle of your life you are in
- To show you how to make the most of the cycles and opportunities you will experience in your life
- To reveal your innermost needs and wants
- To determine when to move, buy or sell a property
- To help you with your career path
- To help you with relationships with friends, partners and work colleagues
- To help determine if someone is the right person to have in your life, whether it be a relationship, friendship or a new acquaintance
- To reveal what name is best for you to use in your life, since your name and how the world perceives you is governed by numbers. Numerology can help you to determine whether or not you should use your christian name, middle name and surname. It can assist you with the choices of whether or not you should abbreviate your name or go by a nickname or whether to add the initial of your middle name to enhance your numerological power throughout your life.

Once you look at all of the possibilities that numerology can do to enhance your life, you will soon wonder why you didn't delve deeper into understanding how it all worked sooner.

Numerology can help you understand the whole picture of who you really are. Numerology can reveal the diverse sides of your personality and how each aspect combines as one to create the person you really are. With this complete understanding, you are able to make the most of your strengths and talents.

It is important to remember that everything throughout the universe vibrates at its own frequency. By working out and understanding the vibrational frequency of any object, you can establish the nature and energies associated with it.

By using the principles of numerology in your name and date of birth as basic data, you will be able to determine the predominate frequencies of yourself and those around you.

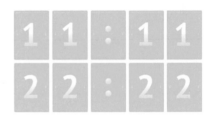

How to do numerology calculations

In numerology, all numbers are reduced to a single figure from the number 1 through to 9, except for the special master numbers that are only divisible by the number 11.

11, 22, 33 and 44 are the master numbers – 11 and 22 have the most power. 1, 2, 3, 4, 5, 6, 7, 8, 9, 11, 22, 33 and 44 represent the major vibrational rates associated with people's characteristics.

Numbers are reduced by simple addition. The number 13, for instance is reduced by adding 1 + 3 = 4. Similarly, the number 1960 can be reduced by adding 1 + 9 + 6 + 0 = 16. The 16 can be further reduced by adding 1 + 6 = 7.

Letters in individuals' names are converted to numbers and then added together. Each letter is designated a number. Pythagoras believed that: 'Numbers are the first things of all nature'. It was Pythagoras who devised an alphabetic code to assign a number to each letter. By using his alphabetic code, it is possible to analyse any word or name to understand the power that is hidden within.

These numbers determined by the code in turn are also added together and then reduced to a single figure. For example the letter A resonates at the number frequency of 1, the letter B resonates at the number frequency of 2, the letter C resonates at the number frequency of the number 3 and so on. The following table shows the numbers assigned to all 26 letters in the English alphabet devised by Pythagoras.

1	2	3	4	5	6	7	8	9
A	B	C	D	E	F	G	H	I
J	K	L	M	N	O	P	Q	R
S	T	U	V	W	X	Y	Z	

Your significant numbers

There are four significant numbers that we have with us throughout our lives. Some of these numbers may change during our lifetime especially if you are female and change your surname due to marriage. You may decide to abbreviate your name or decide to use a nickname which will also alter your numbers.

The four numerology numbers you have throughout your life are as follows:

- Destiny number – also known as your karma number
- Day force number – also known as your personality number
- Birth force number – also known as your life path number
- Personal year numbers.

Then there's also your house number. So how do you work out each of these powerful numbers that are connected to your life?

Your destiny or karma number

Your destiny number is worked out by translating each letter in your birth name (as it appears on your birth certificate). This is the name that you were given at birth and appears on your birth certificate. Pythagoras believed that each letter of the alphabet vibrated at a specific numerical frequency. Pythagoras devised the Pythagorean Chart. You will need to use the chart provided to find out which frequency your destiny number vibrates at.

For example, if you are a male who at birth was given the name John William Smith, your name resonates at the frequency numbers of:

1+6+8+5+5+9+3+3+9+4+1+4+9+2+8=77

As you need to keep adding the numbers together until you reach a single figure you will continue with another additional sum of:

7+7=14

As you still have to add the figures you will continue to add the final two numbers together to reach your final number of 5.

1+4=5

Your name number is called your destiny number. This means that the name John William Smith resonates at the frequency of number 5. As a person using the full name of John William Smith, it will mean that John can be impulsive, get bored easily, is likely to take risks and can be very adaptable to change.

It is important to remember that most people don't use their whole name during their entire life. Many of us don't use our christian name, middle name and surname together when acknowledging who we are.

Many of us choose to drop our middle name when we are addressed by others, making our middle name's energy obsolete. Are you aware that using your middle name or even just the first initial can make a significant difference to your life? It is also important to note that many females will change or hyphenate their names when they are married. By doing so their numerological chart can alter significantly.

Here is a list of what your destiny number will mean to you:

1: As a Destiny Number 1, you are a true individual; you are likely to work at the head of a group or for yourself. You don't like being told what to do. You are a born leader not a follower. You like to have time to yourself for contemplation.

2: As a Destiny Number 2, you prefer to be with people and not spend time alone. People with a Destiny number of 2 are popular and work well in partnerships. You like harmony and fairness. You always see both sides to things in a situation. Work in a vocation in which you can be a negotiator.

3: As a Destiny Number 3, friendships are a big importance in your life. You wish to live life to the full and like to make those around you happy. You do tend to have a jealous side, which you need to keep an eye on. Your tendency to be too laidback can hold you back from reaching your full potential.

4: As a Destiny Number 4, you have an amazing ability to be calm and insightful. While others around you are in chaos, you can put things in perspective. You are organised and methodical in life. You are a perfectionist and expect the most from yourself and those around you.

5: As a Destiny Number 5, you are a person who requires constant change and freedom. You are known to be impulsive. You are bestowed with intuition which will serve you well in life. When your abilities are functioning at full potential you will be able to multi-task. However, as you have a tendency to get bored easily, you will need to learn to finish one task before beginning the next.

6: As a Destiny Number 6, you are endowed with a great sense of responsibility and sensitivity. You are thoughtful and often self-sacrifice to be a support to others. You are gentle, kind, sympathetic and loving, and you have the ability to see the beauty within things that is lost on others.

7: As a Destiny Number 7, you have an analytical outlook on life. You are scientific yet have a very spiritual side to your personality. Finding the truth to how things work is your passion and you may become involved in investigating, analysing and discovering wisdom. You tend to hide your emotions and you enjoy working alone and at your own pace.

8: As a Destiny Number 8, you are an ambitious and goal-orientated person. You are determined and will always achieve your goals. Money and material matters are important to you – you like the finer things in life. Try not to let money and power become more important than your loved ones.

9: As a Destiny Number 9, you have the gift of compassion and worldly understanding. You are a spiritual person who wants to save the world. You are gifted with a great imagination, and creative and artistic abilities. You are sensitive to the needs of others and a born counsellor.

11: As a Destiny Master Number 11, this number gives you the desire to follow a spiritual path where you can focus your energies. You view the world from a different perspective to most people. You may make sacrifices for your family, and you want to change and improve the world for everyone. Your vision is so clear that at times you may become frustrated as others don't vibrate at the same frequencies as you.

22: As a Destiny Master Number 22, you wish to change the world for the betterment of others. You are the number that has the ability to make things possible. You are stubborn and determined and will never give up until your goals are achieved. You do have a tendency to let little things irritate you, so try to learn to let go.

Your day force or personality number

Your day force number is determined by what day you were born on, in any month. Each day of the month has its own personality traits. There are similarities between people who are born with the same day force number, and the energy between people born on, for example, the 4th, 13th, 22nd or 31st of the month – since each adds up to 4 – is also similar, but not exactly the same. A person born on the 22nd of the month is a Master Number, which gives this day a significant difference to the other days that add up to 4 in a month.

Just to reiterate, your day force or personality number is your *actual* day of birth – for example, if your date of birth is 13/4/1963, it's the 13 that is most relevant here.

This number – the day of whichever month you were born – is the most important number of all. When we react to any situation instinctively, we do so with the personality

traits of our day force energy (personality number), as this is, in a sense, our day-to-day number. It has a bearing on our natural talents, choice of colours and individual style, and the way other people see us in frequent situations. In many ways, even the people closest to us only know us slightly, and it is this 'daily' side of us they see most often.

Born on the 1st day of any month

You are original, dynamic, strong-willed and stubborn. You are a born leader and do not like to be told what to do. You are sensitive but have a tendency to keep your feelings hidden. You like to spend time alone. You are imaginative and creative, with good design ideas. You definitely need to work independently or for yourself.

Born on the 2nd day of any month

Your energy is of peace, love and harmony. You are sensitive, quite emotional and you crave affection. You don't like being by yourself. You are loving and social which allows you to make friends easily. Everybody loves you. You can spread your energy too wide, getting involved in too many unimportant matters. You can also be prone to depression or moodiness. You have a tendency to be nervous in large groups.

Born on the 3rd day of any month

You are endowed with lots of energy and vitality. When you are in a good mood, you can be the life of the party. Your talents lie in working with people. However, you can be prone to times of moodiness and melancholy. It is important for you to keep motivated, otherwise you can lose momentum and tend to be quite sedentary. Working in the arts, writing and entertainment professions would suit you best. You can have a tendency to wait for things to come to you in life, when in fact you need to be the one who instigates them. You are an affectionate person who can be very sensitive. Try not to let jealousy or your need to control others become an issue in relationships.

Born on the 4th day of any month

You are bestowed with the gift of self-discipline, honesty and hard work. You have innate spiritual gifts that if acted upon will serve you well in life.

You are creative, artistic and practical with your endeavours. You are honest and trustworthy, and people rely on you to get the job done. You are interested in health and hygiene. You are stubborn and can be set in your ways. You have a tendency to hold in your stress, which can manifest in stomach issues, headaches and shoulder tension. Try to relax and focus on what you can achieve in life. You will be surprised by what hidden talents you have.

Born on the 5th day of any month

You are a hard worker who enjoys being with others. You are versatile and love to see how things work, though you do have a tendency to get bored easily. You are physical and love your freedom. Emotions are important to you – you are a loving being who needs to be loved in return. If you don't have undivided attention from a partner, you will become bored and move on. Travel will be a big part of your life, as you don't like being stuck in the one spot for too long. A career choice should be something that gives you lots of movement and mental stimulation where you are not bored by mundane chores.

Born on the 6th day of any month

You have a love for family, friends and are homely. You have a deep love of nature and anything you do in life is devoted to assisting others. You have a humanitarian side where you self-sacrifice to make a difference in life. You are extremely sensitive and strive for peace in your surroundings. You can be stubborn and will stand up for what you believe in. You are gifted with children and the elderly. Everyone loves you; however there is a risk in life of not achieving your own personal goals, as you are too busy helping others achieve their own. You can achieve anything you put your mind to, but you must remember you need to have balance in your life.

Born on the 7th day of any month

You are bestowed with an important incarnation. Your qualities as a perfectionist and individual are very strong. You are drawn to all things spiritual. However, there is also a scientific side to you that needs proof, which gives you the balance of healthy scepticism. You can be stubborn and self-centred at times, so try to be aware of these negative qualities. You don't always like working with others, as you prefer to be the boss. You are highly analytical and enjoy researching subjects to find the hidden truth. You are well respected by your peers.

Born on the 8th day of any month

You are a very lucky individual, since the number 8 is connected to the symbol of infinity as well as money and abundance. If you can learn to use your executive abilities, you will succeed in business. It is important to make the most of the opportunities that come your way. As 8 is the money number, it can either mean you can make money through your own hard efforts or it can cost you money if you are not careful. You can be accused of being a show-off, as you like to make an impact on others. You like to have the best you can afford. Your number is a karmic number connected to the spiritual and psychic world. You are very psychic, and if you listen to your gut feeling, you will rarely be wrong.

Born on the 9th day of any month

You are endowed with a humanitarian side to your personality. You are intellectual, artistic and a born counsellor. You are sensitive and compassionate to other's needs. You are creative, imaginative and artistic with the gift of writing and music being some of your stronger skills. You are extremely psychic with a strong sense of clairvoyance. You are happiest when you are helping and guiding others. Your number gives you the need for privacy and solitude. You love to be with people, however at times you prefer to be like a hermit crab, needing to withdraw into your shell to re-energise your soul after giving so much of your time and energy to others.

Born on the 10th day of any month

Being born on the 10th day of the month gives you extra independence. You are a born leader who has executive abilities and leadership qualities. You do have a tendency to be dominating in many situations. You have great power and you will not be walked over in life. You are willing and able to stand on your own two feet. You are idealistic and look at different ways to improve the world around you. Be careful not to start things and not finish them. The mundane bores you and you are happy to allow others to look after the finer details to finish the job.

Born on the 11th day of any month

As you were born on the 11th day of the month, you have the energy of a Master Number in its purest form. Being bestowed the energy and power of a Master Number also comes with added responsibilities throughout your life. Your determination is something that others will envy. You are extremely psychic, yet you have strong analytical qualities. You can be over-sensitive and a perfectionist who suffers anxiety when dreams don't become reality. It is important to stay focused on your dreams, as anything is possible with this number. An 11 can succeed in any field that puts them before the public.

Born on the 12th day of any month

With a birthday on the 12th day of the month, the energy of your 3 personality number means you are extremely visual and artistic. Choosing a vocation that allows you to work in the arts especially film or television would be of great advantage to your career. You are similar to those born on the 3rd day of the month, as you love to party and need to be social. You do need lots of stimulation, as you can tend to become bored and impatient with others. You can also be quite moody and melancholy which is something you need to keep an eye on.

Born on the 13th day of any month

You are a born organiser. You are pedantic and can be an absolute perfectionist, which can irritate others around you. You find it hard to delegate as nobody will be able to do the job as well as you. On the positive side, you are someone who can be trusted and will never let others down. You are creative, artistic and spiritually minded. You may also be gifted musically. Music is also something you crave to have around you to soothe your soul. You can be easily stressed and tend to suffer headache, shoulder and stomach issues.

Born on the 14th day of any month

Born on the 14th day of the month gives you lots of energy, similar to those born on the 5th. You are a physical person who needs a partner who will give you undivided attention in a relationship. Otherwise, you will become bored and look for love elsewhere. You are bestowed with stronger spiritual gifts than those born on the 5th. You are highly social and love being with others. You can be a little bit of a rebel, as you like taking risks. You are gifted at being able to turn your hand to many different vocations. This being said, you love travel and freedom, and a desk job would bore you.

Born on the 15th day of any month

You are bestowed with gentleness, patience and kindness. Family means everything to you and at times you are prone to be selfless to make sure those around you are happy. You are a wonderful parent and you love working with children and the elderly. You make an excellent teacher or carer. You strive for peace and harmony and become stressed if your surroundings are not settled. You are a born counsellor who is sympathetic to work colleagues and friends. Be careful not to burn yourself out, as you give so much and don't always focus on yourself.

Born on the 16th day of any month

You are bestowed with psychic gifts. On the negative side you have a tendency to over-analyse your hunches and don't always follow the signs. If you learn to follow your first impressions, you will rarely be wrong. The 16th day of the month can give you a sense of isolation, and you usually prefer to work alone. You are stubborn and independent, and you need time alone to meditate and recharge your batteries. It is important not to focus on past difficulties as this can cause you to worry and become melancholy. You are emotional and loving, but you may find it hard to express your feelings to others.

Born on the 17th day of any month

You are lucky financially, like those born on the 8th. Being born on this day, you will be gifted in the business world and will be successful with almost any projects you put your energies into. You are extremely ambitious and goal orientated; you can be relied on to get the job done. You can be quietly calm, yet ruthless when it comes to business. You are spiritually minded and are born under a version of karmic number 8. You can be sensitive and at times aloof, you may find it hard to show your feelings to those you love.

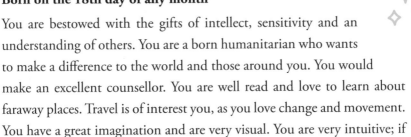

Born on the 18th day of any month

You are bestowed with the gifts of intellect, sensitivity and an understanding of others. You are a born humanitarian who wants to make a difference to the world and those around you. You would make an excellent counsellor. You are well read and love to learn about faraway places. Travel is of interest you, as you love change and movement. You have a great imagination and are very visual. You are very intuitive; if you follow your gut feelings you will rarely be wrong.

Born on the 19th day of any month

You have a karmic connection to this life and your last. You have karmic lessons you need to learn that will make you independent and strong. This number can also give you many challenges in your life. You may have to stand on your own during this lifetime, as you have a tendency to be a loner. You are stubborn and independent, and you have a tendency to be short tempered, impatient and moody with others. This can cause issues with friends and family. When you focus, you can achieve anything you try to do. You are artistic and intuitive, and you love to work on your own undisturbed by others. At times you love the limelight and at other times you can be reclusive.

Born on the 20th day of any month

You are bestowed with the gift of sensitivity and emotion. You are social and thoughtful towards others, which allows you to make friends easily. Everybody loves you. You don't like to be alone; you prefer to be in a relationship. You can have a tendency to become moody and depressed, as you are a born worrier. When you are working with the positive energy of your number, you can achieve anything you set out to do. You are extremely patient and always finish things to the highest possible standard.

Born on the 21st day of any month

You are full of life and have a love for music. You can become restless if you are stuck doing a mundane job. You need lots of affection, however you can become moody which can be a challenge for your partner. In a relationship you need to choose an understanding partner who is happy to leave you alone to recover from your moods, otherwise there will be misunderstandings. You are artistic and have a wonderful imagination. You love to work with others as you need to bounce your ideas off those around you.

Born on the 22nd day of any month

A birthday on the 22nd is a master number birthday. You are born with a strong psychic ability. Your number is that of an old soul who has lived previous lives on Earth. You are knowledgeable and very capable of doing any job you undertake. You can be trusted to continue any project you begin until its completion. You can be stubborn and a perfectionist, and you tend to worry a lot. You are more likely to leave home and work either overseas or away from your place of birth, as you love travel and adventure. You would enjoy any vocation that allows you to work for the greater good of others.

Born on the 23rd day of any month

You are energetic, imaginative and idealistic, and you have wonderful creative ideas if only you can focus enough to bring them to fruition. You have lots of energy but sometimes try to spread yourself too thin. You tend to start a lot of projects but do not always finish them. You are a loving being who loves to be with people. You don't like being alone as being with others brings out the best in you. You are likely to travel the world as you love adventure and excitement.

Born on the 24th day of any month

You are endowed with longevity and focus. You are a born peacemaker and crave harmony. You are devoted to family, like those born on the 6th. You are protective of loved ones and your home life is extremely important. On the negative side, you can become jealous and tend to find faults in others, while not seeing any faults within yourself. Love and affection is of utmost importance to you, both giving and receiving. You can have financial success if you focus on your dreams and make them a reality.

Born on the 25th day of any month

You are highly intuitive, yet gifted with a scientific mind, which makes you look at life logically. You are a deep person who at times finds it hard to express your emotions. You can be quite moody and are sometimes misunderstood because of this. You are a private person who can come across as cautious and reserved. You lack faith in yourself and underestimate your true gifts. If you focus on your dreams, you may surprise yourself by what you can achieve in life.

Born on the 26th day of any month

You are lucky to have the energy of number 8 in your life. As 8 relates to money and finance, you will be lucky in business if you pay attention to the finer details. Money will come to you as a result of your own hard work. If you are inclined to laziness and don't stay focused, your life won't be as abundant. You have wonderful managerial and organisational skills and you love to be the boss. You would prefer to work for yourself or be in charge, as you like to delegate menial tasks to those around you. You like the finer things in life – material belongings are important to you. You are quite intuitive, knowing what will and won't work in business.

Born on the 27th day of any month

You are caring and empathetic to others. You are a born counsellor and everyone will come to you with their problems. As you are very selfless, you will need to try and not take on other's problems, as this will affect you personally. It is important to avoid being around negative people, as you will absorb their energy. You are creative and artistic, with a strong imagination. Any vocation in an artistic area will make your heart sing. You are a natural born psychic, with great wisdom and insight into the spiritual world. You love to be around people, but due to your caring nature, you may need time alone to re-energise your batteries.

Born on the 28th day of any month

You are an independent person, stubborn and determined. You have high expectations in life, for yourself and others. You love freedom like the other 1 personality numbers, and you love to be the boss or at the head of the group. You can be prone to being a worrier and may focus on the negatives instead of finding the positives in life. However, when you are focusing on the positives, you are a born leader who will forge the way for others to follow.

Born on the 29th day of any month

A birthday on the 29th of the month is also a master number 11 birthday. You are an old soul that has experienced many lifetimes. You are idealistic, imaginative and creative, with great leadership skills. You have spiritual gifts you should learn to explore throughout your lifetime. If you work with these gifts, you will be a great inspiration to others. You like to be around others and don't always like to be alone. You can tend to be a bit of a daydreamer who, if unfocused, will dream about your ambitions instead of achieving them. It is important to not let your tendency to worry take over your life as you over analyse, and this makes you doubt the gifts you were born with.

Born on the 30th day of any month

You are someone who needs freedom and self-expression. You can be social, like the other 3 personality numbers, and you hate feeling like you are too restricted. You are a true individual who can be stubborn and emotional. It is enlightening to realise that your opinion is not always the only one. If you can follow the positives in your number, you will discover you have great dramatic and creative gifts you can use in your vocation. It is important to stay positive though, as you can be prone to moments of melancholy and depression. Meditation is a wonderful outlet for you.

Born on the 31st day of any month

You are bestowed with great organisational skills, you are practical, energetic and a hard worker. You are the person that people will come to, to get the job done. A loyal person, you remember the kindness that others bestow on you during your life. You are a born worrier, which means you need to keep an eye on your stress levels. You are prone to headaches, shoulder and stomach issues. When you are stressed, listening to or playing music can be your greatest friend. You are spiritually minded with a healthy scepticism that keeps both sides of your life in perspective. You have an interest in health and hygiene. You are gifted with healing abilities. If you choose to work with your psychic side, you will be surprised by what you uncover.

Your birth force or life path number

To work out your birth force or life path number, you need to add all of your birthday numbers together. For example, if your birth date is 30/12/1990, then you would add this up, so that: 3+0+1+2+1+9+9+0=25. Then add the number 25 together: 2+5=7.

Your birth force number stays with you throughout your lifetime – it doesn't ever change. Your birth force number is connected to your spirit, and it will give you glimpses of the potential directions you may choose during your lifetime. Your birth force number can reveal what challenges you may experience during your life. It can also give you an indication of what vocations you are best suited to. By understanding your birth force number, you will also be able to uncover what your strength and weaknesses are.

Date of Birth:

30th December 1990

30/12/1990

3+0+1+2+1+9+9+0=25

2+5=(7)

Your birth force number has more of an influence than any other numbers in your life.

Birth force 1

You are an original! You are truly independent, a strong individual who is courageous, stubborn and a creative achiever. Your journey in life will take you down the road of independence. You prefer to work for yourself or to be in charge. You like to spend time alone to re-energise your batteries.

You are a true leader who will have many opportunities in life to demonstrate your leadership abilities to others. It is your strong pioneering spirit, courage and determination that will get you through in life. You will be followed by others during a crisis, as you are calm and organised when needed.

Birth force 1 is a masculine number that endows both men and women with this number strength and determination to get the job done. With this birth force number, you need to be selective in relationships, as you need to choose a partner who is happy to allow you to shine in the limelight. However, you also need to be aware that your partner does need you to show them some attention or they will feel they are being neglected.

A Birth Force 1 number gives you the ability to be successful in any career choice that allows you to use your unique ideas, inner strength and pioneering spirit!

Birth force 2

You are extremely sensitive, with a strong spiritual quality. You are a born peacemaker who seeks balance and harmony in all aspects of your life. You are highly intuitive with great visionary skills.

You make friends easily, and you are a kind and loyal friend. You are someone who always sees the best in everyone. You are very giving and need to understand that not everybody is as nice as you. Try not to let people take advantage of your kindness.

You are neat and tidy, with an interest in all things healthy. You don't like change, which can hold you back at times in life. You tend to worry about making mistakes, so instead of being brave and giving things a go you won't start them at all.

You would make a great counsellor or teacher, or you would do well in any vocation where you can be a peacemaker or negotiator, as you are a born diplomat. You prefer to work with others, as you love to be around other people and can become withdrawn if you are left to work on your own.

Birth force 3

You are a born communicator with great literary, speaking and acting skills. You work best when you are amongst company. You like to be in the limelight and love the attention others give you. You like to live life to the full, not really worrying about what tomorrow brings.

You are gifted with a wonderful imagination and artistic talents, and you are very creative. You have the ability to inspire others. You can be ambitious, intolerant and impulsive, lacking patience with others who do not view the world as you do. You don't like to be stuck doing a vocation that ties you down and makes you feel repressed.

You have a tendency to get bored and lose interest in things if they don't happen as quickly as you would like them to. You are prone to moodiness and melancholy, which is something you need to keep an eye on. You are a sensitive soul who tends to take things to heart. In relationships, you need to have a partner who can cope with your popularity. Try not to be too dominating in relationships – you need to keeps things in balance.

Birth force 4

You are practical, determined, reliable, balanced and down-to-earth, with a calming influence that is noticed by those around you. You are someone who can be relied upon, as you are the person who others come to, to get the job done. Your determination and focus makes you a master builder in society. You are a highly talented person who is a perfectionist. People who are born with this number often succeed in entrepreneurial and management areas in the business world.

Once you have made a decision, nothing will change your mind. Some people may think that you are stubborn, but it is the standards you set that will never be compromised for anyone. You are practical and are wonderful at organising and managing your time with projects.

You are extremely loyal and devoted. It is important in relationships that you find a partner who is as loyal and loving as you are. Birth force 4s don't always have a large number of friends, preferring to have a few close friends that will be with you for life. You do tend to stress a lot about things you can't control, so try not to focus on what you can't change. Otherwise, you may end up suffering from stomach issues, headaches and shoulder problems.

Birth force 5

You are energetic, highly progressive, adventurous and multi-talented. You have a positive attitude to life and you want to make the world a better place for all who live in it. You have a strong humanitarian side and are compassionate towards others.

It is important for you to learn how to multi-task as you become bored with the mundane side of life. You have a tendency to be impatient, starting projects yet not always finishing them. If you can keep focused, you can achieve in any area you set your sights. Those born with this number usually travel, needing to keep the mind stimulated by new horizons. A vocation in film, writing, travel or sales would suit you, as you love to be with people. Working at a 9–5 job where you are stuck at your desk would bore you.

In relationships, you don't like to be too restricted or tied-down. You need to have a partner who is romantic, giving you their undivided attention, otherwise you become bored and lose interest. You need to have a partner who understands your need for freedom and movement.

Birth force 5s tend to make great partners for other birth force 5s, as they understand the freedom each other needs in a relationship.

Birth force 6

You are a compassionate, sympathetic and peace-loving being. Your goal in life is to be of assistance to others. You are a born counsellor who is happiest when nurturing and guiding others. You need to find balance in your life between giving and receiving, otherwise you will become too self-sacrificing.

You would make a great teacher, doctor, nurse, care giver or social worker, and of course, you make a wonderful parent. You are extremely sensitive to others' needs. Family members often rely on you to sort out any differences in a harmonious way.

People born with this number are loyal and loving partners. You have a tendency to attract partners that are often needy and somewhat weaker than yourself. You thrive on nurturing and looking after them. It is important to focus on your own hopes and dreams at least sometimes. Otherwise, you will feel bitter about others taking advantage of your generous loving nature.

Birth force 7

You are gifted with great investigative and analytical skills, a wonderful imagination and a philosophical outlook on life. You are extremely intelligent and a complete perfectionist. You set high standards for yourself and those you work with.

You are a highly spiritual being, with heightened psychic abilities. If you follow your intuition, you will rarely be wrong. However, you also have a healthy sceptical side, and are always looking for scientific outcomes in life.

You are a deep thinker who has a need for time to be with your thoughts and ideas. You don't have a wide circle of friends as you prefer to be selective with friendships. When you accept a friend into your life, their friendship will usually last a lifetime.

You are a private person who resents intrusion and questions about your personal life. You can have a tendency to be suspicious of others and overly critical at times. Try not to be too rigid in your ways as there are always two sides to every story. You can be quite moody, fluctuating from highs and lows.

Birth force 8

You are endowed with the gift of power and confidence. Birth force 8 is a karmic number that has given you knowledge and life experience from your previous lives here on Earth. You are highly intuitive which serves you well when making decisions in life. This gift is also useful in helping you read other people.

You also truly understand what the material world can offer you, as well as understanding that finances alone will not bring you complete happiness.

As your birth force number is connected to money and finances, you can be successful with business enterprises. You are a born leader who is extremely inspiring to others. You are a dedicated worker who can be prone to workaholism. It is important to be aware of this side of your nature.

On the negative side, your dedication to being successful in life can become an obsession. This can cause you to put your need for material success before your family and loved ones.

Birth force 9

You are a born humanitarian who wants to make a difference in the world. You are a compassionate soul who feels the pain of others as though it is your own. Music touches your soul, connecting to your deep spiritual awareness. You are extremely intuitive, with the gift of seeing the truth within others.

You are creative, artistic and imaginative. You have the ability to write poetry, music or even work in the media in the fields of film and television. You would also make a wonderful teacher as you are patient and an inspiration to others.

You are a person who makes friends easily, as people are drawn to your captivating nature. As you are a born counsellor, you tend to be the person everyone comes to for assistance. You will need to protect yourself from becoming too involved in others' issues as this will drain your energy.

You like to have time to yourself, which friends and loved ones don't always understand. Be careful not to isolate yourself from others. Throughout your life, your spiritual side will become more pronounced.

Birth force 11

You have been given the gift of true spiritual insight. You will need to grow into the gifts this birth force number brings as you grow older. At a younger age you may not understand why others don't see the world through the same eyes as you do. You may feel as though you are a black sheep, when in fact you are the sheep with a golden fleece.

You are a highly inspirational human being who can achieve anything you set your mind to. The trick is to understand what you truly possess within yourself. You are courageous, never giving up on your goals. Some may think you are simply stubborn, however you are someone who starts a task and always finishes it with utmost perfection.

During your lifetime you will experience many challenges that will only make you stronger and more understanding of the ways of the world. In relationships, it is important to find a partner who is spiritually minded like yourself. Together, you will be able to conquer the world. In fact if you don't live your life acknowledging your spiritual gifts you may not find true happiness. You were born to inspire others.

You are so talented that there are many career choices for you in this lifetime. Your gifts can bring you before the public in the form of acting, writing, public speaking, teaching, metaphysical studies or research.

Birth force 22

You are a visionary. This gift also comes with karmic debts you need to work with and understand during your lifetime. You have been born with an inherent spiritual side that needs to be explored. You are happiest when you are working with your spiritual gifts.

You also have the gifts of an executive who will fundraise for the goodness of others. Part of your life's path is to do good for others, whether through charity work, fundraising or campaigning for others. Whatever it is, your path needs to be for the greater good of the world. You do like the best life has to offer, however you also understand it's about giving your best to those in need.

You are a perfectionist who expects the best from others as well as yourself. You do have a tendency towards intolerance. Try not to be impatient with others who do not view the world as you do. You are always quick to view the world from a higher perspective, while others do not have the insight that you do. The most important thing for you in this life is to leave a legacy, as your life will be incomplete if you don't feel you have achieved some sort of accomplishment.

Your career paths are endless. Remember – anything you put your mind to can become a reality if you stay focused.

Birth force 33

You are modest and extremely sensitive. You have a deep sense of service to others and the community in which you live. You have experienced many challenges in your life. You are a born empath and your deep sense of purpose to helping others can leave you prone to being taken advantage of, so be mindful to protect yourself. You are patient and gifted with children and the elderly. You would make a great nurse, carer, healer or counsellor. You have the ability to see beauty where it can be lost on others.

Birth force 44

You are a powerful achiever in the world. This is also one of the rarest birth force numbers. The number 44 is the number of manifestation. You have extraordinary insight in your life and the ability to manifest your dreams and ideas into reality. You can see the balance between the spiritual and material worlds. You have a way of implementing better ethics in the world, whether it be in business, education or on a world scale. You are strong, and like the base number 8, you are well read and balanced in your way of thinking. As a 44 you need to feel you have a sense of purpose in your life, otherwise you will feel unfulfilled. Money comes easily to you, but you will need to use it wisely. Your life offers you great rewards, however you will need to make considerable effort to reach them.

Your personal year number

A personal numerological cycle lasts nine years. At the end of the cycle it will end and start all over again. Your personal year number is worked out by adding the day of your birth to the month of your birth and then adding the current year number.

For example: If you are born on the 13th day of April and the year is 2021, you would add up the numbers as per the example below: 1+3+4+2+0+2+1=13

As you need to keep adding the numbers together until you reach a single figure you will continue with another additional sum of:

1+3=4. This then means you are in a 4 personal year.

It is important to remember that your personal year starts from the month you were born, not from the first day of the current year you are in.

Personal year 1

A personal year 1 is a time to begin a new nine-year life cycle. You will undertake many changes and the unsettling energy of the previous nine years can follow you into the first few months of your personal year 1. The beginning of the cycle can be quite lonely, as you may have experienced some changes or endings in friendships and personal relationships. You may have moved house recently or changed your vocation. A personal year 1 is a time for you to rely on yourself and find your inner strengths and exert your independence. It is a time to plan your future and to plant seeds of the life you would like to cultivate in the future. Towards the end of this year, you will feel more settled and focused on the future.

Personal year 2

A personal year 2 is a year where partnerships of a romantic and business kind will come to the fore. It is important to follow your intuition to make the right decision on how to proceed in these areas. If you are single, love usually blooms at this time. If you already have a partner, this is a time that your relationship can become stronger and more permanent. A personal 2 year is a time where you may feel that your life has slowed down after the quick-paced year you experienced in your personal year 1. Use this time to plan and focus on your goals coming to fruition. A personal year 2 is a time where you need to be patient and diplomatic. Do not try to force outcomes; gentle persuasion is far better than being pushy and over-bearing. This is a time of balance and compromise in all areas of your life.

Personal year 3

A personal year 3 is a year where you can expect celebrations, profits and rewards. A personal year 3 is a busy year where all your hard work of the past will come to fruition. The last two years have been spent planting the seeds and working towards reaping the benefits of all your hard work. This cycle can be a very social time in your life, where new friendships can emerge and you are feeling much happier and more settled than in the past. This is a year where romance is in the air; it is a time where you could experience a whirlwind love affair that could result in an engagement or wedding. This is also a fertile cycle in all areas of your life. You need to be alert as there could be news of a pregnancy. Be aware of all that this cycle has to offer you. If you don't make the best of this cycle there could be a delay in your desired outcome.

Personal year 4

A personal year 4 is a cycle that focuses on hard work and attention to detail. It is a time where you will be challenged both emotionally and in a business sense. If you can stay positive and focused on your abilities, new opportunities will present themselves and you will be noticed. This cycle can be a time when you are in the limelight and offered opportunities that may not have been available to you in the past. It is a great time for business, and you may be noticed by your peers for your systematic and driven work ethic. A mentor may even come into your life offering guidance and inspiration that will alter your future path. A personal year 4 can be a time where legal elements may be brought to your attention, so make sure you pay attention to any paperwork that requires your attention. If you work methodically and calmly during this cycle you will be surprised by the achievements and progress that is made during the year. Most importantly stay focused on the tasks at hand.

Personal year 5

A personal year 5 is a cycle where there is a lot of movement in your life. It is a time where you have a lot of energy and the opportunity to travel, change your lifestyle or have more time for yourself and those close to you. It can be a time where you may think about moving. A personal year 5 is a positive time, and you will experience abundance, pleasure and romance. It is a time to give birth to ideas and a time of fertility, so be aware of the possibility of a new addition to your family. A personal year 5 is even more romantic than the personal year 3. It will be evident to friends and colleagues that you are in your zone and a pleasure to spend time with. If you have been on your own this is certainly a time for romance to blossom and to meet your soulmate. This is also a cycle when a love from the past may reappear in your life. If this occurs you will discover that you have grown and the romance could progress to a more permanent connection than was possible in the past. This is a highly creative time for you in both your personal and business life.

Personal year 6

A personal year 6 is a settled time in your life. It is a time when you will focus more on emotional and financial security. Marriage is connected to this cycle so it may be an area of your life that will be more relevant than in the past. Your family becomes a priority in this cycle – their happiness becomes paramount and you may put more energy into your home environment. You may decide to purchase a property or make changes to your current domestic arrangements. This is a positive time to find a new abode that is exactly what you have been looking for. You may decide to renovate or make cosmetic changes to your living space. This is a year to follow your creativity and show your hidden talents. It may be a time where you decide to take lessons and explore your inner artist. This is certainly a creative time for you both personally and in your business life.

Personal year 7

A personal year 7 can be a very demanding year. It can put a lot of pressure on you both mentally and physically. You may feel restless and want to make changes in your life. It is a time where you may question your path and you won't know what you want from one minute to the next. It is a time to work on remaining focused, as you will tend to be scattered and unmotivated. Try not to be too hard on yourself; use this time as a period to manifest your goals and visualise them into reality. A personal year 7 is also a time to pay attention to your health. It may be a time where you decide to make some changes to your fitness regime or you may be tested with health issues. This is also a cycle where legal issues come to the fore, they will be connected to business, investments and house options. It may be as simple as you looking into refinancing or getting a home or car loan. Make sure you pay attention to the fine print and remember to dot your i's and cross your t's. Try to focus your energy into the positive side of this cycle to survive the challenges that will present themselves during this cycle.

Personal year 8

A personal year 8 cycle is a karmic year. It will be a time where all of the positive things you have done in the past will be rewarded. It is also a time when all of the negative things you have done will come back to haunt you. A personal year 8 is usually a cycle where good news and positive outcomes take place. If you are single, this could be a wonderful time for you to meet your significant other as it is a time when your soulmate can connect with you. Pregnancy is also strongly connected to the personal 8 year. As this cycle is a karmic year, it has a connection to past lives and could result in a reincarnation link of parents and children. This cycle is also a money year, so follow your intuition in connection to your finances and business decisions. If something doesn't feel right, do not proceed. The positive side to this cycle is to remind yourself that like attracts like, so focus on what you really want in your life.

Personal year 9

A personal year 9 cycle is a time of endings and clearing out. It can be a challenging time, as change will be forced upon you whether you want it or not. All areas of your life will be tested, friendships and relationships will be questioned and possibly come to an end. If you were thinking about moving or changing your living arrangements, this is the time that it will come to the fore. It is a time to not go against the flow, as this will only make the cycle ahead challenging and upsetting. Try to think of this cycle as a time of change for the better. If a relationship wasn't working out, it is time to let it go so that a better one will enter your life. Your vibration is going through significant changes, and you may be growing in a new direction away from friendships that no longer serve you well. If you have been thinking about changing your vocation, now is the time to do so. Use this year to plan what you do and don't want in your future life, and embrace the future possibilities.

Personal year 11

A personal year 11 cycle is a master number year. It is a time of hard work that will afford you greater opportunities than in a personal year 2. Don't waste this cycle on the things that you can't achieve; focus on all the things that you can. This is a time to trust your intuition and move forward. There will be great opportunities that present themselves to you at this time. Be brave and take the first step. This is a time to show your talents and hidden strengths. Goals that you may have thought were unattainable are now available for you to pursue. A personal year 11 is also a time for you to find your soulmate; in the past you may have been too concerned about looks and appearances. This is a time to realise that connecting with a partner on a deeper soul level is much more important. This is a time to focus on the positives – focusing on the negatives can delay your journey. Believe in your own abilities – you have nothing to lose and everything to gain.

Personal year 22

A personal year 22 is master number cycle that offers great opportunities and progress. This cycle has similarities to a personal year 4, but it is amplified due to its master number influence. The energy of the cycle is on a grand scale. If you wish to change jobs, it won't simply be a similar job to what you were doing previously. This is a time to really be noticed and given credit for being an expert in your field. You are full of inspiration and ideas at this time, and your peers will stand up and take notice of your expertise. It's a time to put yourself before the public; there may be opportunities for you to work in media or on the stage. Don't hold back, believe in yourself. Travel can become a priority at this time. You may not simply go to a holiday resort; you are more likely to undertake a spiritual journey to an ancient civilisation or to a destination that is off the beaten track. Do not worry about finances at this time, as the cycle is one of abundance and if you are meant to go on the trip, the finances will appear. This is a time to embrace your spiritual and intellectual knowledge.

Your house number

The way to find out the numerology of your house is quite simple. Add the digits of your house together and reduce them to a single figure. For example, if your address number is 1234 Short Street, simply add 1+2+3+4 = 10, then 1+0 = 1. The numerological number for your house is 1.

If you live in an apartment block, then add all the numbers together and reduce them to a single figure. For example, if your address is Apartment 20, 2150 Short Street then add up 20 + 2150 = 2+0+2+1+5+0 = 10, then 1+0 = 1 to get your single number of 1. By simply adding 2+1+5+0 you will get the energy of the building as well.

The numbers in your address are part of what determines the energy or vibration that surrounds those who live within the home. All homes have their own individual energy. Every property will have both positive and negative energy affecting it. It is important to understand which house numbers are good for you to live in and which numbers to avoid.

Your house number can be a big influence on your surroundings and the life you lead. There are no good or bad numbers for you, however there are four karmic debt house numbers that are best avoided if you don't want to live in challenging surroundings. These karmic debt numbers 13, 14, 16 or 19, and they have energies that will affect your personal life by placing obstacles and challenges before you.

It is good to remember that challenges are not always a bad thing to experience, as this is how we grow and progress through life.

House number 1

A number 1 house is usually an individual type of property, with different décor to other houses in the neighbouring area. A number 1 house attracts you to it because of its individuality, and its energy allows the people who live within it to have their own space. In fact, many people who live in a number 1 home tend to spend a lot of time alone and don't tend to have many visitors. This home also suits people who wish to work from home.

House number 2

A number 2 house is always busy and full of life. It's a wonderful house number for newlyweds and couples, as it is a house to be shared and enjoyed. It's also a house for people to entertain in. Friends will love to drop by for a visit as they will be drawn to the calm, positive energy within. The energy of a number 2 house functions best if there isn't any clutter and décor is minimalistic.

House number 3

A number 3 house is a happy place to live. It's a wonderful home for those who are creative and artistic, as the energy within the house is always happy and upbeat. This is a house to party in, and it's a wonderful place for communication. It's also great for larger families, as 3 homes tend to be more extravagant than some of the other house numbers. A number 3 house often goes through many transformations including renovations, extensions and landscaping additions. Those who live in a number 3 house are wonderful gardeners.

House number 4

A number 4 house is a wonderful home for the family. This house number is extremely grounded, creating security for family life. Those who dwell within this home tend to like routine, order and stability. A 4 house is usually a good investment, as there aren't too many issues that arise within this house number. A 4 house is usually a well-built structure and is connected to the earth. Most 4 homes have beautiful gardens that attract owners who like to keep their home and garden neatly manicured. This number is also great for owners who like to achieve in their working life.

House number 5

A number 5 house will undergo many changes and owners – people will come and go. If you wish to have a peaceful and serene existence within your home, this is not the property for you. It's a wonderful number for an investment property though. But if you want this house number to be your permanent residence, it may be a place that you travel away from often. This house number requires a lot of attention and may require money to be spent on it to bring out its full potential. A 5 home is great for newlyweds or a couple, as it's a wonderful number for romance and pleasure.

House number 6

A number 6 house is a great home to raise a family. It's a safe haven with great security and peace for the children. A 6 home usually has a wonderful kitchen, as this is a house that is perfect for entertaining friends and family. The energy of a 6 house can vary from a harmonious and tranquil place to a place of conflict, as this home involves family matters and emotions. It's a house for communication and is wonderful for running a home business. Most people who move into a number 6 house usually live at the address for many years. It's also a property with a wonderful garden.

House number 7

A number 7 house is a spiritual home – peaceful, quiet and great for meditation. In fact, it's a great place for any kind of spiritual work, usually with a great library and beautiful furnishings. People who live in 7 properties generally spend a lot of time alone, due to the peace and quiet. A number 7 house is renowned for water problems though. It's extremely important to check the plumbing, drainage or leaky showers before moving into this number property as there will definitely be some kind of water issue.

House number 8

A number 8 house is a wonderful investment property. It's a house from which to make money. An 8 house is well built with a feeling of grandeur and status about it. For those who like money, power and success, this is the house for you. The only problem is that money can become an obsession for those who live in this number house. It's great to be successful; however, it's also important to take time to enjoy life.

House number 9

A number 9 house experiences many changes within it. It is a property owners will often travel away from. This house number may have many different residents and doesn't have the warmth of a family home. The residents who live in a number 9 house face many challenges in their lives. They have to work hard to get ahead in life. The residents who live in a number 9 house are giving, and are often looked to for assistance by others.

CHAPTER 21

PSYCHIC CHILDREN

EVERYBODY IS PSYCHIC – FROM THE MOMENT we are born we are aware of and connected to the spiritual world. We are born with amazing, untapped gifts from above.

Some of these gifts are the 'clairs' we have discussed in previous chapters: clairvoyance, clairaudience, clairsentience, claircognisance, clairempathy, clairtangency, clairalience, mediumship abilities and the ability to see auras. Some people will be endowed with all of these gifts while others may only have one or some of these abilities. Many of these gifts work in conjunction with each other and are gifts that we actually take for granted.

There is a saying that messages come 'from the mouths of babes'. Children have a direct line to spirit. Our children are the innocent messengers who connect with those from above. Children's psychic awareness is most pronounced in their younger years – up to ten years of age. When children start to interact with people outside of the family and begin to participate in kindergarten and primary school, they are often told that the invisible people they see and hear are not real and merely a figment of their imagination. Some children are more open to spirit than others, and it isn't until they discover that they are not like everybody else that they begin to shut down and ignore their abilities, fearing they will be ostracised by others.

Children are not born with a filter system. It is most important to listen to their wants, needs and fears. If your child reports they have an invisible person who comes to visit them and looks like a deceased relative, or if they tell you they have an invisible friend, it is important to listen to them as they are telling you the truth.

How many times have you heard your young child giggling and interacting in another room as though they are playing with someone, yet when you go in to check, there is no one else there with them. As babies, they may even put their arms up as if they want to be picked up by an unseen person. This is because they are psychic and can connect to the spiritual realm.

Don't be alarmed that there is anything wrong with your child. Young children can see people in spirit as clearly as they see those in the living. They don't know that the people they are seeing are actually people who are in the spirit realm (deceased).

Young children are aware of their guardian angels and loved ones. It is only when they get older and go to school that they realise who and what they are seeing and communicating with are beings not seen by most adults.

It is such a shame that most of us shut down our special gift of psychic sight and communication as a child. How wonderful it would be if we all continued to have our spiritual awareness from childhood to our final years. It would certainly make life a lot more interesting, and we wouldn't need to invest so much time in remembering what we already know.

Many times our children will make contact with loved ones who are long passed. They may talk to you about speaking with a person who they were named after in spirit, even though they have never met that person in life. When our children connect to these people, they are making contact with their ancestral angels, guardian angels and spirit guides. Our loved ones in spirit make an enormous effort to be present in our children's lives, even though they may have passed long before your little one arrived on Earth.

When your child begins to talk and communicate with you, it is always important to listen to their hopes, fears and ideas. If your child tells you they don't like somebody they meet, it is for a reason. You may have a friend or relative that frequently comes over to your home who may be nice to your child, but there is something your child just doesn't like about them.

The reason your child is telling you this is because the person's vibration may not resonate at the same vibration as your child's. Children can pick up the energy of people they meet much better than you would think. Children can be better judges of character than we are as grown adults. Children are innocent and don't use a filtering system when telling you what they see in a person. They will just tell you how it is.

If your child does express this type of communication to you about someone they don't like, it would be a good idea to look further into why they are telling you this. They are expressing this feeling to you for a reason.

Another common issue parents of young children report is of them having trouble sleeping alone in their bedroom as they have a fear of the dark. They will even report they are frightened of the invisible people who visit them in their room. It is important to listen to your child's fears, as they are telling you the truth about what they can see and hear. As an adult you may not be able to see these invisible beings in the room, however they are very real to your child.

As a child it can be traumatising being sent into a room (especially a bedroom) where they don't feel safe and protected. There is a misconception that ghosts/spirits only come out at night. This is not always the case. Spirits are creatures of habit – if a person who is now in spirit tended to be in a particular room in the house, they may continue to be there after their death. This is common for people who live in a property that is historical or has had previous owners who have passed.

So don't think that your child will be fine to be in the scary room during the day as they may still suffer the same fears they do at night. Beings in the spirit world tend to visit when the child is alone. It is not because they want to frighten your child, it is because the child will be more aware of their presence as they will have their undivided attention.

In some cases, a loved one in spirit will come to visit your child while they are playing happily in their room by themselves. They come to visit to give your child messages of reassurance their love has not ceased since they passed. They may even give messages to the child to pass onto their parent. How many times have you been given a message from your child telling you that someone you love and miss dearly is talking to them trying to get your attention?

The spirit being your child is seeing could also be the child's ancestral guide or guardian angel who comes to reassure and protect them from any negative spirits that may be frightening them.

Signs your child is psychic

- Your child has an invisible friend.
- Your child sees and communicates with deceased loved ones.
- Your child is frightened of the invisible people or dark shadows they see in their bedroom.
- Your child is frightened of the dark.
- Your child sees lights or orbs in their room.
- Your child sees ghosts.

- Your child gives you messages from those in spirit.
- When you take photographs of your child, there are unusual anomalies in the picture.
- Your child tells you about their past lives.
- Your child tells you that you are not their real parent.
- Your child tells you they have another name to the one you have named them.
- Your child sees and communicates with the fairy realm.
- Your child has a great imagination and tells you amazing stories.
- Your child sees auras around people and describes the colours they see.
- Your child is drawn to a certain time in history or to places they have never been before – for example, your child tells you about their life during the war in England.
- Your child has an interest in angels and spirits.
- Your child has healing abilities.

So now you are aware of what to look for with the little old souls who surround you, what can you do to assist them with their spiritual journey?

As a child, you too may have felt that you were different, and you may have had your own invisible friend or spirits. Did you ever feel alone and like others didn't understand your life experiences, even though you knew they were real? This may be because you too were a child who saw and heard spirit, but nobody believed your 'stories' even though they were real.

Now is the time to be the nurturing parent, care giver or caring relative who can help the child in your life. You don't want them to grow up feeling and experiencing the same things you did as a child. In this day and age, it is more acceptable to speak about the spirit realm. There are more people who have had spiritual experiences than haven't.

Firstly, it's important to reassure your little spiritual child that you are listening to their fears and questions about who and what they are seeing. If they tell you there is a person in their room that is scaring them, be as patient and understanding as possible. If your child is old enough to verbalise what is going on, ask them if they can tell you about the spirit person. Either ask them to draw or describe what the person looks like. If you have a loved one in spirit you think it might be, show your child a picture of them and confirm if it is or not. Talk to your child about the wonderful memories you have of the person in spirit. Tell your child about your loved one's life, so they begin to understand who this person is. This will help to allay any fears your child might have of their visitor from spirit.

As your child grows, so will their connection to spirit. Keeping a special diary to record all of the events that take place as your child grows will help your child to progress. When children reach a certain age, their spirit friend may just disappear or they may stop talking about them. This can happen as your little one no longer needs guidance from their spirit helper or they may feel concerned that their friends will not understand their special gift.

It is important to note that by encouraging your child to talk about their invisible spirit friends, angels, spirit guides and friends from the fairy realm will not cause them any harm. It is better to be aware and if possible to talk to your child about what they are experiencing, so they are not frightened of their gifts. It will be up to your child whether they choose to work with their gifts when they get older.

Power is knowledge, if you understand what is happening, it is easier to understand how and what to do about certain situations that may arise as your child grows.

Ways to help your child be protected by their angels

The most important way to assist your child is to teach them about their guardian angels and spirit guides. If you speak to them frequently about these unseen positive beings, they will be able to access the higher realms of spirit with ease.

Take the time to look for the signs from above. Children love to go on adventures, so plan a trip into your backyard or local park to look for signs that their special friends in spirit are nearby. A wonderful way to connect with the angels is by taking a picnic blanket or towel with you, so that you can lie down on it and look for angel signs in the clouds above. Your children will be surprised by what beautiful messages appear in the clouds when you look for them. The angels have been known to appear in clouds on many occasions, whether it be the image of an angel, feather, lost loved one or pet in spirit.

Taking your child on an angelic treasure hunt is another fun way to connect with spirit. Go outside into the garden to look for feathers, butterflies, dragonflies and, if you are really lucky, four-leaf clovers.

When you and your child have collected your special treasures from the angels, take the time to make a beautiful box to keep the treasures in. You could also make a collage, scrapbook or photo frame in honour of the angels. Placing this special memento in your child's room will remind them of the angels each day.

Teaching them how to protect themselves with white light is extremely important. I suggest that you begin the white light protection process when your child is having their nightly bath or shower. If your child prefers to have a bath, adding some bubble bath to the water will make it a fun and uplifting experience.

Run the bath, adding the bubble bath. When your child is sitting or floating amongst the white fluffy bubbles, tell them that their angels are putting a beautiful cocoon of protection around them from heaven.

Explain to them that floating amongst the bubbles is what it is like for the angels to float amongst the clouds. Giving your child a physical experience when calling in their angels will help remind them that every time they are amongst the bubbles, they are safe and protected by spirit.

If your child prefers to have a shower you can teach them to imagine the water coming out of the shower-head as an angelic forcefield that washes away any fears, negativity and worries. Your child may wish to imagine their favourite colour showering down upon them to help them to feel more protected.

The more often you and your child practise these protective white light rituals, the stronger their connection to the angelic realms will be. Learning to white light will also help your child if they experience any bullying.

Each night when your child goes to sleep recite a protective prayer with them, or you may choose to do it on their behalf, so that they will feel safe and protected when they are alone in their bedroom at night.

Playing ambient music or lullabies can assist your child when they are going off to sleep. It can become a nightly ritual that will help them to settle down and reconnect with their angels.

Regularly cleansing your home, paying extra attention to your children's bedrooms will lift the vibration and rid your home of any negative vibrations (see chapter 3 for how to cleanse your home).

Some children like to wear a pendant, talisman or crystal to help them feel protected. This item doesn't have to be expensive. It can be as simple as a christening medal, a cross, an angel charm or a crystal on a leather thong from a new age store. The item may also be something that belonged to a precious loved one who has passed over and your child was close to. Let your child choose what item they are drawn to, as this will give it more meaning to them. If your child wants to wear a crystal pendant, ask them to feel different ones to see which one 'speaks' to them. Crystals usually pick out their owners, which strengthens the connection.

You may wish to have a picture of your loved one in spirit in the room to confirm to your child they are looking after them. Each night when they go to bed, you can ask the person to protect your child while they sleep.

For example, asking their nanna to be with them throughout the night.

A night-light is a good idea for little ones who are afraid of the dark. It is comforting for them to see the light in their room if they wake up in the middle of the night.

If your child is very young, it is a good idea to have a video baby monitor in their room, especially if they are waking up in the middle of the night or having trouble sleeping. The cameras on baby monitors are good at picking up spirit energies. You may be surprised by what you see. There have been many cases of parents reporting seeing their child playing and talking with someone in their room. Do not be surprised if one of your loved ones in spirit has come to visit and protect your little one during the night.

Some children grow out of their spirit friends and their psychic gifts close down as they get older, while other children have their psychic gifts with them their whole lives. If this is the case, it is important that your child learns to work with spirit on a positive level, so that they are guided and protected by their angels and spirit guides throughout their life.

Teenage children and the spirit world

As your child reaches their teenage years, they may lose their connection to spirit. However, this can be the most important time of their life to stay connected and be guided by their angels and spirit guides. The teenage years are extremely vulnerable times for your child. It is a time of self-discovery and understanding of what the world around them has to offer. During this period of your child's life, they will question many things about themselves, their friendships and belief system.

It is also a time when their spiritual GPS system can come into play. Your teen's gut feeling tends to re-awaken itself at this stage of their life. The only problem is they don't always understand what their gut feeling is or how to use the messages they receive. If you can assist your child in understanding the different signs or feelings they experience within themselves during this journey, they will be better prepared for their future. It will also strengthen their guidance and help them to be protected by their angels and guides.

It is important to discuss with your teen that there is a reason if something doesn't feel right. For example, your teen is asked to go to a party, and they get a weird feeling in their stomach that makes them feel like they want to be sick, or they may feel like they have an upset stomach. The feeling can be heavy and unsettling for no apparent reason. People receive this type of feeling as a warning about something. It is our inbuilt warning system, or as I like to call it, our spiritual GPS, warning us to be careful about something even though we don't quite know what it is. The warning could be your teen needs to be careful of other people who will be at the party, or it could be a warning that people attending will be drinking underage. If on the other hand the feeling is uplifting, exciting or like butterflies in the stomach, then this is confirmation that the experience will be positive. It is giving your teen the green light that everything will be OK.

The feelings that your teen picks up don't always resonate in their 'gut' or stomach area. Feelings can also be in their heart – a heavy or light feeling in the heart space or their heart racing. Feelings can manifest in goose bumps up the back of the spine, arm or face, or it could be a feeling of being unsafe, being watched or just unsettled. Discuss these types of feelings as it could be something that can save them from a life-threatening situation in the future. How many times have you heard they didn't do something because it didn't feel right? For example, a teen may be asked if they want a lift home with some friends but they declined because it didn't feel right. Unfortunately, the friends in the car were involved in an accident and were injured. If the teen was in the car, they could have been injured or killed.

Your spiritual teen may also start to hear voices when they have decisions to make about things in their life. When I talk about voices, I am not indicating that this is connected to any mental illness or schizophrenia. You may wish to speak with your teen about this. Explain to your teen that when they are making decisions about what is the wrong and right thing to do in a situation, they may hear their higher self, spirit guide or guardian angel giving them advice on what is best to do.

This information will come to them in the form of words, phrases and guidance. The guidance can be heard in your teen's own voice or words can appear to be male or female (this is from guides and angels). Let them know that the first information they receive is always the correct guidance to follow. It is when they over-analyse things and try to think rationally that they can start to interfere with the right decision.

Do's & don'ts for spiritual teens

Here are some helpful tips you can pass onto your spiritual teen, or if you are reading this book and you are a teenager, then I hope you find this helpful.

Do's

Think positive thoughts and try and always look at the good things you have in your life. Sometimes things don't always go the way you want them to; it is only when you look back on this type of situation that you will realise that everything happens for a reason.

Think about one great thing you have in your life each morning when you wake up. You may wish to use some positive affirmation cards to give you a positive message for the day.

Notice the signs from your guides and angels – for example, feathers, coins etc.

Meditate to lift your vibration each day. It will enhance your connection to your spirit guides and guardian angels as well as giving you spiritual clarity.

Use your imagination to manifest and create your world. Remember, if you think negative thoughts, that's what you will attract into your life. So from today onwards, only think about the positives you want to have and achieve in your life. Be patient and watch the changes around you. If you find this type of thought change a bit of a challenge, ask your guides and angels to assist you.

Be brave and let your spiritual light shine.

Ask as many questions as possible about the spirit world. Knowledge is power.

Be inspired. Pay attention to inspirational guidance from your spirit guides and guardian angels.

Be aware of your dreams. This is how you can receive guidance from your spirit guides and guardian angels.

Pay attention to how people who come into your friendship group feel in your gut. If you meet someone and you don't feel comfortable with them it is a sign from your built-in spiritual GPS system to be cautious with the friendship. You don't have to be unpleasant to the person – however, be cautious of them until they prove themselves to you.

Be patient with spirit. Your spirit guides and guardian angels need time to help situations heal and improve.

Remember you are a unique spiritual being who is having an earthly experience. Enjoy your journey.

Keep a diary of the messages, feelings, visions and guidance you receive from your angels and guides. I am sure you will be surprised by what guidance they have to offer you.

Don'ts

Don't think you are too old to be guided from above – your assistance is only a thought away.

Don't play with Ouija boards, especially at parties or while using alcohol or substances. Ouija boards are not a toy; they are a gateway to the spirit world. Negative entities and energies can reside at this vibration, and they can open you up to the lower astral plain. Ouija boards can allow entities to attach to your auric field.

Don't wish anything negative towards another. Remember what goes around, comes around.

Don't get caught up with the crowd. If something doesn't feel right, don't do it. When you go against yourself you will be disappointed by the outcome.

Don't be frightened to ask your spirit guides, loved ones and guardian angels in spirit to help you with guidance and reassurance. After all, that is what they are there for. It is better to consult them when you are not angry or upset as your vibration will drop and you will find it hard to hear them from above.

Don't consult your psychic tools when you are angry – for example, don't use your cards, pendulum, divining rods etc. when you are angry, as your vibration will be lowered and you won't receive clear messages from above.

Don't over consult any psychic tools if you don't receive the answer you want.

Don't cast spells or incantations on anybody else for your own personal gain.

Don't listen to negative thoughts or voices you feel or hear. If you experience this type of thing call in your spirit guides and guardian angels. Consult chapter 6 on psychic protection for more information on this.

Ways for teens to meditate

When you are a teenager, the last thing you want to do is sit still. The exceptions to this are of course when playing a game on the computer, surfing the web, Facebook, texting or on the phone.

Your teen can meditate by walking, playing sport, going to the gym, listening to their phone/music, while swimming or riding their bike or skateboard.

If you find that your teen does get stressed, encourage them to do an activity that will change their focus. As they are at an age when their hormones are changing and developing you may find that they can become quite moody, angry or withdrawn without warning.

The following guided meditations are also a beneficial way for your child to connect to spirit.

Whether or not your teen is on their spiritual path, they will experience these changes throughout their teenage years. It is important as their parent that you are their greatest supporter. Be there to listen to their hopes and fears. Guide them along their spiritual path, picking them up when they feel challenged.

More and more children are opening up to the spiritual world. Being a psychic child can be a lonely path. It is a time when they will feel like a black sheep amongst their friends. It will take them time to realise that they are a gifted spiritual being with a higher purpose in their life. Nurture and guide them along the way. Things will not always be easy, although they will be enlightening. Together you will discover the many hidden treasures the universe has in store for your child.

PROTECTIVE PRAYER FOR YOUR CHILD

Dear guardian angels and spirit guides
(you may add the names of any loved ones in
the spirit world at this point of the prayer).
I ask for you to protect and guide (your child's
name) tonight. Please fill (child's name)
room with loving angelic light. I ask that
(child's name) angels, guides and loved ones
surround (him/her) in a beautiful fluffy cocoon
of white light that protects (him/her) while
(he she) sleeps. (Imagine the cocoon to be like
a sleeping bag made of fluffy cotton wool).
I ask that you guide (child's name) during
(his/her) dream state and to protect (him/her)
from any nightmares or night terrors. I ask
that (child's name) meets you during (his her)
dream state and experiences the protective love
and guidance you share with (him/her).
I thank all of the angels, spirit guides and
loved ones in spirit for their presence and
protection in my (child's name) life.
I send you all love and light.
Amen

Meditation for teens

Doing a daily meditation is a wonderful way to calm your mind and feel at peace within yourself. If your teen is stressed due to schoolwork, exams, friendships or just coping with being a teenager, introduce them to meditation. Daily meditation is a good habit for them to get into. By them taking a little 'me time' and meditating they will be able to reconnect with their higher self, allowing them to see their problems and fears from a different perspective.

Creating a spiritual meditation journal is a wonderful way for your teen to record their thoughts, messages and guidance from above. The journal doesn't have to be an expensive book, it could be as simple as an exercise book or notebook. There are lots of great stationery stores that have inexpensive books with great covers that your teen would love.

Prior to each meditation, it is a good idea to write down what question your teen would like answered through their meditation. It is important to remind your teen that the answer may come as a thought, symbol or vision. It could also arrive as a feeling or inner knowing.

At the end of the meditation, remind your teen to write down whatever guidance they have received during the meditation. They may not pick up any messages, they may simply feel calmer and more relaxed. If this is the case, remind them that is what they needed to receive at that time.

Ask them to write a positive affirmation about their experience in the journal if they have one.

Your teen may wish to undertake this simple meditation before beginning their day:

- Find a quiet place to sit and relax. You may wish to sit outside in the garden or you may have a sacred space where you feel safe and protected. Gently close your eyes and slowly breathe in. Visualise breathing in positive uplifting light. As you breathe out, imagine you are exhaling any negative emotions you may be experiencing at the moment.
- Breathe in positivity and light.
- Exhale any negativity that you may have around you. Imagine you are ridding yourself of any emotion that does not belong to you.
- Once again, breathe in the light.
- Exhale any residual energy that is still attached to you.
- Visualise a beautiful bright white light surrounding your entire body. Now watch as this light expands to make you glow from its brightness.
- Look down at your feet and see this protective light entering your body via your feet. Watch as the light slowly moves up to your base chakra.

- As the energy reaches your base chakra, it turns a brilliant red. The light continues to move and reaches your sacral chakra turning a brilliant orange. The light continues up and reaches your solar plexus turning a brilliant yellow. Feel the energy filling your body and continuing to move up to your heart chakra turning brilliant green. Allow the energy to progress and move up to your throat chakra turning brilliant blue. As you feel the energy moving along your body, notice if there are any blockages you may need to spend more time on. If there is any resistance, visualise the light cleansing and clearing any blockages. Watch as the energy now moves up to your third eye turning a brilliant indigo. Continue to see the energy reach your crown chakra and turning a brilliant violet.

- Take a few moments to feel the light filling your entire body with cleansing purity. Feel the energy expanding throughout every part of your body, allowing you to be reconnected with your inner self.

- A feeling of lightness now surrounds your entire body. An overwhelming feeling of calmness and protection washes over you. Sit quietly in this peaceful environment and begin to look around at your surroundings. In the distance, you can see a beautiful shimmering light making its way towards you. Watch as the light moves closer and closer towards you. Do you recognise the being of light? Does the being remind you of someone you have met before? Is this being a loved one in spirit who you miss and would like to make contact with? Pay attention to how you feel as the being comes towards you. Does the being look like your guardian angel or spirit guide?

- The being now sits down beside you in your sacred space. Think about any questions or concerns that you may wish to share with this being. You may simply wish to ask them their name and enquire about what guidance they wish to share with you. The information they share with you may come in the form of words in your mind, you may hear them speak, or you may feel the connection as the knowledge flows within you. Don't worry about how you pick up the information from this being; it is more important to pay attention and remember everything they share with you.

- Pay attention to what the being looks like. What colour hair do they have? What eye colour do they have? Is the being male or female? What is the being dressed like? Do they have any wings? Ask them their name. Are they wearing any perfume or fragrances? It is important to remember these points about the being as it will help you to reconnect with them in the future.

- Once you and the being finish communicating, thank them for sharing their knowledge and guidance with you. Let them know you would like to meet up with them in the future at this special sacred space.

- Watch as the being gets up and slowly walks back into the direction from which they came. As the being leaves, they take with them any worries or fears you may have been experiencing. Your worries and fears dissolve into the light as the energy of the being slowly withdraws into the brightness.

- Feel the protective spiritual light that now completely surrounds your entire body, giving you the feeling of warmth and protection.

- You are now at peace, calm and relaxed to begin your day ahead. Know in your heart whenever you feel uneasy or stressed that you may return to this sacred space to reconnect with the being and release any negativity you may be feeling.

AFFIRMATION

I feel protected, calm and relaxed with the
knowledge that I am not alone. I acknowledge
the connection to my spirit guides, loved ones and
guardian angels in the spirit realms. My spiritual
beings are only a thought away – I believe in their
positive energy and guidance.

CHAPTER 22

WHAT IS A NEAR-DEATH EXPERIENCE (NDE)?

A NEAR-DEATH EXPERIENCE OR NDE is an overwhelming psychological experience that can occur when a person is close to death, in the process of dying or pronounced clinically dead.

People who have NDEs often report that they no longer feel any pain or suffering during their experience. Many people report feeling light and at peace with a heightened awareness.

The appearance of white or golden light is commonly reported by NDE experiencers, coming down from above from what many people would call heaven. The light can be in the form of a protective comforting experience contained within the sky or clouds. The light can be accompanied by beings of light that come from within it to guide and assist the NDE experiencer.

A classical NDE is often described as a sense of movement at great speed through a long dark or tunnel-like space with a bright pin-hole of light at the end of it. As the person journeys further and further into the tunnel, the pinhole of light increases, becoming brighter and brighter, often surrounding the person with a radiance of love and light. Often noises such as a whirring, buzzing or ringing sound is heard by the person having the NDE.

Some people who have experienced an NDE with this tunnel of light experience describe travelling through the tunnel alone and being met at the end of it by a supreme being, angel, spirit guide or loved one. Others have reported being accompanied throughout the entire journey with a being they may or may not have known during their life.

Some people report arriving in much more beautiful surroundings than they have encountered here on Earth. They report the colours being brighter and more colourful than any they have experienced on Earth.

Still others report arriving at a destination where there are cities and buildings, and/or what is known as the 'Halls of Learning', where they are instilled with higher knowledge.

Another common type of NDE is when the experiencer travels up through the clouds into space and the cosmos. They are aware of the connectedness of all things. They may experience going through black holes and then coming back into space having a clear view of the universe. It can be as though they are a satellite travelling through space and time. Experiencers may report the feeling of total calmness and euphoria within their being. Many people cannot put into words what they saw during their journey through space, as they find it hard to comprehend.

Others have reported the feeling of separating from their body at the time of a great trauma. For example, being in a car accident, undergoing a medical operation, or while experiencing a life-threatening event such as a heart-attack, drowning or stroke. Women have also had similar experiences when they are in a highly emotional state such as going through childbirth, even though they are not close to death.

Some people may be guided on their journey by angels, spirit guides, beings of light or a supreme being. (The being could be in the form of Christ or another deity, depending on the experiencer's cultural and religious belief.) When they meet up with those in spirit, the communication is by mental telepathy or mind-to-mind communication rather than verbal communication.

It is not uncommon that people meet up with their deceased loved ones. Some of these loved ones may be relations they have never met during

their lifetime on Earth. The person only knows of them due to family photographs or family history. When the experiencer returns back to their life on Earth, they have a greater connection and understanding that their loved ones are always with them.

Many people who have NDEs report witnessing the entire event as if they were watching it from a higher perspective. There have been cases when a patient is undergoing an operation, and they experience an NDE. The patient can relay exactly what happened during the operation, describing what conversations took place during the time of their NDE. Some experiencers have reported they were able to see what was on top of the cupboards in the room when it was not possible to see them from the operating table.

Another common occurrence is for experiencers to undergo a life review. During this experience, the person is shown glimpses of their lifetime from their birth to the current day. They can be shown highlights and even the lowlights of their lifetime on Earth. The experiencer can be given the choice of whether or not they wish to return to their life or cross over to the spirit realm.

During this time the family left behind can be shown to the experiencer, which is often why the person makes the decision to return to Earth and continue on with their life here. Sometimes the person is told by a being/s in the spirit world it is not their time and they need to go back. The experiencer can feel a reluctance to return to life, as they feel the immense love and peacefulness while in the spirit world.

I must point out that a minority of people have reported having a negative experience during an NDE. This could be experiencing a feeling of powerlessness, fear, anger, despair and being frightened by the experience. Some report the feeling of being in a place of darkness and nothingness. They describe the experience of feeling like they are being judged and in great distress. The experience is of negativity and worthlessness where the person felt lost and alone.

Sometimes experiencers have witnessed evil spirits or entities who are frightening to the experiencer. The experiencer is shown all of the negative things they have done during their life and it isn't until they surrender and ask for assistance from a higher being that their negative experience ends, and they are met by a being from the light.

After people have returned from an NDE many have reported a spiritual awakening. Some people choose to change their birth force after such an experience. Others report coming back from their NDE with psychic gifts such as clairvoyance, clairaudience, claircognisance, clairsentience and mediumship.

Many scientists dismiss NDEs as a chemical reaction in the brain after the heart stops, causing a reduction of oxygen to the brain. Scientists would have us believe that due to the neurotransmitters of the brain shutting down, people mistake this experience as an illusion of a spiritual vision or heavenly afterlife experience.

There certainly is a lot of evidence to support that in many people's minds, an NDE is an actual experience and not just a chemical brain reaction. To the many people who have experienced their own NDE, this scientific explanation is not acceptable. It does make you question why so many people around the world all report similar experiences if an NDE wasn't in fact a real experience.

It is interesting to note that NDEs have been reported all over the world throughout time. NDE experiences have been reported by both religious and non-religious people, regardless of their belief system, culture or educational status.

People who experience NDEs can come back enlightened, with a different perspective on life. They can return to life with the knowledge of what their life's purpose should be. Many wishing to do something with their life that is for the greater good of humanity. This experience can also make the experiencer feel alone and isolated due to their unique experience. The most positive result of a person who experiences an NDE is their understanding of life after death is a reality and not simply a hope.

My own experiences of NDEs

I have now experienced seven NDEs during my life. Each of these experiences has deeply influenced me and it has changed my life forever. I had my first NDE when I suffered with bronchopneumonia at the age of three and was put into hospital. My earliest memories were of being in a hospital ward with lots of other children lying in cots and beds. I will never forget lying in bed coughing uncontrollably and wanting to see my parents. The most vivid memory of this dark time was of a beautiful female being coming and sitting and holding my hand and telling me I was going to be okay. The being was calming and glowed with a gorgeous ethereal light that was almost too bright to look at. I had never seen anything so beautiful, and it wasn't until I had other experiences that I began to understand I had been touched by an angel. The beautiful being patted my head and helped me feel safe and calm, even though I couldn't breathe properly. As an adult, I understand that this being was my guardian who saved my life.

In 1976, I was 13 years of age, I had a grumbling appendix and I was rushed to hospital as the doctor feared that my appendix might burst. At the time, I was quite excited, as it felt like I was going on an adventure, and I hoped after the operation I would finally feel well and not have to put up with the constant stomach cramps and pain. Little did I know what a life-changing event I was soon going to experience.

On the morning of the operation, I was given a pre-med injection to relax me, before I was taken to the operating theatre. This is the last thing I remember until after the operation. In the afternoon, the nurse woke me up and took my blood pressure. The pain was so intense I wondered how I could have ever been excited to have an operation. After the nurse left the room, I began to drift off into a strange dream-like state. I felt my body lifting off the bed, and I felt like I was floating on the surface of a pool. The strangest thing was, I was looking down at my body still lying in the hospital bed.

I tried desperately to get back down to the bed and back into my body, but I felt as if I was a cork floating on the top of the water, and I kept floating back up to the ceiling of the hospital room.

I saw the nurse come back into the room to recheck my blood pressure. She looked concerned, and I saw her ring the buzzer. Another nurse came rushing into the room with an oxygen bottle.

I suddenly woke up safely in the bed with an oxygen mask on my face. The nurse was looking at me with a panicked expression on her face. At that point, I thought I had just woken up from a weird dream.

It wasn't until the following day when the doctor came to check on me that I was told that something had gone wrong during the night and my heart had stopped. The doctor ran some tests but they all came back normal; he couldn't explain what had happened to me.

After this experience I always knew that I had a greater purpose in this life, but at that point I never truly understood what that gift was to be.

To be honest, this experience made me feel very isolated, and I felt like an outsider amongst my group of friends. What I had experienced was not widely spoken about in the 1970s, and it made me look at life differently and also feel like I didn't belong.

I did try to tell some of my closer friends about what I had experienced, but they didn't understand. I began to look at the world through different eyes and my greatest connection was when I went to the beach, and I was swimming in the ocean at peace.

When I went back to school, I discovered the most wonderful book in the school library by Dr Raymond Moody called *Life After Life*, released in 1975. This book helped me immensely after having my NDE experiences. In 1976, NDEs were not something many people had ever heard of or experienced on a personal level.

It wasn't until 1996 that I experienced my next NDE. I was pregnant with my third child and I had caught a virus. I was extremely unwell and had to be rushed to the hospital as I went into labour two months earlier than my due date. When I was at the hospital, I was given an injection of pethidine for the pain, when suddenly I could feel myself leaving my body. I kept telling my husband to shake me, as I could feel myself floating up towards the ceiling of the room, and I knew that I was about to go.

The nurse came in and gave me some oxygen and asked me to calm down. The next thing I remember was being up amongst the clouds and floating. I looked back towards Earth and then I saw a vision of my husband with my two boys and a baby girl (who I had not yet given birth to).

What was quite confusing was that I saw my husband dressed in a soldier's uniform from the First World War and my children were dressed in clothes from the same era. I now look on this experience and realise that, even though I was experiencing an NDE, I was also seeing a glimpse of my past life with my current family.

After spending over a week in hospital, the birth of my daughter was delayed, and she arrived around her original due date. She was born perfectly healthy which was a blessing to me.

One year later, I was to experience my most vivid and frightening NDE. I had to have a major operation, and I kept having visions that this time I was going to die. I relayed my fears to my husband and he just thought I was being overly anxious. I was so concerned about what I saw that I prepared my will the day before the operation, in case I did die during the surgery.

On the day of the surgery, a nurse came to wheel me on a trolley into the operating theatre. I felt very emotional and I couldn't stop thinking about my vision. When I arrived in the operating theatre, I began to cry, and my doctor and the anaesthetist asked me what was wrong. I told him I was a psychic and I had had a vision that I was going into the light. They both looked shocked, and I asked them to look after me to ensure that I came back.

When I awoke from the surgery, I was in the recovery room some hours later. The room was so crowded with spirits that I felt like a couldn't breathe. As I was in so much pain, I was transferred to the high dependency unit. I had been administered a drip for the pain on my left hand. The nurse told me if the pain got too much, all I needed to do was push a button that was taped to my hand and the machine would automatically administer a dose of morphine in my drip.

I once again told the nurse that I was going into the light, she turned and smiled at me and said, 'Not on my shift!'

Over the next few hours, the pain became unbearable, and I did push the button. But unbeknownst to me, I was allergic to morphine and I had a reaction to it. I began to hallucinate and I could see worms crawling under my skin. I wanted to rip my skin off and I could see devils floating in the room.

The nurse sat with me and held my hand to settle me down; suddenly, I had the feeling of flying and I was quickly rushing up out of my body. I felt so free and alive, I wasn't in any pain anymore and I felt incredible. There was a shaking sensation and then I was floating into a black-purple haze. I felt very calm. I then entered a long black tunnel. I felt out of control as I swished this way and that. There was a little pinhole of light in the distance; I abruptly came out and I was flying out into the universe.

I could see stars, nebulas and planets floating at high speed. Time would slow and everything would go into slow motion, then suddenly it would speed up again and I was propelled forward again. I felt like I was an astronaut without a spacesuit. Sometimes, the vibration was so strong I felt like my body was going to break apart.

I then went back in a black-purple swirl and there was another pinhole of light ahead of me. The light was getting bigger and bigger and I could see people moving ahead of me. I didn't feel frightened – I felt overwhelming calm and I desperately wanted to see what was at the end of the tunnel with the glorious light.

Suddenly, all of the movement stopped, and I was completely surrounded by light. When my eyes adjusted, I could see lots of people smiling at me and I was guided to a beautiful meadow.

Between me and the meadow, there was a waist-high hedge and a gate in the middle of it. People were lined up before me and one by one they went through the gate. When it was my turn to go through the gate, I was told I wasn't allowed to go through because if I did, then I would have to stay. I truly wanted to stay as it was so peaceful and calming in this heavenly place. Everything seemed to be brighter in colour than on Earth and the feeling of love was indescribable.

I was told to turn around and look down and I could see my husband and three children point up to where I was. I could hear them say that 'Mummy is up there', then I felt myself suddenly falling very quickly. I suddenly woke up in total agony, back in my hospital bed feeling like I wanted to be somewhere else. I had just experienced what it was like to die, and I wanted to go back there so I didn't have to feel the pain anymore.

The nurse came over to me and began to shake me. I asked her to stop but she said she needed to keep me conscious as she said my heart had stopped. She said that I had had an allergic reaction to the morphine and I had stopped breathing.

I was in hospital for another three weeks and when I returned home I was still quite unwell. I couldn't sleep, so I hired a lot of video movies to watch. One of the movies was *Contact* starring Jodie Foster. From the moment I began watching the movie, I couldn't take my eyes of the screen. I felt highly emotional – some of the scenes in the movie were exactly what I had experienced a few weeks before in the hospital bed. The shaking, the moving quickly, the peacefulness, travelling through the universe, seeing the stars and planets, and the meeting of higher beings. This movie felt like it was made for me. It all made complete sense – I had been to heaven.

Since that NDE, I have had another four NDEs. All of them have been brought on through illness, and all have come about through having medical procedures, usually involving an anaesthetic. I have suffered with many health issues over the years, and I have come to realise that this is just a bump in the road and part of my journey. If it wasn't for these experiences, I don't think I would work as a psychic medium.

What I have come to understand is that each of these experiences have all been profoundly different, yet the essence has always been the same. I have learnt to be more mindful and compassionate to others and my job is to be of service to others. I know that there is definitely life after life.

I have lost my fear of death, but it has made me realise how fragile we all are and how we should all make each and every moment count.

Creating memories is the most important thing we can do with our loved ones and friends, as when we die that is all that will come with us. Money and belongings are left behind. The love in our hearts lives on forever.

Common elements reported during NDEs

- The sensation of the soul leaving the body followed by the feeling of floating, experiencing speed and movement.

- A feeling of overwhelming calmness and peace. This feeling can be followed by the experience of immense love and belonging.

- Many experiencers report seeing a brilliant bright light and a tunnel with light at the end of it. Some experiencers report travelling through to the end of the tunnel of white light.

- Most commonly, experiencers report meeting higher spiritual beings. These beings can be connected to the experiencer's own religious beliefs. Other experiencers report meeting key figures who meant a lot to them during their life, such as passed relatives, friends and loved ones.

- Most people who have experienced an NDE undergo a life-changing experience. They usually have a greater respect for life and those around them.

- Many people come back with spiritual gifts they were not aware of prior to their NDE. Many experiencers report new-found psychic gifts and healing abilities they didn't have before their experience.

Reasons people become psychic after an NDE

As I have mentioned in prior chapters everyone is psychic in one shape or form. A person who experiences an NDE undergoes a life-changing or, shall I say, life-challenging experience. Many who have NDEs cannot physically put into words what they witnessed and felt during their time in the spirit world, although they know that they have experienced something that is life changing.

However, it is a time when they return to source and many of the blockages, worries, doubts, fears and insecurities they experienced in their life before their NDE disappear. They return with a new and greater understanding of life and what it should and could be. Many return with the knowledge that there is life after life and their fear of death disappears.

They also come back with heightened spiritual gifts that may have been lying dormant within them prior to their experience. An NDE can re-awaken their psychic gifts of clairvoyance, clairaudience, claircognisance and healing abilities.

Most people who have had an NDE report that they return spiritually awakened and enlightened. They have come back with a sense of purpose to assist and heal others.

Some experiencers of an NDE report being given their psychic and spiritual gifts from their spirit guides, angelic beings, ascended masters and even God.

What is an out-of-body experience (OBE)?

An out-of-body experience is when the astral body temporarily leaves the physical body, allowing the human consciousness to travel freely through time and space without the restraints of the physical body. People who have experienced an OBE describe the feeling of floating and of weightlessness, similar to what it would be like for an astronaut in zero gravity. People who have an OBE are able to perceive the physical world from a heightened perspective outside of themselves.

OBEs tend to occur when a person is close to falling asleep, in deep meditation, sleep deprived or while they are entering into a lucid dream state. It is interesting to note that not all people who have an OBE do so while they are in some form of sleep state. There have been reports of people having an OBE experience while they are driving a car or while they are undergoing extreme exercise such as running a marathon.

It is not uncommon for those who have experienced an OBE to describe the same type of feelings and visions as those who have experienced an

NDE. Most people see and feel themselves floating up and out of their body. They can see themselves floating or hovering above their physical body while their body is in a sleep or dream state. Some report seeing a silver cord between themselves and their physical body as they travel up into the higher astral realms onto the astral plane.

It is reported that if the silver cord between the physical body and spiritual body is severed during an OBE or NDE, the experiencer may pass. The five stages that people experience during an OBE are very similar to what people experience during an NDE.

There are five stages that take place when someone experiences an OBE:
Stage 1 – (withdrawal stage) is where the experiencer falls into a state that is very similar to when you are falling asleep. This is known as the withdrawal stage, and it is where the experiencer drifts from physical consciousness and begins to separate from their physical body.
Stage 2 – (cataleptic stage) is where the experiencer may fall into a trance-like state. They may be aware of physical sensations surrounding their body

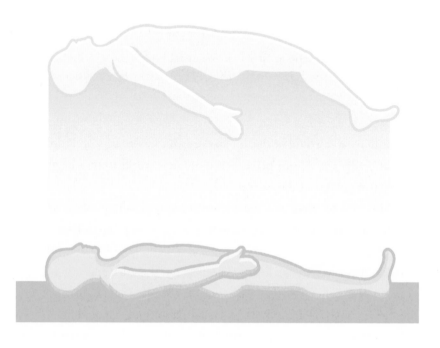

such as a pulsing or vibrating sensation. The experiencer may experience a feeling of heaviness and/or a feeling of being weighted down. They may even feel like they are enveloped by a black velvet void.

Stage 3 – (detachment stage) is where the experiencer feels like they have dis-engaged from their physical body while still connected by the silver cord. (The silver cord has been seen by many experiencers; some report that it shines like Christmas tinsel, while others report that it looks like a bright silver tube of light that is connected to the physical body similar to that of an umbilical cord.) The experiencer may feel as if their spirit body is rising and separating from their physical body.

Stage 4 – (astral stage) is where the experiencer is free to travel to other realms, either on the physical or spiritual plane. This stage is a fragile time for the experiencer, as some people may look down upon their physical body and suddenly feel themselves falling, causing them to wake with a sudden jolt. For those who stay connected to the astral realm, the journey becomes quite vivid. The experiencer can travel to places or planets they have never seen before. The experience is viewed from above as though the experiencer is moving through space and time. The speeds travelled at this stage are extremely fast.

Stage 5 – (re-connection stage) is where the soul re-enters the physical body and the experiencer becomes aware of their re-connection to their physical body once again. An OBE usually only lasts up to two-to-three minutes, yet to the experiencer it may feel as if they were gone for a prolonged period of time.

Many experiencers return to their physical body feeling that something profound has taken place. They may even return with a completely different outlook to the world than they had before the experience.

Please note: Not all experiencers will go through all five stages to experience an OBE.

An OBE can happen spontaneously and with practise can be self-induced. People who practise meditation and have a strong connection to the psychic realm are better at inducing this type of phenomena.

How many times have you awoken after having a vivid dream and felt that you were falling down from above? You may even have felt as if you were floating above your body and dropped back into bed. You wake up in your bed wide-awake with your heart beating profusely. This experience is an OBE.

What is the difference between an NDE and OBE?

When someone experiences an NDE they are not in control of what they are experiencing, unlike when someone experiences an OBE. When a person experiences an NDE, they are usually close to death, pronounced dead, in a coma, their heart has stopped or they are unconscious.

During an OBE the experiencer is usually in a dream state, lucid dreaming or in a deep meditative state. The person experiencing an OBE is not under any life-threatening event.

A person who experiences an NDE is given a choice of whether or not they wish to continue their life on Earth or whether they wish to pass and join the spirit world. With an OBE, the experiencer leaves their body for a short period of time and then routinely returns to their body. Many times, an OBE is put down to a vivid dream or even a nightmare.

Most people who return from an NDE, experience a life review and return to life significantly changed and enlightened by their experience. Those who have experienced OBEs report feeling enlightened by their experience, however, the changes for someone who has had an NDE are more profound.

CHAPTER 23

WHAT IS THE CERT METHOD?

OVER THE YEARS I HAVE HEARD mention of the CERT Method or CERT Rule. People I have met over the years who have trained in this method to enhance their mediumship skills undertook their training within the Spiritualist Church or at the Arthur Findlay College in England.

The CERT Method was devised by a Welsh medium named Stephen O'Brien. The initials CERT are an acronym for the four vital components for gathering information from the spirit realms and relaying it to a client during a mediumship reading.

CERT stands for:

C=Communicator

E=Evidence

R=Reason

T=Tie it up

C = Communicator – This step is about identifying who the spirit is and receiving vital information and descriptions about the person in spirit so the recipient can identify who is coming through with the message. The communicating spirit will confirm if they are male or female, and whether or not they were a child or adult at the time they passed. They may share with you what they passed from or the symptoms they had at the time of their passing. The communicator may give you their first and last name or just an initial to clarify who they are. Do not be disappointed if you don't always receive the name, as the spirit will give you other information to identify themselves to the recipient. The communicator may show themselves to you so that you can describe physically what they looked like – eye colour, hair colour, height, build – and they may indicate what relationship that had with the recipient such as a relative and their role within the family, or if they were a friend. They may even take you back in time and show you glimpses of their life, so they can be identified.

E = Evidence – After step 1 and the spirit being identified by the recipient, the spirit will continue to give more evidence that can be validated. The evidence step is a point where the medium is able to ask the spirit to share information with the recipient in the form of memories and personal experiences that only the spirit and the recipient would know. The spirit may come through with mannerisms, personality traits, sayings, signs, symbols, birthdates, hobbies, songs and other important information to the recipient. Some of the information the medium may receive may not make any sense at all to the medium at this point. It is extremely important that all information that is given to the medium by the spirit be communicated to the recipient, as these facts will help validate the spirit's existence in the spirit realm. The medium should always give the messages verbatim, as the information you share will be extremely detailed and accurate. Providing evidence to someone during a reading is an important part of the process of validating that a loved one in spirit is really coming through.

R = Return – After proof has been received from the spirit to identify who they are, it is important for the recipient to know why the spirit has returned to them and what messages they wish to share with them. It is at this point the medium will ask the spirit why they want to make a connection with the recipient. The spirit may simply communicate with the medium that they want the recipient to know they are always with them, and to remind them that even though they are in spirit they are still available for emotional support for the recipient from the spirit realms. The spirit may also want to let the recipient know that they are aware of what is taking place in the recipient's life on Earth, such as knowing the arrival of a new baby into the family, a new home or a family member getting married. During a private session, the spirit may give private and detailed information to the recipient. Whereas, during a public demonstration, a spirit may share messages that will be of benefit to the whole audience about the reality of the existence of life after death.

T = Tie it up – This is the final step where the medium will conclude the reading. Think of a reading as a journey that is shared by the medium from the spirit to the recipient. The reading is broken down into segments of contact, proof, messages and conclusion. As the tie-up is the end of the reading, use this time to tie up any loose ends that came through during the reading. You may decide to revisit important points of evidence that you spoke of during the reading. It is also an opportunity where information that the recipient may not have understood during the reading can now be pieced together. For the final conclusion of the reading, ask the spirit if they have any uplifting messages or final words of love they would like to share with the recipient to end the reading on a positive note.

CHAPTER 24

WHAT IS SPIRIT PHOTOGRAPHY?

PEOPLE HAVE REPORTED SEEING SPIRITS and ghosts since the beginning of time. There has always been hope that our loved ones will always be with us even after their death. Many people feel spirits around them, however, they also want to see tangible proof.

The history of spirit photography

In the 19th century, people would have their photograph taken, and it was around this time that some of the first spirit photographs were captured.

Spirit photography originated in the United States. It was first introduced in 1862 by William H Mumler, who was a photographer from Boston.

Mumler took a photograph of a man named Dr Gardner, and on the photographic plate, an image appeared of the doctor's cousin who had died 12 years earlier. The doctor wrote about his experience, and due to this, spirit photography became popular with spiritualists of the time. The spiritualists used this photography as a means to prove life after death. There is still much controversy about whether or not the photographer was real or fraudulent, as some of Mumler's photographs did capture the spirits of lost loved ones while others contained the images of living models.

In the 1850s and 1860s, photographers began to experiment with new effects, and they began to take double exposures, and some dishonest photographers realised they could use these techniques to capture the image of dearly departed loved ones and insert them into the portrait of an innocent victim, tricking them into thinking that their loved one had returned from the grave. This was a great money maker for these unscrupulous photographers and it also gave spirit photography a bad name.

The authorities tried to prosecute Mumler for his fraudulent photographs, but there was insufficient evidence to prove that he was a fraud and the charges were dropped. It is thought that Mumler did in fact capture genuine images of spirits on film, although he did also double expose images to keep up the demand and make a tidy profit.

During this time in history, the spiritualist movement became popular, and it was quite common for people to sit in a séance with a medium to make contact with a departed loved one. Sir Arthur Conan Doyle, the author of the Sherlock Holmes series was an avid supporter of early spiritualism. He was also a great believer in spirit photography.

When a medium would participate in a séance, there were reports of a fog or clear white, light-coloured viscous substance that was said to exude from the body of the spiritualist medium. The medium would usually be in a trance-like state and the substance, known as ectoplasm, would materialise into the shape of spiritual bodies, faces and hands, and it was said to be the spirit of a loved one in spirit returning from the other side. At the end of each séance, the ectoplasm would disappear and return back to the medium's body.

English spiritualist medium Ada Deane was well known for her spirit photography. In the 1920s, she took a photograph and on the photographic plate an extra face appeared in the image. This image was to launch Deane's psychic career, and she became highly sort after in the spiritualist movement. Deane went on to take many images, only to be classed a fraud when images she took had the famous faces of people of the day.

She was said to have used images that were taken from newspapers and to superimpose them onto the photographic plates. The faces in the image seemed to be surrounded by a cottonwool substance, while others looked to be a cheesecloth or muslin type material.

I have personally seen some of Ada Deane's images in an exhibition at the Sydney Centre for Photography in Paddington, and some of the images did look fake, while others had anomalies in them. I guess we will never know how many of the images from these times were fake or real. What is important is that these pioneering photographers have opened the conversation, and it has inspired many of us to embark on a journey to see if it is at all possible to capture images of spirits of the dead in photographs.

Before I went to the exhibition, I had a vision that I should take some photographs of the spirit photography including an image of Sir Arthur Conan Doyle. Conan Doyle himself had come to me and he told me clearly that he wanted me to take a photograph and he would show up in the image. I was excited by the prospect of being able to capture his image.

In the early 2000s, digital photography was still quite a new way of taking images, and the cameras were expensive. I saved up and was extremely excited to get my first digital camera in 2002. It was a Sony Cybershot 2.1 Mega Pixel camera a dear friend of mine purchased for me in the US.

As digital cameras no longer needed film, and the image was stored on a memory card, it was possible to see the image as soon as it was taken. Previously, I had taken thousands of images on an SLR film camera and had to patiently wait until they were developed at the local chemist shop to see if I had captured any anomalies or not. Some of the locations I had limited access to, so it was hit and miss as to whether I captured anything or not.

Many dollars and many unexciting photographs of abandoned haunted houses and cemeteries later, I was excited to discover that it was possible to view the image immediately. Not to mention it was a lot less expensive than film.

When I arrived at the spirit photography exhibition there was a large sign stating there was to be no photography. I was not to be put off by this as I had a vision and I wanted to see if it was going to come true. I quickly took four images and I was extremely shocked by what I had captured on the camera. Yes, Conan Doyle did appear in one of the four images. Two images had anomalies in them which was very exciting. Unfortunately, I couldn't take anymore images as the security guard came into the room, so I quickly put my camera away and left before I got into any trouble.

Anomalies caught on camera

At night as a child when I would try to sleep, I would often see whitish coloured balls of light moving around in my room. These coloured lights were extremely fast, and at times, I could also hear muffled voices accompanying the lights. These experiences made me feel frightened of the dark, as these unexplained lights never seemed to leave me alone when I was trying to go to sleep.

I tried telling my parents about the happenings in my room, but they told me I had an over-active imagination. It wasn't until I participated in a television series called *Scream Test* that I finally understood what these balls of light actually were.

Scream Test was a show about the paranormal. The premise of the show was to take contestants to some of Australia's most haunted locations and literally scare the wits out of them, while asking them to try and capture any paranormal evidence on film.

We were given a video camera, temperature gauge and an EMF tester to use while we were locked in each of the haunted rooms in the dark. We were asked to record any temperature changes, electromagnetic fluctuations we felt in the room, while the camera crew tried to scare us. When I look back now, it was an interesting concept and something that didn't help my fear of the dark.

The two locations I was taken to were Maitland Gaol and the Sydney Quarantine Station at Manly. Maitland was one of Australia's most brutal gaols and closed down in 1998. The Quarantine Station was closed in 1984. Both these locations are extremely haunted, and there have been many deaths at both. During my time on *Scream Test,* I began to see the balls of light like I had seen when I was a child. I also physically saw ghosts of deceased prisoners and poor immigrants who had come to Australia from overseas searching for a new life.

The experiences I had during the filming of the show actually gave me more questions than answers as to what I was seeing, feeling and experiencing, and it started me on a quest to capture tangible evidence in photographs.

When I first began to take spirit photographs, I really didn't know what I was doing. The internet was not as big a network of information as it is today. There was limited information about spirit photography, and there weren't a great deal of books you could find on the subject.

What I have discovered is there are different types of paranormal anomalies that do show up on SLR film, Polaroid Instamatic film, digital, video and our smart phones. Orbs are also commonly seen on surveillance cameras and baby monitors with video cameras. With today's technologies, there are many opportunities to capture the paranormal quite readily.

I have found that different types of cameras and phones capture spirit energies in different ways. Now, let's discuss what those differences are and what they are called.

Orbs

An orb is a ball of light or a light anomaly that looks like a full moon. Orbs have been known to feature the faces of departed loved ones, and they can come in many sizes and colours. Orbs are reported to be the energy of a deceased person, spirit or ghost. It is possible to see them with the naked eye, as well as through a camera and on video.

They move extremely quickly, and they can show up in many places. They are often captured in graveyards and haunted locations, and at family events and sacred sites. Orbs are known to communicate with mediums and some think that they have their own consciousness.

I have had many experiences with orbs, and I have been able to communicate with them in the same way as I would with a deceased person. My belief is they are the soul of a person who has passed over and they use the form of an orb to move between the spirit realm and earth realms. They communicate in the form of telepathic thought and they can hear what the living are saying and thinking. I have undertaken many experiments with orbs and asked them to show up in an image in a particular spot, and the orbs have done exactly as I have asked.

Orbs have been known to fly in and out of windows and to mysteriously go through solid brick walls only to appear on the other side.

Orbs generally are white/bluish in colour, however, they have been known to be seen in shades of red, pink, green, gold and purple. Some orbs can be made up of a number of colours. It is thought that different coloured orbs are to do with the different frequencies on which they reside.

Orbs are quite controversial as they can be captured in images and are sometimes mistaken for dust, moisture or rain drops. Lens flare can also be mistaken for orbs which further adds to the controversy. I personally feel they are real, though yes, some orb images can be scientifically explained as environmental elements appearing and are not always the presence of a spirit.

Orbs can be photographed during the day or night, however, they are captured more easily when it is darker and a flash is used to take the photograph. I have discovered that when a flash is used, the orb will reflect off the light and is frozen in time in the image. Orbs like to connect with the camera, and they have the ability to drain the camera batteries almost instantly. When communicating with spirit energies, they have told me they get stronger from connecting to the power of physical objects. Some orbs are extremely fast and can move at lightning speed.

The newer and bigger flat-screen televisions we have in our homes are certainly attractive to orbs. I have captured many images of orbs on my television whether it is turned on or off. As a lot of televisions are in standby mode even when they are turned off, it makes sense that an orb will still be attracted to the energy coming from the screen. My television does seem to have a mind of its own, as the orbs have the ability to physically turn on my television even if we are upstairs asleep in bed.

Orbs tend to be more prevalent during different cycles of the moon. During a full moon, for example, I have captured a large number of orbs that have then accumulated and turned into ghost fog or what is also known as ectoplasm. The ectoplasm then turned into the image of a spirit being.

Ghost fog, spirit mist or ectoplasm

This form of spirit energy is closely connected to the orb phenomenon. Ghost fog, spirit mist or ectoplasm is seen as a mist or a fog that can mysteriously appear out of nowhere. It appears to look like it is swirling and it can be white, blue, grey or black in colour. The fog usually appears floating above the ground and can move quickly and disappear. It can also be captured with orbs within it, which gives the impression that orbs can gather and join together to manifest into the fog. It is also common for the fog to become so dense that it then turns into a full-bodied apparition.

The early spiritualist mediums were known to exude ghost fog or ectoplasm out of their mouths or from behind them when the materialisation of a spirit would take place.

Ghost fog or ectoplasm is commonly seen outside at historical sights, battlefields, sacred sites or graveyards. It is possible to see this phenomenon with your eyes and it can easily be captured on video and through your smartphone. Once again, using a flash is recommended, as this form of spirit energy also reflects off the light of the flash.

This type of energy can be attracted to mediums as it seems to want to connect with them and communicate with them. In the *Ghostbusters* movies, ectoplasm was seen to be sticky green slime that ghosts would cover unsuspecting humans with.

From my own personal experience with ectoplasm and orbs, there is a temperature change and the area surrounding me becomes cold. I also smell a damp earthy scent, similar to what you would smell if you were to go under a house or in a damp location.

Vortexes

Vortexes are another form of spirit energy that can look like a spiralling strand of light. This type of spirit photograph is not as common as an orb or ghost fog. This type of phenomenon is also known as a funnel ghost, wormhole or strand. An image of a vortex can be more solid than an orb appears. At times, the vortex can look like strands of DNA floating in the air. Vortexes are thought to have a higher frequency than an orb does, and they are thought to be of a more spiritual nature and more highly developed within the spirit realms. Sometimes images of vortexes are mistaken for camera straps, as they look similar in colour and thickness. This is one of the reasons that vortexes are dismissed and not really understood.

I have captured a few images of vortexes, and they have been different colours – red, yellow, green, blue and white. Some of the images I have captured are quite intricate and beautiful, when studied up close.

Apparitions or ghosts

This type of energy has been captured on many different types of photographic equipment over the years. The image can look as solid as a living person, while other images can also look like a transparent or see-through being. I have personally taken quite a lot of images with spirits or ghosts in them. I feel that the reason the spirits show up in the images is because they want to show proof that an after-life does exist.

I took an image of William Charles Wentworth, a famous English explorer, at his mausoleum in Vaucluse in Sydney on my iPhone. His image was in full colour and clearly showed his suit and tie and the kerchief in his pocket. At the time I took the image, I didn't see anyone before me, but I could feel the energy of someone close to me, which is why I took the image. To my surprise, Wentworth was standing right in front of me looking quite annoyed we had disturbed him by visiting the mausoleum during a ghost tour.

Shadow people

There are a lot of questions about whether seeing or capturing shadow people on film is a good or bad omen. Many people think that seeing a dark energy means that the energy is also dark in nature. We are led to believe that the light is enlightening and the darkness is of a demonic nature. From my own experience, when I have seen dark energies, I have the feeling they are of a negative nature and when I have captured a shadow person, the energy has been negative, dense and of malevolence. The jury is still out as to whether this is a lost soul who wants to make contact from beyond or an entity that wants to make its presence known. I leave this up to you to decide.

I have in fact captured shadow people in a few images and the images were taken at locations that had a brutal past. Could these images be of a poor tortured soul looking for some redemption from the light?

What type of camera to use?

SLR film camera

As I previously mentioned, it's possible to capture images on many different types of cameras. I personally have found it's possible to capture images on a pre-digital SLR camera that uses film. Some of the images I captured on this camera were quite different to what it is possible to capture digitally today.

The positives about this type of photography is that a record is stored or imprinted onto the film negative. This shows irrefutable proof that the image is in fact real. The downside is that using film, especially in this day and age, and getting it developed can be quite expensive. The other downside is that you don't get to see what you captured immediately; you will need to wait until the film is developed. You won't know till you see the image whether you managed to capture anything or not. You might find later you were in the right location but took the image in the wrong spot.

I have captured many ghostly images only to see that if I had focused the camera up a little higher or slightly to the left of the frame that I would have captured an extraordinary image. It can be frustrating when you see a small glimpse of a spirit energy just on the corner of a frame. I am sure that the spirits think it is great fun to play with us here in the living, so they just give us a tease as to their existence.

Polaroid Instamatic

The first Polaroid camera went on sale in 1948 in Boston, United States. This technology was quite ground-breaking, as once you took the photograph, the image would pop out of the front of the camera within a few minutes. The only problem with this technology is there wasn't a negative as film cameras have.

I used this type of technology in 2002 when I purchased a second-hand Polaroid camera from a pawn shop. The camera did manage to capture a few anomalies – quite different to what I could capture on the SLR camera. However, the price of the film at the time made it an expensive exercise. In 2021, it is almost impossible to purchase the film for this camera, and it is even more expensive than it was in the early 2000s. The disappointing thing about this is the images the camera captured were quite amazing.

Low megapixel digital cameras

The images that could be captured with the lower megapixel digital cameras were quite incredible for their time. I was extremely lucky to capture some wonderful images of ghosts, ectoplasm, vortexes and orbs. The downside to these cameras is that the images cannot be enlarged very much, as they become quite grainy and the pixels in the images become distorted.

The Sony Cybershot range were wonderful cameras. When the Cybershot first came out, I probably captured some of my best spirit photographs using it. I also found that the Nikon Coolpix and Kodak Digital cameras also captured some great spirit photographs. The Nikon in particular captured orbs and spirit energy that look almost 3D in nature.

Higher megapixel digital cameras

The Panasonic Lumix range was also excellent for spirit photography. I have a Lumix TZ10, and this camera captured arguably some of my best all-time images of spirit photography. The camera has a Carl Zeiss lens known for maximum image quality. These cameras can be purchased quite cheaply on eBay. My Lumix camera was released in 2010 and it still takes great images in 2021.

Digital SLR cameras

I personally use a Canon 7D and Canon 80D as I also do astrophotography and landscape photography. These cameras take incredible images, and I was extremely happy with the results when I went to Norway and Finland to photograph the Northern Lights.

However, with my own personal experience, these cameras seem to be too technical and too advanced when it comes to doing spirit photography. I have captured only a few orb images using these cameras, even though I have tried to do so on a number of different settings.

I personally feel that the sensors within these cameras are too highly sophisticated, making it difficult to capture the spirit energies.

Smart phones

Most of us have a smartphone, whether it is an Apple, Samsung or an Android. To be honest it doesn't really matter what brand you have. As we are very social creatures and we are all constantly taking photographs, many of the images are taken to upload to our social media accounts or share with our friends. This is a time when more photographs have been taken around the world than any other time in history.

Largely, photography was once for the wealthy, as they were the only people who could afford to pay to have an image taken by a photographer or purchase a camera and have the film developed.

Now, with the digital age we can take as many photos as we like as there is no cost in processing a film, and as we always have our phones with us, it is nothing to take at the very least one photograph a day, and many of us are willing to share our pics with family and friends on our social media accounts.

Video is also a huge part of our lives. Years ago to own a video camera was a privilege and also only available to the wealthy. Now, our phones also contain the ability to film a video with just the push of a button.

The ability to record images has made it even more possible for spirits to show up on video and in photos on a daily basis.

Personally, I use an iPhone and I have been very lucky to capture videos and photos of the spirit realm. It was my dog Sonny who actually showed me that it was possible to see spirit through the iPhone. Sonny is a Pug x Maltese and he has his own personality. He loves to watch television and he likes to play; what I didn't realise was that he also likes to play with ghosts.

In 2010, I had just bought the iPhone 4 which was the first iPhone to come out with a flash. Sonny was running around and interacting with an invisible person. He was showing off and running and looking up at nothing, then he was chasing an invisible thing, and then sitting and looking up and waiting to play some more.

My daughter decided to film him, as he was acting so strangely. It was a rainy day and it was quite dark inside our loungeroom. To all of our surprise, when Shannon started to film the dog, the flash automatically turned on and we could see through the view finder that Sonny was chasing orbs. He was trying to bite them and he was chasing them around as if they were his playmates.

From this point onwards, I realised that to capture orbs on my iPhone I needed to turn the flash on while either photographing or filming a video.

iPhone live photo function

When you are taking photographs on an iPhone, a function called Live appears in the top bar of the iPhone photo screen. The Live icon button looks like three concentric circles. When the Live function is turned on, it turns yellow in colour.

Taking a photograph using Live on the phone will capture a three-second moving image. I have found this to be useful when doing any spirit photography, as ghosts or spirits tend to move quickly, and sometimes you will see them when you take the picture but the camera won't be able to capture the image before it passes by the screen.

The Live function captures multiple images, so it's great for capturing moving orbs, ghosts, vortexes or ghost mist. Once you capture the Live photograph, Apple has now made it possible to separate the frames, and you are able to choose which image you wish to use as the main image. It is also possible to make your Live photo capture a GIF which will highlight the movement of the spirit image. (A GIF is an image that is encoded in graphics interchange format, and can be an animated loop of a number of images that can be viewed as a mini movie.)

I am sure that with your own experiments and trying out different types of cameras and phones, you will be able to capture your own form of spirit photography. There are no rules – spirit photography is all trial and error. What works for one person may not necessarily work for another. Stay open-minded and try different forms of photography to see what actually works best for you.

The one thing I have failed to mention in this chapter is the reason a spirit appears in your photographs is because they want to connect with you. Be mindful of this, and when and if you decide to try and capture spirits on film, communicate with them first – ask them if they would like to make contact and be open to the messages you receive via clairaudience, clairsentience and clairvoyance.

CHAPTER 25

PSYCHIC DO'S & DON'TS

DEVELOPING YOUR PSYCHIC ABILITIES and using them to tune in and do readings for others comes with huge responsibilities. Doing a reading for a client can be an emotional and life-changing experience for the client, so it's important to work within ethical guidelines while doing your work. Conducting a reading for a client needs to be clear, concise and honest.

It is of utmost important to tell the truth to the client, and not sugar-coat the information you receive. You, as the reader, must remember that you are the messenger, not some magical being who can wiggle their nose or wave their hand to make everyone's dreams come true. It is important for both parties to have realistic expectations of what is expected during a session.

Sometimes when I do a reading, I will see that there are challenges that may eventuate in the person's future. This being said, not everything is set in stone, and the client still has free will to make their own choice of what actions they will undertake to achieve the final outcome. My guides might show me the client walking down a road which then splits off in two or three different directions. My guide will then give me a view of what could happen if the person chooses to go in this or that direction. I have had clients ask me to tell them which one they should choose. My answer to them is to choose which one feels most comfortable when they feel it in their heart or their stomach (solar plexus) region. Again, if it doesn't feel right or sit well with their gut, this is a sign they should rethink the situation.

Spirit does love to use parables when they communicate with me. Usually in this situation, I will hear the words, 'Be careful what you wish for, you just might get it!' or 'All that glitters is not gold!' Meaning that the person may want something very much, but it may not be in their best interest, and the path could be more difficult than they expect. It could also mean it's all about timing, and if what they're wanting doesn't happen now, the timing may not be right, and it is better to wait until the path ahead is much clearer and easier to follow.

Personally, I feel that a reading should offer balanced information that can highlight the positives people have in their lives. Sometimes we become too obsessed by what we don't have.

It is good to remind the client that energy attracts energy or like attracts like. If the person is constantly negative, angry or depressed, this can drop their vibration and attract more of the same energy into their life. Remind the person that by trying to be more positive, their life can change dramatically. Manifestation is such a powerful tool and the best part about it is, it's *free*, and only costs you your energy and devotion.

There are times in a reading when I can see that the person could have some challenges ahead of them, and it's good to give them some information to help them deal with what's ahead. But it's also important how you deliver that information. I have had clients come to me who have had readings from other psychics and mediums, and they have told me some terrible stories of the negative information the person has given them during the reading.

The saying, 'Being forewarned is forearmed!' holds true – meaning, it is better to be prepared and take appropriate steps to manage the challenges that could arise. But it's also important to focus on the positive and be helpful. Say, for example, I am doing a reading for a client and I can see that there are some legal issues that could arise for the person. I may be shown the image of a contract and then I see the person shaking hands with someone, then I see the hand being pushed away or the contract being ripped up. In this instance, I would say to the person that if they are doing anything with contracts to check the fine print before signing. I would advise them to look further into the person who they are doing the business dealings with or to think carefully if this contract is in their best interest.

It's not in anyone's interest to scare them with the way you deliver the information you receive.

Setting boundaries

Sharing your psychic abilities can be rewarding as well as challenging, and at times, demanding of your mental and spiritual health. Those who are not as enlightened as you may become excited about your newfound gifts. You may find that people around you constantly ask or demand you tune in for them and give them a message. What you both need to understand is you need to set boundaries. When I say this to you, it is not that I want you to feel bigger or better than those around you. It is more that you understand you have a gift and you need to respect it – and so do others.

You are a human being, and you are not here to provide entertainment to others. Some people can expect far too much from a psychic or a medium, by expecting them to be able to fix any problems in their life. They do not want to be responsible for their current situation and they want someone to do it for them. They may want you to give them the winning Lotto numbers, the winning horse at the races or advice on where they can buy the lucky Lottery ticket. There are times in life when someone is on a luckier cycle in their life, but I am sure that spirit is not just sitting around waiting for you to supply the lucky numbers to your clients. Money can't buy happiness. If someone seeks you out for this type of reading, then they are being unrealistic.

Since beginning my journey as a psychic medium, I have had to set my own boundaries. At first, it was fun to go out and do readings when I went to events with friends. However, this quickly changed when nobody was interested in me as just being part of the friendship group and having a lovely time with my friends. Some of the people I knew became more and more demanding of me.

I found myself not wanting to go out anymore. As soon as I arrived at a friend's house for a barbecue, I would be surrounded and suddenly the most popular person there. People would start to take off pieces of jewellery and quickly push them into my hand and ask me to read them. I became quite embarrassed by this as my husband would get annoyed with me and say why can't you leave your work at home. I feel obliged that I had to read for everyone who asked, as some of them would get upset if I refused. I really did want to leave my work at home – I didn't want to be doing readings 24/7.

The phone was constantly ringing, and friends and friends of friends were always asking my advice and wanting a reading. It wasn't until I began to value myself that others began to value me.

Once I told people that this was now my job and I was going to charge for a reading, this type of behaviour from some of my so-called friends stopped. My true friends understood and they were fine and respected me for my decision. Those who only wanted me for what I could give them either respected me and chose to book in with me for a reading, or they became angry or I didn't hear from them again. At first, I felt hurt that some people I thought were friends didn't respect me or understand the energy I had to exert to do a reading. I came to understand this was all part of my spiritual advancement, learning to understand what was best for me to protect myself and my energy. Many people who work in an area of giving service to others will know that it can be very draining when you are constantly giving. I do love to give, but I also need time to recharge my battery so that I can be at my best.

I have been told on many occasions that I was given this gift for free, so I should do readings for free to help others. When I thought about this statement, I did feel guilty. However, my guides gave me a clear and poignant message: 'Energy = Outcome'. When you engage in giving your energy for an outcome, there must be some form of an energy exchange in return. The energy does not always have to be monetary; it could be as simple as a person giving you a hug, a thank you card or a bunch of flowers. I find that when there is no reciprocation, the person has the least amount of respect for your gifts.

I choose to work on unsolved police cases pro-bono when asked to assist by the police. I think of this as my way of giving an energy exchange to loved ones who are suffering and a way of giving back to the universe. However, I do charge for readings, as this is my full-time job, and this is where I have had to set my boundaries.

As time goes on, I am sure you will set your own boundaries and decide what is best for you. Don't get me wrong – I did appreciate that I was able to practise and hone my skills in those early days. It was just disappointing that people began to use me for my abilities and did not appreciate my friendship.

Setting your requirements before doing a reading

Having a list of requirements that you wish to undertake before beginning a reading is a good way for you and your client to understand what is expected from you.

Entering into a consultation with a client means that you need to be able to concentrate and focus on the information you receive.

If I am doing a personal reading, I have guidelines that I set in order to conduct a reading. You may choose to use this as a guideline for yourself – feel free to change and tweak it to what feels right for you.

I only allow one person into the session at a time, unless I am doing a reading for a family who have lost a loved one – for example, parents who have lost their child, or siblings who have lost their parents.

Otherwise, I find that there is what I call a 'psychic bounce' where a number of spirits come through and the information can bounce between the different participants. Psychic bounce often happens when people are sitting in close proximity to each other. When the doorway to spirit is open, the strongest and loudest personalities usually try to get the most attention during the reading. This can make it harder for the more gentle and quiet energies to make contact with their loved ones.

A reading can be a very private experience, and I find that it can be uncomfortable for both the reader and the client when information comes through that is only for the person being read for at the time.

If clients have a friend who comes in the room with them and wants to be read as well, it can make things awkward as not all of the information should be heard by both parties.

Clients need to understand that the reason you are not seeing them with a friend is to protect everyone's privacy.

I don't allow people to eat or drink when I see them for a personal reading as they become too distracted during their reading and you do not have their undivided attention.

I find that when people write and take notes, they close off, and it makes them more difficult to read. They are concentrating on writing and not on the new information I bring through for them. I ask them to take the notes at the end of the reading when it is fresh in their mind.

It is important for you to be focused and dedicated to your client during their session, so minimising distractions gives the client the best possible reading.

Do's:

- Take time to prepare yourself before a reading.

- Be patient. It takes time and patience to develop your connection to spirit.

- White light yourself before commencing.

- Focus on the positives when doing a reading.

- Be honest and truthful.

- Be mindful of how you deliver information.

- Be compassionate as the information you share can be very emotional.

- Nurture your gift and take time out for yourself.

- Set boundaries with your clients. Just because you have a gift, it doesn't mean you are on tap 24/7.

- Meditate and be grounded.

- Be respectful of other people's privacy.

- Be clear about the type of readings you do so that a client understands what to expect.

- Be punctual and be mindful of your client's time.

- Treat your client as you would like to be treated.

- Ensure that you clear yourself properly at the end of each reading and release the energy of the emotions that have come up for the client.

- Always disconnect the connection between you and your client at the end of the reading.

- Wash your hands at the end of the reading to break contact.

- Do spend time in nature to restore your natural state of being. Allow the light to surround and heal you.

- Do not feel that your only purpose on this earth is being of service. You are allowed to enjoy your life. Take some down-time and have fun. It will help you to have a better connection to source energy.

- Do clear the area in which you work regularly.

Don'ts:

- Don't try and rush your journey. Spirit will only give you as much as you can handle when you are developing your psychic abilities.

- Don't let your ego get in the way. You are the messenger who spirit is using to pass on the message, it is not your personal opinion.

- Don't do readings unsolicited.

- If you see any medical issues, remember you are not the doctor, advise the person to visit a doctor.

- Don't predict a death. Sometimes, seeing death is symbolic and not representing an actual death. It may be an indication that something is coming to an end and a new beginning is on the horizon.

- Don't see a client too often. Sometimes clients become too dependent on a psychic medium and they want you to do readings for them on a weekly basis. This is not healthy for either of you.

- Don't over-extend yourself. If you try to book in too many clients in the one day, you will wear yourself out and you may not be tuning in as best you can for each client.

- Don't claim to be 100% accurate. No reader is ever 100% correct all of the time.

- Don't invite spirits home with you. You don't want to get an attachment from a lost spirit or ghost.

- When you do a reading for a client, let them know they have free will. A reading is a glimpse into the past, present or future. If they decide to take a different path, their outcome could change.

- Don't be manipulated by the client to tell them what they want to hear. Some clients come to you for a reading and expect for you to change their life to their desired outcome. You are a messenger not a magician. Say, for example, your client has broken up with their partner and their partner is not coming back into their life. You are not responsible for the partner's decisions. It doesn't matter how many other readers the client has seen prior to seeing you. You can only tell them what you see, you can't change the outcome.

- Don't feel guilty when you do a reading and the client tells you they already know what you have told them. When you are doing a reading for a client, you are tuning into their energy. If, for any reason, you tell them what they already know, this is no reflection on your abilities. It is a sign from spirit that you are tuning into them and spirit has already given them the same message.

- Don't answer your phone when you are with a client – they are paying for your time.

- Don't eat or drink (except if you need a glass of water) during a reading.

GLOSSARY

Akashic records – Spiritual data believed to be stored and accessed via the astral plane. The records contain the history of all that has happened on Earth since the dawn of time.

Angel – A spiritual being who is a messenger from the heavens.

Angel numbers – Number sequences given to us from angels to offer divine guidance and deliver messages through their meaning.

Ascended master – A spiritual being who has lived on Earth and achieved enlightenment who works with the living as a spiritual teacher.

Astral plane – A spiritual realm or celestial sphere where humans reside before birth and after death. It is a high frequency where spirits and angels reside.

Astral travel – The ability to leave your physical body while still alive and project yourself to connect with the astral plane.

Aura – An electromagnetic energy field that surrounds the physical body and is made of seven layers.

Automatic writing – Writing or teachings that are received from the spiritual realms.

CERT Method – A method mediums use to do a mediumship reading.

Chakra – A Sanskrit word that means spinning wheel. The body contains seven main chakras that reside from the base of the spine to the top of the head.

Channelling – The ability to receive communication from the spiritual and angelic realms to offer divine guidance.

Clairalience – The ability to receive information through smell, such as fragrances, cooking smells or odours. Translates as 'clear smelling'.

Clairaudience – The ability to hear beyond normal senses and use your sixth sense to hear messages, guidance and voices of beings in the spirit realms. Translates as 'clear hearing'.

Claircognisance – The ability to experience a 'light bulb' moment where you spontaneously receive information about something or someone without prior knowledge. This is not connected to the other psychic clairs, such as sight sound, sensations or psychic touch. Translates as 'clear knowing'.

Clairempathy – The ability to feel emotions, thoughts and symptoms of another person or in the heart chakra. Also known as empathy. Translates as 'clear emotional feeling'.

Clairgustance – The ability to receive psychic information through the sense of taste, without having the actual item in your mouth. Translates as 'clear tasting'.

Clairsentience – The ability to receive messages from the spirit realms via your feelings, usually in the solar plexus chakra, located in the stomach. Translates as 'clear physical feeling'.

Clairtangency – The ability to receive information from inanimate objects such as a watch, ring, photograph or antique item. Also known as psychometry. Translates as 'clear touching'.

Clairvoyance – The ability to see beyond the normal senses of sight and use your third eye to see signs, symbols and beings in the spirit realms. Translates as 'clear seeing'.

Crystals – A semi-precious or precious stone said to have powerful spiritual/healing properties.

Deity – A god or goddess considered to be divine or sacred and who possesses sacred spiritual knowledge.

Déjà vu – A French word meaning 'already seen' – a feeling that someone has already seen or experienced something before it actually happens.

Dowsing – The ability to tune into or 'divine' (find) a particular object using a pendulum or divining rods.

Ectoplasm – A white or grey substance a physical medium can secrete while doing mediumship. It can also be a plasma or fog-like substance that can be seen before a spirit takes form.

ESP (or extrasensory perception) – The ability to perceive information about something without using your normal five senses.

Ghost – The disincarnate figure or a spirit of a person who is deceased. A ghost can also be the spirit of someone who doesn't realise they are dead.

Ghost mist – A fog-like substance, also known as ectoplasm, that can appear in spirit photography. It can also be the substance that a ghost or spirit uses in order to manifest into human or spirit form.

Grounding – An important process to assist you to be connected to the earth to allow you to release any negative energy back into the earth and to assist you to be connected to the higher energy realms.

Guardian angel – An angel assigned to be your protector while you are on Earth and to accompany you into the next life.

Frequency – A spiritual level in which different spiritual beings reside – the higher the frequency the higher vibration the beings reside on. When we lift our frequency, we connect to the higher astral plane.

Kirlian photography – A method of photography that captures the human aura and that of living plants, animals and objects.

Mandala – A sacred image or design that can be used as a focus point in meditation.

Meditation – A spiritual practice that allows us to relax our mind and body. Meditation can allow you to connect to your higher self and to higher spiritual beings such as spirit guides and guardian angels.

Medium – A gifted spiritual person who can make contact with people who are deceased and deliver messages from the deceased to those in the living.

NDE (or near-death experience) – A life-threatening experience that can occur when a person has died or is close to impending death and they return back to the living. This experience allows the experiencer to die and return from the dead, often coming back with new-found psychic abilities.

Numerology – An ancient form of divination where everything in life is connected to numbers. Numerology can be used to forecast upcoming events, personality traits and your life.

OBE (or out-of-body experience) – When a person's soul separates briefly from their physical body and connects to the astral plane.

Orb – A ball of light or a light anomaly that looks like a full moon. Linked to the paranormal, deceased and ghosts, orbs can be seen with the human eye and captured in photographs.

Ouija board – Also known as a spirit board. Ouija boards are used to help the living make contact with the dead.

Pendulum – An object that is hung from a chain or piece of string and used for divining answers, using questions that require a 'yes' or 'no' response. A pendulum can be made from crystal, metal or wood.

Psychic – A person who can see, sense and feel outside of the normal senses. A psychic can see the past, present and future.

Psychic circle – A group of people who sit together in a circle to connect with higher beings, to gain spiritual wisdom from the spiritual world.

Premonition – When someone sees a vision about something that will happen in the future.

Psychometry – The ability to hold an item and see pictures, feel emotions, see the history associated with an item and also people in spirit who are connected to the item and the owner who owns the item. Also known as clairtangency.

Reincarnation – The belief that a person can be reborn into a new life after their death.

Remote viewing – The ability to view a place, location or person through using psychic ability.

Séance – A group meeting used to make contact with spiritual beings and the dead.

Sensitive – Someone who can sense the feelings and emotions of others. A sensitive can also sense when spirits are close by.

Soul group – A group of people who have been together in previous lives who decide to incarnate at a similar time in the future.

Soulmate – Someone who you have been connected to in previous lifetimes. A soulmate can be a romantic partner who you have been with previously.

Spirit – A non-physical being who shows their existence of life after their death.

Spirit fog – An anomaly that can be seen via your eyes or captured in a photograph. Spirit fog is proof that there is existence of life after death. Also known as ectoplasm or ghost fog.

Spirit guide – A spirit being who is assigned to you to guide your soul throughout life's journey.

Spirit photography – Photography that aims to capture a ghost, orb, spirit mist or ectoplasm on a camera or recording device.

Symbol – A message or sign that can have a mystical or hidden meaning from the spiritual realm to guide you psychically.

Synchronicity – The occurrence of events happening simultaneously that form some type of symbolic meaning to an individual.

Telepathy – The ability to send and receive information through thoughts to another person.

Third eye – The third eye is the chakra that is located above your eyes and in the middle of your forehead. This is the energy centre where you can channel and receive psychic information.

Trance – A state in which a psychic or medium can enter to channel communication with beings in the spirit world. While in this state, a psychic or medium can receive higher knowledge from the spiritual realms.

Unworldly – Not from this world. Could be connected to spirits, beings or knowledge that is from the planes of the universe.

Vibration – An energy frequency that a soul resonates at, which can be a positive or negative frequency. It is a state of being that a person, place or thing can reside within.

White light – A protective energy that can be called upon by all beings for assistance, protection and healing.

JOURNALLING NOTES

Sectioning your journal

This section is to be used as a guide when you start to record your spiritual journey. I can't stress enough how important it is to record your progress while working with this book. In the future your spiritual journal will become a very valuable resource to refer back to.

Below are suggestions for how and what to record in your journal. It is up to you how you proceed with this. You may wish to separate your journal into different sections or under different headings so that you can come back to the information easily when you need to. These sections might include the following:

- Symbols
- Guides and guardian angels
- Names
- Number sequences
- Colours
- Affirmations

- Fragrances
- Drawings
- Psychic phenomenon
- Feelings
- Sounds and songs

Some questions to consider when you are journalling

Spirit guides and angels

What angel numbers do you see?
What angel symbols have you received from your angels?
When you meditate what does your spirit guide look like?

- What are they wearing?
- Are they male or female?
- What type of colour and hairstyle do they have if they have hair?
- What is their eye colour or any other distinctive facial features?
- What part of the world or universe do they originate from?
- Are they wearing any jewellery or sacred symbols?
- Is there any particular colour that you pick up with them?

Clairvoyance, psychic signs and symbol

- What are you seeing?
- Are there any symbols, any scenery, different types of vegetation?
- What colours are you seeing?
- Are you inside or outside?
- Are you up or down?
- Do you see a house, people, animals etc?

Clairaudience

- What do you hear?
- Do you hear any voices?
- Do you hear music?
- Do you hear your own voice or someone else's?
- Do you hear a male or a female voice? Is it young or old? Do they have an accent?

Clairsentience, clairempathy and clairtangency

What are your psychic impressions when you tune in to a person or an item:

- How do you feel?
- Are you happy, sad, excited, depressed, light, heavy?
- Do you feel any pain in your body or any sensations, headaches, sore back etc?
- If you do, what side of the body?

Clairgustance and clairalience

- Do you smell anything? For example, any perfumes, aftershave, cooking smells, cigarette smoke, alcohol, aftershave, bush or floral smells, the ocean, wet or damp, dirt, dead fish, boot polish etc.

- Do you taste anything? For example, any food, coffee, cake, chocolate, cigarette smoke, alcohol, salt, sweet or sour etc.

Numerology

What are your numbers?

- Date of birth
- Day force
- Birth force
- Current numerological cycle
- Birth name and your numbers

ABOUT THE AUTHOR

DEBBIE MALONE

Sydney-based Debbie Malone is an internationally acclaimed and highly respected psychic, clairvoyant, medium, psychic detective and spirit photographer, who over the past 30 years has been investigating and developing her abilities.

Debbie has seen and sensed spirit since a child. She has experienced seven near-death experiences (NDEs) and at the age of 28 had a miscarriage. Due to these experiences, her unique abilities were heightened and brought to the fore, and she has been able to give insight into what she experienced as well as making contact with those in spirit. Since then, Debbie has provided the link for thousands of people to communicate with their loved ones who have passed on. Clients have reported a sense of closure and healing by being able to connect to their loved ones.

Debbie is a columnist for *New Idea* magazine and regularly runs workshops teaching students how to tune into their own higher self and how to become attuned with their spirit guides and guardian angels. She is a best-selling author, and has written four books: *Never Alone*, *Clues From Beyond*, *Awaken Your Psychic Abilities* and *Always With You*; and the creator of a series of best-selling Angel cards: *Angel Whispers, Angel Wishes, Angel Reading Cards, Guardian Angel Reading Cards* and *Psychic Reading Cards*.

Debbie's books *Never Alone* and *Clues From Beyond* document some of the work she has done with Australian Law Enforcement over the past 30 years. Debbie assists police Australia-wide to bring new light on unsolved murder investigations and missing persons cases. The information Debbie receives has been very successful in providing new lines of inquiry, criminal profiles, and identikits of perpetrators through working with police identikit artists and through using an identikit app to provide images of suspects.

Due to Debbie's mediumship abilities, she can make contact with the deceased victim and provide insight into who, what, when, and why the crime was committed.

Debbie is regularly interviewed on television, radio, and national print.

www.debbiemalone.com

f ⊙ @debbiemalonebtw